Walter Pater

Edinburgh Critical Studies in Victorian Culture

Series Editor: Julian Wolfreys

Volumes available in the series:

In Lady Audley's Shadow: Mary Elizabeth Braddon and Victorian Literary Genres
Saverio Tomaiuolo
978 0 7486 4115 4 Hbk

Blasted Literature: Victorian Political Fiction and the Shock of Modernism
Deaglán Ó Donghaile
978 0 7486 4067 6 Hbk

William Morris and the Idea of Community: Romance, History and Propaganda, 1880–1914
Anna Vaninskaya
978 0 7486 4149 9 Hbk

1895: Drama, Disaster and Disgrace in Late Victorian Britain
Nicholas Freeman
978 0 7486 4056 0 Hbk

Determined Spirits: Eugenics, Heredity and Racial Regeneration in Anglo-American Spiritualist Writing, 1848–1930
Christine Ferguson
978 0 7486 3965 6 Hbk

Dickens's London: Perception, Subjectivity and Phenomenal Urban Multiplicity
Julian Wolfreys
978 0 7486 4040 9 Hbk

Re-Imagining the 'Dark Continent' in fin de siècle *Literature*
Robbie McLaughlan
978 0 7486 4715 6 Hbk

Roomscape: Women Readers in the British Museum from George Eliot to Virginia Woolf
Susan David Bernstein
978 0 7486 4065 2 Hbk

Walter Pater: Individualism and Aesthetic Philosophy
Kate Hext
978 0 7486 4625 8 Hbk

Jane Morris: The Burden of History
Wendy Parkins
978 0 7486 4127 7 Hbk

London's Underground Spaces: Representing the Victorian City, 1840–1915
Hwang Haewon
978 0 7486 7607 1 Hbk

Thomas Hardy's Legal Fictions
Trish Ferguson
978 0 7486 7324 7 Hbk

Moving Images: Nineteenth-Century Reading and Screen Practices
Helen Groth
978 0 7486 6948 6 Hbk

Forthcoming volumes:

Her Father's Name: Gender, Theatricality and Spiritualism in Florence Marryat's Fiction
Tatiana Kontou
978 0 7486 4007 2 Hbk

British India and Victorian Culture
Máire ni Fhlathúin
978 0 7486 4068 3 Hbk

Women and the Railway, 1850–1915
Anna Despotopoulou
978 0 7486 7694 1 Hbk

Visit the Edinburgh Critical Studies in Victorian Culture web page at www.euppublishing.com/series/ecve

Also Available:
Victoriographies – A Journal of Nineteenth-Century Writing, 1790–1914, edited by Julian Wolfreys.
ISSN: 2044-2416
www.eupjournals.com/vic

Walter Pater

Individualism and Aesthetic Philosophy

Kate Hext

EDINBURGH
University Press

For Rufus Foster-Carter

© Kate Hext, 2013

Edinburgh University Press Ltd
22 George Square, Edinburgh EH8 9LF

www.euppublishing.com

Typeset in 10.5/13 Sabon by
Servis Filmsetting Ltd, Stockport, Cheshire,
and printed and bound in Great Britain by
CPI Group (UK) Ltd, Croydon CR0 4YY

A CIP record for this book is available from the British Library

ISBN 978 0 7486 4625 8 (hardback)
ISBN 978 0 7486 4626 5 (webready PDF)
ISBN 978 0 7486 8358 1 (epub)

The right of Kate Hext
to be identified as author of this work
has been asserted in accordance with
the Copyright, Designs and Patents Act 1988.

Contents

Series Editor's Preface   vi
Acknowledgements   viii
Note on Editions and Abbreviations   x

1. Introduction: Individualism and the 'aesthetic philosopher'   1

2. Empiricism and the Imperilled Self   24

3. Subjectivity and Imagination: From Hume to Kant via Berkeley   44

4. Metaphysics: Pater's Failed Attempt at Atheism   64

5. Sense and Sensuality: Caught between Venus and Dionysus   85

6. Pater's Copernican Revolution: The Desiring, Dying Body   109

7. Evolution and the 'Species': The Individual in Deep Time   130

8. The Moment and the Aesthetic Imagination   146

9. Ethics, Society and the Aesthetic Individual   165

10. Conclusion: 'the elusive inscrutable mistakable self'   183

Bibliography   190
Index   208

Series Editor's Preface

'Victorian' is a term, at once indicative of a strongly determined concept and an often notoriously vague notion, emptied of all meaningful content by the many journalistic misconceptions that persist about the inhabitants and cultures of the British Isles and Victoria's Empire in the nineteenth century. As such, it has become a by-word for the assumption of various, often contradictory habits of thought, belief, behaviour and perceptions. Victorian studies and studies in nineteenth-century literature and culture have, from their institutional inception, questioned narrowness of presumption, pushed at the limits of the nominal definition, and have sought to question the very grounds on which the unreflective perception of the so-called Victorian has been built; and so they continue to do. Victorian and nineteenth-century studies of literature and culture maintain a breadth and diversity of interest, of focus and inquiry, in an interrogative and intellectually open-minded and challenging manner, which are equal to the exploration and inquisitiveness of its subjects. Many of the questions asked by scholars and researchers of the innumerable productions of nineteenth-century society actively put into suspension the clichés and stereotypes of 'Victorianism', whether the approach has been sustained by historical, scientific, philosophical, empirical, ideological or theoretical concerns; indeed, it would be incorrect to assume that each of these approaches to the idea of the Victorian has been, or has remained, in the main exclusive, sealed off from the interests and engagements of other approaches. A vital interdisciplinarity has been pursued and embraced, for the most part, even as there has been contest and debate amongst Victorianists, pursued with as much fervour as the affirmative exploration between different disciplines and differing epistemologies put to work in the service of reading the nineteenth century.

Edinburgh Critical Studies in Victorian Culture aims to take up both the debates and the inventive approaches and departures from convention that studies in the nineteenth century have witnessed for the last half century at least. Aiming to maintain a 'Victorian' (in the most positive sense of that motif) spirit of inquiry, the series' purpose is to continue and augment the cross-fertilisation of interdisciplinary approaches, and to offer, in addition, a number of timely and untimely revisions of Victorian literature, culture, history and identity. At the same time, the series will ask questions concerning what has been missed or improperly received, misread, or not read at all, in order to present a multi-faceted and heterogeneous kaleidoscope of representations. Drawing on the most provocative, thoughtful and original research, the series will seek to prod at the notion of the 'Victorian', and in so doing, principally through theoretically and epistemologically sophisticated close readings of the historicity of literature and culture in the nineteenth century, to offer the reader provocative insights into a world that is at once overly familiar, and irreducibly different, other and strange. Working from original sources, primary documents and recent interdisciplinary theoretical models, Edinburgh Critical Studies in Victorian Culture seeks not simply to push at the boundaries of research in the nineteenth century, but also to inaugurate the persistent erasure and provisional, strategic redrawing of those borders.

Julian Wolfreys

Acknowledgments

Without the love, support, and expertise of many friends and colleagues this monograph would not have been written.

In 2002, when I was an undergraduate at the University of Warwick, Martin Warner told me that I should – no, must – read Walter Pater. It is a pleasure to thank him here for his suggestion. At the University of Exeter, the warm support, friendship and guidance of Regenia Gagnier who supervised my PhD on Pater, has been invaluable. Since taking up my current post at Exeter, my colleagues have been unwavering in their help and support. Principally I would like to thank Peter Faulkner, Nick Groom, Jason Hall, and Alex Murray for commiserating with me on my tussles with Pater.

Further afield my research on Pater and aestheticism has brought me into contact with many of the scholars whose work I engage with in this study. The field of Pater Studies is a warm and vibrant place for an early-career scholar and I have benefitted greatly from becoming part of it. I am especially grateful to Laurel Brake, Andrew Eastham, Lesley Higgins, Lene Østermark-Johansen, and Carolyn Williams. Beyond the field of Pater studies, I am also indebted to Peter Evans, Hannah Lewis-Bill, and Charles Page for their friendship, inspiration, and (not least) for offering welcome breaks from dear Mr Pater.

As Editor of the Edinburgh Critical Studies in Victorian Culture series, Julian Wolfreys deserves not only thanks but praise for his astute, kind, and helpful advice and support. Another eminent professor of Victorian Studies told me, as I was nearing the end of my PhD studies, that 'single author studies are dead'. I will be eternally grateful that Julian and Edinburgh University Press take a different point of view. His belief in the value of this single author study has been essential to its publication. At the stage of development and production, I am very grateful to Jackie Jones, Jenny Daly and Christine Barton for their kindness and efficiency. Sections of this book have appeared in print before, and publishers have generously allowed me to reproduce revised sections from: '"Of the Things Sweet to Touch": Walter Pater and the Tyrannies of Sensation', originally published in the *Journal of Pre-Raphaelite Studies* (Spring 2010 [19]: 55–67), and 'The Limitations of Schilleresque Self-Culture in Pater's Individualist Aesthetics', which was published in *Walter Pater Across the Arts* (Lesley Higgins and Elicia Clements (eds), Basingstoke: Palgrave Macmillan, 2010, pp. 285–302).

The life of the mind is all very well but I could not have finished this study without great practical help. Whilst working on it I gave birth to my little boy, Rufus, and a few months later started my first full-time academic position, which has made life very busy. In this period my mum, Claire Hext, has been unwavering in her support as baby-sitter extraordinaire to Rufus.

My greatest debt though is to Aidan Foster-Carter, the sweetest of critics, who has lived with Pater for almost as long as I have.

Note on Editions and Abbreviations

It has been de rigueur in studies of Pater to reference Macmillan's *Complete Works*, but this edition has not been reprinted since the middle of the last century and is no longer readily available. For the reader's convenience, I have chosen to use modern critical editions wherever possible. This has not been possible in the cases of *Greek Studies*, *Miscellaneous Studies* or *Essays from the Guardian* because these works are out of print at the time of writing. I have only abbreviated works by Pater.

A	*Appreciations, with an Essay on Style*
AL	'The Aesthetic Life'
BB	*The Book Beautiful*
D	'Diaphaneitè'
GL	*Gaston De Latour*
GS	*Greek Studies*
HP	'The History of Philosophy'
IP	*Imaginary Portraits*
L	*The Letters of Walter Pater*
M	*Marius the Epicurean*
MS	*Miscellaneous Studies*
PP	*Plato and Platonism*
R	*Studies in the History of the Renaissance*
WM	'Poems by William Morris'

Walter Pater, by Simeon Solomon (1872)

Chapter 1

Introduction: Individualism and the 'aesthetic philosopher'

Art is the most intense form of Individualism . . .
Oscar Wilde, 'The Soul of Man Under Socialism' (142)

Beyond and above all the various interests upon which the philosopher's mind was ever afloat, there was one subject always in prominence – himself.
Walter Pater, *Gaston de Latour* (54)

The faltering centre of Walter Pater's aesthetic philosophy is his conception of the individual. The individual, and not art, is at the very heart of his aestheticism. Amid the storms that assailed subjectivity in mid-Victorian culture, Pater's aesthetic is a portrait of humanity 'in its uncertain condition' (R 39); an admission that we may be but 'a tremulous wisp constantly re-forming itself on the stream' (R 151), spiritually desolate and ever possessed by conflicting desires. Yet still it is animated by the quiet Romantic ambition that self-identity in the modern world may be reconceived through aesthetic experience. *Walter Pater: Individualism and Aesthetic Philosophy* explores Pater's individualism, both intellectual and personal, and how this individualism is formed through his attempt to redefine the scope of philosophical thought under the conditions of modernity. As it does so it asserts that Pater is the philosophical centre of aestheticism, and explores his significant interventions in the relationship between the individual and art, and 'philosophy' and 'literature', as they underwent significant revision in mid to late nineteenth-century Britain.

In every one of Walter Pater's essays, 'imaginative portraits', and novels, he is in some sense looking for what he calls 'the elusive inscrutable mistakable self' (HP 23). This endeavour – never concluded, never resolved – is given most prominence in his manuscript essays, where he writes:

And if we know so little it might be urged of the supposed substance of one's own mind how much less can we really penetrate into the minds of others of whose whole inward existence in a strictly logical estimate of facts nothing really comes to us but a stream of material phenomena as of ourselves to ourselves but the stream of the phenomena of our own elusive inscrutable mistakable self. (HP 23)

This unpunctuated passage from 'The History of Philosophy' (c.1880) flows out in a stream of consciousness, with Pater's writing barely keeping up with his thoughts as he attempts to come to terms with the isolation of the individual and 'the elusive inscrutable mistakable' nature of other people and of ourselves. In the same essay, his thoughts trail off as he wonders at 'the idea of the mind itself or of the <u>ego</u> or of personality or will[1] or of the soul or spirit of man as it is variously named' (HP 19; Pater's underlining). His irresolution about how to conceive the distinctive self here is as striking as it is touching: after almost twenty years of contemplating and writing about the individual he is still uncertain about its nature. With examples like this no doubt in mind, Carolyn Williams speaks for many of Pater's critics when she suggests that the inherently troubled individuated self in Pater's writings becomes 'irrelevant' (1989: 17). Whilst the individual is not and cannot be for Pater an unproblematic entity, it is not though 'irrelevant'. In truth, Pater returns again and again with an intense curiosity to explore the vicissitudes of the individual: the nature of subjectivity, the substance of personal identity, spirituality, the dangers of desire and the limitations of epistemology. He is captivated by the situation of the modern individual: in a world where all we can be certain of is the truth of our impressions, we are left unable to understand the nature of the *self* who is having these impressions and – worse still – life is left vacuous by the empirical-scientific dissolution of metaphysics.

Walter Pater: 'the mask without the face'

The nature of the individual is an ironic enquiry for Walter Pater. For whilst the endeavour wrought out in his essays and imaginary portraiture is to explore the conditions of individualism and the constituent parts of the individual, Pater is himself shrouded in mystery. Henry James, who did not know him well but understood him acutely, remarks that 'He is the mask without the face, and there isn't in his total superficies a tiny point of vantage for the newspaper to flap his wings on' (293; sic).[2] The biographer's art is all but lost on Pater because we will never understand his heart through his ostensible words or deeds; he did not want us to and he has delicately achieved his aim. He was not given to confidences, being 'cautious, reserved and shy in his relations even with his friends' amongst whom his 'extremely affectionate disposition took the place of expansiveness' (Gosse 1913: 265). Neither did he keep a diary and his letters are brief and unrevealing. As he apologetically admits to various correspondents: 'I write so few letters!'; 'Letters are such poor means of communication'; 'I am but a poor letter-writer' (L 52; 80; 128). As though he sought to emulate '[Prosper] Merimée's superb self-efface-ment, his impersonality' (MS 24), he ensured that few if any saw behind his masks. He was J. Alfred Prufrock in many ways; his intense inner-life hemmed within by a shyness and meticulousness nagging always 'Do I dare / Disturb the universe?' The only way to glimpse behind the mask is in a sideways glance through his literary art and the few telling moments and habits of his life of which we have some knowledge. Pater is quoting Merimée when he writes, '"It has always been my rule to put nothing of myself into my works" (to be *disinterested* in his literary creations, so to speak), "yet I have put too much of myself into them"' (MS 23–4). Like Basil Hallward in *The Picture of Dorian Gray* (1891), Pater might have been speaking of himself (Wilde 1999: 2). As the epigraph of the current chapter suggests, Pater always kept himself in prominence: to work out what it means to be an individual under the conditions of modernity was always, for him, a personal enquiry, inextricable from his attempt to understand himself.

In some sense Mrs Oliphant is quite correct when she writes in her review of Pater's *Studies in the History of the Renaissance* (1873),

> It is in furtherance of the grand pursuit of self-culture that he writes, treating all the great art and artists of the past, and all the centuries of men, as chiefly important and attractive in their relations to that Me who is in the centre of the dilettante's world. (1873: 606)

Yet this supreme 'Me' is effected and affected with a seriousness that eludes Mrs Oliphant's sardonic tone. Pater grapples within a philosophi-cal paradigm of epistemology, which had become both insistent and fraught, to defend the individual as the centre of being against contem-porary cultural and philosophical forces that threatened to dissolve it into nothingness. Furthermore, he offers to reconcile his readers with their finitude and to show them that they are more than mere prisoners: be it prisoners of history, the Darwinian 'species', Victorian society, modern technology, or rational thought. Reflecting on modernity in *The Renaissance* he asserts that 'not less than ever, the intellect demands completeness, centrality' (146). He is understating his point here, for he believed – or at least wanted to believe – fervently in the centrality, or even 'lordship', of the creative subject (R 132). 'Pater's vision of the human condition,' Murray Pittock has recognised, 'is one which stresses the autonomy of the human spirit: that which we create ourselves, and are the measure of our own value' (1993: 15–16). All told, Pater agonises over this vision. Autonomy is hard-won against the extraneous forces, primarily God which he parodies as 'a sort of mythical personage without us, with whom we can do warfare' (R 148), the necessities imposed on us by society and its ethics, material conditions in their eternal flux, and the self-destructive impulses that may possess one. His writings are a wondering quest to explore how it is possible to achieve autonomy under the conditions of modernity through aesthetic experience.

Pater's Late-Romantic Individualism

Out of Pater's hesitating consideration of the individual there emerges what I will call his 'late-Romantic individualism'. This is a term I define through Steven Lukes' seminal work, *Individualism* (1973), and conceive through the dialectic of what Lukes calls 'German individualism' and 'Victorian individualism'. Developing out of German Romanticism, German individualism connotes 'uniqueness, originality, self-realization' (Lukes 17) whilst 'Victorian individualism' emphasises the individual's economic and political freedom from State intervention (Lukes 32–9). Pater's individualism and that which he influences emerges from a tension between the desire to assert individualism centred on 'uniqueness, originality, self-realization' and a contemporary context in which the individual was defined, contrastingly, in socio-political and economic terms. It is Pater's negotiation of these tensions and his attempts to define the individual despite the forces of self-dissolution that form his late-Romantic individualism. Therefore, Pater's late-Romantic individualism must be understood, in the current study, to stem not only from Germany: for as Nikolas Kompridis has shown in *Philosophical Romanticism* (2006a), such a tendency forms and reforms itself across Germany, France, and Britain from the late-eighteenth century to the twenty-first century. Not bounded by national or temporal borders like the problematic term aestheticism, Romanticism is an especially nebulous spirit as the nineteenth century progresses. It continues to define the individual according to those qualities of 'uniqueness, originality, self-realization' expressed through aesthetic creativity and appreciation, inherited from the late-eighteenth century. At the same time Romantic individualism takes its vitality from its untimely character: always, throughout history, conscious of itself as out of step with its tumultuous age. This is particularly the case in the late-nineteenth century when the Romantic spirit was transfigured into aestheticism.[3]

Pater's late-Romantic individualism is utterly defined by its position at the schism between Promethean individualism and the ways in which modernity forces a radical reconception of what it means to be an 'individual'. He is torn: unable to give up his belief in the Romantic individual, yet profoundly touched by the insistent realities of Darwinism, the fragmented experience of time, the death of God and subjectivity in the modern world. Looking back to Wordsworth and Schiller and forward to Proust and Woolf, Pater stands at a watershed: as one who must attempt to understand the nature of the cultural and intellectual transition taking place in the late-nineteenth century and define its implications for art, one's conception of self, and subjectivity.

To some extent it is understandable that his Conclusion to *The Renaissance* has led critics such as Carolyn Williams and Angela Leighton to suggest that Pater does not believe in individuality. Though the individual may appear flawed, conflicted, and under threat of dissolution in the Conclusion, the present study will argue that in fact the individual is persistent and vital, indeed at the very centre of Pater's flawed aesthetic. Pater's 'commitment to engage with and assimilate "modern thought" and then to turn it against itself under the auspices of aestheticism', as Carolyn Williams (1989: 27) perceptively puts it, is at its most fervent in fact when he considers the individual. If, at times, this individual becomes absorbed into the flux, this is part of Pater's exploration of how individuality is assailed by modernity; part of his endeavour to understand these conditions in order to forge an alternative and distinctly modern conception of individualism. In contrast to Oscar Wilde – Pater's self-anointed disciple and another figure whose philosophical seriousness is largely ignored – who would explore the 'myriad of lives, myriad sensations' of the individual conceived now as 'a complex multiform creature' (1999: 139) in the knowledge that there is no simple, permanent essence of self, Pater hankers still after some such unifying essence and the means to make one's self whole.

Walter Pater: 'the aesthetic philosopher'

In a minute there is time
For decisions and revisions which a minute will reverse . . .
T. S. Eliot, 'The Love Song of J. Alfred Prufrock'
(1917: lines 48–50, 13)

One of the further reasons why the Paterian individual has been so often neglected or misunderstood in the past has to do with the way in which critics have framed Pater's work. It is Pater the stylist and, more recently, Pater the purveyor of male-male desire, which have been the subject of the critic's gaze; Pater the thinker is an altogether rarer concern. In one of my favourite digs, which could stand for many others, Angela Leighton quips that 'Pater is good at memorable nonsense' (2005: 67) and, similarly, Denis Donoghue declares that 'Pater was indifferent to ideas' (1995: 306), even as Richard Wollheim argues that, in fact, we must begin with Pater's philosophy if we hope to understand him at all (1995: 24). Academics such as Billie Andrew Inman (*Walter Pater's Reading*; 1981), Carolyn Williams (*Transfigured World*; 1989), and Andrew Eastham (*Aesthetic Afterlives*; 2011) have done much to bring to life the philosophical dimensions of Pater's writings; and her above comment notwithstanding, Angela Leighton's *On Form: Poetry, Aestheticism, and the Legacy of a Word* (2007) has itself contributed to elucidating the relationship between Pater's philosophical ideas and form (31–54). Even so, too many critics only skirt the edges of Paterian thought whilst engaged in quite other discussions, or else restrict their scope to just that most famous of passages: Pater's Conclusion to *The Renaissance*. This will not do. In order to understand the dynamics between the individual, modernity and art that underpin Pater's works, and grasp the full intellectual significance of Pater's place in the late nineteenth century, the critical scope must be broadened to include his lesser-known and unpublished works and, crucially, to consider the philosophical influences and ambitions that define his contribution to literature and the intellectual culture.

And yet the question raised by Angela Leighton's dismissive comment on the quality of Pater's thought must be addressed. Certainly, the nature of his thought is idiosyncratic: shifting, apparently contradictory and, in places, tinged in purple. It is not what philosophical thought is meant to be. But this is, in part, the point. If we grant that he is a little like J. Alfred Prufrock, we should grant too that there is a touch of Nietzsche about him too. Though it is Wilde's epigrams and paradoxes that most closely echo Nietzschean form, it is Pater who could most legitimately be called Nietzsche's brother in arms against established philosophical forms and ethics.[4]

There is an endearing and altogether characteristic incongruity between Pater's assertion that 'we will hardly have time to make theories about the things we see and touch' (R 152) and the way that he devoted his career to this endless task. His endeavour, always, is to explore what kind of philosophical discourse might be possible under the conditions of modernity. In his anonymous review of 'Poems by William Morris' (1868), he writes:

It is a strange transition from the earthly paradise to the sad-coloured world of abstract philosophy. But let us accept the challenge; let us see what modern philosophy, when it is sincere, really does say about human life and the truth we can attain in it, and the relation of this to the desire of beauty. (309)

In the career which took off with this review, Pater's writings represent his acceptance of this challenge as he attempts to fuse the desire for beauty with sincere exploration of the human condition as he sees it in the third of a century (1860–1894) during which he lived and wrote. He is an idiosyncratic thinker; there is no denying that. He did not believe in objectivity, eternal truths or philosophical systems, nor did he believe that rational discourse can ascertain moral values. Yet this does not mean that his thought is nonsensical or a merely stylistic performance. As I shall suggest, intellectual rigour is crucial to Pater's literary art. Thus he applauds the achievements of Violet Paget's *Euphorion* (1884),[5] writing to her: 'I always welcome this evidence of intellectual structure in a poetic or imaginative piece of criticism, as I think it a very rare thing, and it is also an effect I have myself endeavoured after, and so come to know its difficulties' (L 54). Humphry Ward recalls that Pater 'was severe on confusions of thought, and still more on any kind of rhetoric. An emphatic word was sure to be underscored and the absolutely right phrase suggested' (Benson 1906: 25). This aspiration to the exact expression of rigorously worked-out thought is in accordance with his vision of art as a perfect fusion of form and content (R 88). It is thus his own credo that he attributes to Flavian in *Marius the Epicurean* (1885): 'The happy phrase or sentence was really modelled upon a clearly finished structure of scrupulous thought . . . [and] this rare blending of grace with an intellectual rigour or astringency, was the secret of a singular expressiveness in it' (M, I, 154; 157). Flavian's preoccupation with the fusion of beauty and intellectual thought characterises Pater's own literary art. It is not that he sacrifices the intellect to beautiful form, for he understands that these are inseparable. Indistinguishable. Yet whilst the development of Pater's style has been discussed extensively by his critics, of his exploration of ideas there is much left to say.

Falling Between Schools

One of the problems in recognising Pater's contribution to ideas in the late nineteenth century is that – as befits someone so preoccupied with the individual self – he does not belong to any school of philosophical thought that would allow the critic to easily fix him in a formulaic phrase. Here Gerald L. Bruns is helpful in suggesting that 'Life-Philosophy' – a term borrowed from Carlyle's *Sartor Resartus* (1836) – characterises much philosophical thought in Victorian Britain:

> 'Life-Philosophy' [. . .] is, a set of ideas, beliefs, attitudes, and feelings whose structure is that of experience rather than system, a life-pattern or 'plot' that disposes a set of meanings by revealing how a particular mind came to create them and that accordingly makes these meaning accessible through the experience of character itself. (1975: 907)

Through his imaginative portraits Pater exemplifies the Life-Philosopher. During his career British philosophy was in a period of transition. Pater saw himself as a participator in this transition, especially in the early part of his career when he positioned himself at the vanguard of intellectual thought: he published 'Coleridge' (1866), 'Winckelmann' (1867), and 'Poems by William Morris' (1868) in the *Westminster Review* which was 'the mouthpiece for advanced theological and philosophical thought' (Seiler 1999: 3). Pater looks back to the practical intelligence of Ancient Greek philosophy, then recently reasserted at the centre of the Oxford curriculum by Benjamin Jowett, to address how we are to live in the modern world. In part for this reason, he addresses what we would now call problems of identity from a perspective quite distinct from that of his contemporaries. As I have put it elsewhere, this was 'a period of modest transition and expansion in British philosophy'. Whilst Utilitarian, Empirical and Idealist schools of thought, established in the late eighteenth century, provided the grounds for the most compelling works of the century on practical questions of political economy, ethics, society, and the methods and aims of science Pater shied from direct engagement with such concerns. Still he was one of the first and most significant figures to reconceive the scope and style of philosophical discourse in light of the external challenges that threatened its authority. 'Increasing uncertainty had surrounded the scope, nature and purpose of philosophical discourse in the course of nineteenth-century in Britain' (Hext 2012: 702). At a time, then, when the systematisation, dogmatism, and atemporal of philosophical discourse seemed increasingly out of step with the shape of life as it was lived, Pater took philosophical ideas and worked them through in full knowledge that ideas could no longer be systematised or brought to conclusions.

Pater is usually identified, of course, with 'aestheticism', yet this is problematic. Not only are those so labelled a rather disparate group, but this move can be a distraction from the significant dimension of Pater's work that reconsiders the nature of philosophical ideas and form. It also prioritises the hedonistic Walter Pater that others wished him to be.

Perhaps he had entertained the thought of becoming such a man early in his career, but in truth he never did; nor, to reiterate, was he part of any school or movement. Up to the late 1870s this autonomy was in large part due to his strong instinct for self-preservation against the forces of authority and censure in Oxford, discussed in Chapter 6. Thereafter an eccentric if not paranoid element also enters in, for the same reason that he remained surprisingly and deliberately ignorant of his contemporaries: a morbid fear that he would lose his style – and even himself – in the influences of others. His friend, Edmund Gosse, recalled after Pater's death in 1894,

> Pater did not study his contemporaries; a year or two ago he told me that he had scarcely read a chapter of Mr. Stevenson and not a line of Mr. Kipling. 'I feel from what I hear about them,' he said, 'that they are strong; they might lead me out of my path. I want to go on writing in my own way, good or bad. I should be afraid to read Mr. Kipling, lest he should come between me and my page next time I sat down to write.' (265)

Pater shied from the influence of other writers, just as he shied from intimate friendships, as though ever fearful that 'Our collective life, pressing equally on every part of every one of us, reduces nearly all of us to the level of a colourless uninteresting existence' (D 157). Still it is quite correct to see Pater as a key fragment in the 'kind of looking-glass world' of Oxford, 'through which all of the intellectual, cultural, scientific, and political issues of the day were reflected' (Higgins 2006: 33). The question is where and how he figures in this 'looking-glass world', and how to put into perspective his intellectual relationships (with such figures as Benjamin Jowett, Matthew Arnold, Algernon Swinburne, T. H. Green, Henry James, Gerard Manley Hopkins, Oscar Wilde and Arthur Symons); his resistance to contemporary influences; and his engagements with both classical and modern European philosophies. What emerges, I shall argue, is a unique vision: born of immersion in the intellectual and cultural shifts that challenged the equilibrium of self-identity in the late nineteenth century, and refracted through the prism of modern Western philosophy and art.

Here Pater's self-directed education in both ancient and modern philosophies is fundamental. His programme of reading, begun as an undergraduate at The Queen's College, Oxford, between 1858 and 1862, was a self-imposed and selective regime which combined the conventional with the unconventional; it included a wide range of empirical, German Romantic and transcendental Idealist, and ancient Greek philosophies as well as histories of philosophy. One can see why these epochs and schools appealed to Pater: the Greeks offered him a practical philosophy of living, the empiricists foregrounded sensation as the basis of epistemology, and the German Romantics and Idealists were the first both to take art seriously as a philosophical concern and to place the individual at the centre of the universe.

The least conventional element here was Pater's interest in German philosophy. At that time 'anyone suspected of being influenced by German scholarship was assumed to be unorthodox' by many at Oxford, as this suggested association with the criticism of religion by Feuerbach and Strauss (Annan 2001: 64). Quite likely this was part of the attraction to Pater and his interest was intensified by several visits to Heidelberg, where he had an aunt. Yet quite soon this suspicion was superseded by a renewed interest in German culture and thought at Oxford, led by the Oxford Hegelians such as T. H. Green. His contemporaries duly acknowledged the young Pater's expertise in this field. Thomas Wright remarks that Pater's knowledge of German philosophy helped him to gain his fellowship at Brasenose in 1864 (1907: I, 211); while years later Lionel Johnson confirmed that still 'he gave much time to the aesthetic theorists of Germany – Winckelmann, Lessing, Goethe, Hegel, such speculations agreed with that cogitating spirit in him' (364). Pater's inaugural paper to the Old Mortality Society in 1864 was on 'self-culture' in the work of Gottlieb Fichte, and it was to philosophy that he returned in his last book, *Plato and Platonism* (1893).

Overall, the Oxford Hegelians participated significantly in making German culture prominent amongst the English-speaking literati, to the point where, by 'the end of the nineteenth century, the leading academic philosophers, both in America and Great Britain, were largely Hegelians' (Russell 2005: 661). However, this does not wholly apply to Pater. He was not an *Hegelian*. Giles Whiteley's *Aestheticism and the Philosophy of Death: Walter Pater and Post-Hegelianism* (2010), Andrew Eastham's chapter, 'Walter Pater's Acoustic Space: "The School of Giorgione", Dionysian *Ander-Streben*, and the Politics of Soundscape' (*Aesthetic Afterlives: Irony, Literary Modernity and the Ends of Beauty*, 2010), and Kit Andrews's essay, 'Walter Pater as Oxford Hegelian: Plato and Platonism and T. H. Green's *Prolegomena to Ethics*' (2011), are the most recent in a distinguished line of critical works which illuminate Hegel's influence on Pater's aesthetics and idea of history. As such, they follow works going back to Anthony Ward's *Walter Pater: The Idea in Nature* (1966).

However Pater's engagement with Hegel is, I suggest, limited. True, in 'Winckelmann' he borrows from Hegel's *Introductory Lectures on Aesthetics* (*Philosophie der Kunst oder Ästhetik*; 1826), which he had read in German in 1863 (Inman 1981a: 49). Yet Hegel's overall philosophy is wholly at odds with Pater's world-view. Hegel's politics, his conception of *right*, his metaphysical vision of art in which aesthetics is ultimately made subject to philosophy and religion in the realm of Absolute Spirit; his belief that thesis and antithesis necessarily resolve into synthesis, and even the teleology in which this idea is formed; all these are profoundly un-Paterian. The integral relationship between self-identity and society which made Hegel central to the British Idealists at Oxford – T. H. Green and F. H. Bradley being the most prominent – was antithetical to Pater's individualism. Pater never could reconcile himself to, what he describes in 'The History of Philosophy', as

> a very imperfect reciprocity between the exacting reasonableness of the ideal [Hegel] supposes, and the confused, imperfect, hap-hazard character of man's actual experience in nature and history – a radical dualism in his system, as to the extent of which he was perhaps not always quite candid, even with himself. (HP 6)

Hence when considering the relationship between the mind of the individual and the universe, Pater entertains not the social self of Hegelian philosophy but the various conceptions of selfhood envisaged by Kant, Hume, Locke, and Schiller.

Pater's long visits to Germany and his capabilities with the language[6] meant that he was well-versed in much more than Hegel. The influence of German Idealism in nineteenth-century Britain should not be equated with Hegelianism, as tends to be the case today. In addition, Kant, Schiller, Novalis, Schlegel, Schleiermacher and Schiller appear in Pater's library records and their thought permeates his writings. Here again, though, his approach to them differs from that of his Oxford contemporaries. Staying true to his own warning against any 'facile orthodoxy' (R 152), he picks out ideas from transcendental philosophy without ever becoming a transcendental Idealist. Instead, as we shall see, he interweaves many of these different philosophies into his aesthetic, often without direct references, and creates in the tissue of his texts an internal dialogue with them. It will not do to subsume Pater under any single thinker, or even any single school of thought: be it the German Idealists or the Romantics, or the French aesthetes, or the philosophers of ancient Greece, or British empiricism, or the Oxford of his own day. He abides by no system or single philosophy, Pater forges his own idiosyncratic, though sometimes faltering, philosophical aesthetic through a nexus of influences; taking threads from here and there to weave from them something new and quintessentially modern.

Indeed, he writes with a strong sense that philosophy in the modern world is precisely defined by the multifarious and fluctuating bric-a-brac character of its age. Like his own characterisation of Plato, we find that Pater

> figures less as the author of a new theory, than as already an eclectic critic of older ones, himself somewhat perplexed by theory and counter-theory [. . .] They are everywhere in it, not as the stray curved corner of some older edifice to be found here or there amid the new, but rather like minute relics of earlier organic life in the very stone he builds with. (PP 2)

Thus his writings are textured with the philosophers that interested him – Hume, Berkeley, Kant, Schiller, Hegel and Herbert Spencer, to name but a few discussed in the following chapters – as he defines a careful dialogue between them and modernity through his own consciousness. What he thereby creates is a new perspective; not a system or orthodoxy, but an unconventional kind of philosophical thought which attempts to come to terms with the fluctuating character of individualism in a world where God, if not yet dead, is in terminal decline. Pater did not write philosophy in any conventional sense and was in no way a conventional philosopher, precisely because he was acutely aware that such ideas as philosophy and the figure of the philosopher are incongruous in a modern, fluctuating, irreducibly subjective world, where system and authority have no place. As he attempts to readdress the question of what it means to be an individual in the modern world, then, he is also implicitly asking what sort of philosophy is possible under the conditions of modernity. And how can literary form, style and imaginative portraiture reconceive the terms of 'philosophy', taking us beyond merely rational discourse to create alternative modes of 'philosophising' the human condition?

Any enquiry into Pater's thought is certainly hindered by the fact that his constructive epistemology is 'passive, confused, shifting [. . .] with distinctions blurred and influences crossed' (Harrold 1935: 110). This is the ironic truth behind his recurrent image of man's 'clear crystal nature' or 'transparent crystal' (D 158; MS 46): in the 'clear crystal' ideal the workings of the individual's mind are plain before the philosophical enquirer, but in practice a Romantic mystique lingers in Pater's account of it. He struggles between his desire to know and his Romantic sense that things are essentially unknowable and beautiful because of their infinite mystery. He is not exactly confused in his beliefs, though they would alter in the course of time, any more than he is he uninterested in ideas. Rather, he is a writer trying to come to terms with his conception of the world and his place within it; and the unassuming way in which he does this makes him, in some ways, Every Man.

This is part of what makes his aesthetic difficult. Its apparent contraditions may suggest a lack of rigour, which is often due to his personal modesty and his understanding that he has no authority to legislate for the world. Pater 'never thought of using ideas as Arnold used them, to win an argument and make people change their lives. Pater did not argue' (Donoghue 1995: 306). Truly, Pater did not argue. Gosse compares him to Renan, whose tendency 'led him to refrain from opposition and argument, and to bow his head in the conversational house of Rimmon' (1894: 266). It is difficult to imagine Pater arguing with anyone, not because of indifference but because of his reserved and gentle nature – which is reflected in his narrative tone. Humphry Ward's recollection (above) implies that Pater distrusted the rhetorical hinges of argumentation for their hollow force and flourish. He chooses instead in his writings to suggest, illustrate and allude to his ideas, rather than assert them to the reader.

In his attempts to pinpoint his own fluid endeavour, Pater often returns to the question of how 'philosophy' might be other than it is.[7] He reweaves philosophy and aesthetic discourses into a new mode of philosophising in essay form to befit the modern world, aspiring always beyond philosophy to art, in his attempt to reconcile discourse with the uncertain, subjective, conditional nature of modernity. He thus becomes characteristic of 'the aesthetic philosopher' that he identifies (R 94). It is no accident that the essay was his preferred form, and the one on which this study will mainly focus. Pater 'associates the essay with modernity, agnosticism, uncertainty, and therefore with a kind of knowledge which does not easily reach conclusions or answers' (Leighton 2007: 28). Truly, the essay is, as Pater reflects, 'that characteristic literary type of our time, a time so rich and various in special apprehensions of truth, so tentative and dubious in its sense of their ensemble, and issues' (PP 120). The essay thus creates a sense of 'final insecurity' (PP 127):

> This is an apology, but it is also a boast. The essay finally leads, not to a point proved but an 'insecurity' achieved. It is the critical genre which can, on the one hand, admit uncertainty, subjectivity, conditionalness, while also, on the other, putting its own shaped form into play as part of its matter. (Leighton 2007: 28–9)

When we scratch the surface of Pater's prose, we may see then that he is attempting to redefine philosophy from within. This is an endeavour that harks back to the Romantics, but above all it begins the process whereby philosophy's 'phlegmatic, "clogged" homogeneity is soon to be broken apart and reformed in the mobile discourse of aestheticism' (Carolyn Williams 1989: 39). What Pater knows for certain is that the time is past for the grand, static philosophical systems which had dominated modern philosophy. He is frustrated with speculative forms of philosophy that take 'fugitive, relative' thought and 'tr[y] to fix it in absolute formulas' (A 72). In this world of unceasing flux we must think and look for truths, but without ever 'acquiescing in a facile orthodoxy of Comte or of Hegel, or of our own' (R 152).

Having thus subsumed philosophy into the artistic realm of the essay, Pater himself chooses literary art, rather than traditional philosophical discourse, as the medium through which to express his own ideas. Imaginative literature maps the vicissitudes of the modern condition:

> For the essence of all artistic beauty is expression, which cannot be where there's really nothing to be expressed; the line, the colour, the word, following obediently, and with minute scruple, the conscious motions of a convinced intelligible soul. (PP 82)

Elsewhere he writes of 'the incapacity of philosophy to be expressed in terms of art' (MS 43). Yet, still, in 'Giordano Bruno' (1889), 'philosophy becomes a poem, a sacred poem' in the hands of the title figure (GL 74);[8] and this is just what Pater aspires to. His is a mode of philosophising like that of Raphael: 'Well! in Raphael, painted ideas, painted and visible philosophy, are for once as beautiful as Plato thought they must be, if one truly apprehended them' (MS 43).

This reminds me of W. B. Yeats' reflection that 'we looked consciously to Pater for our philosophy' (302). But to a far greater extent than those self-defined writers of the next generation whom he influenced – Yeats, Wilde, Symons, Joyce, Woolf – Pater's status as a university academic means that his disciplinary identity is a matter of contestation. The fundamentally philosophical character of Pater's interests and, in particular, his academic involvement in teaching philosophy suggests an organic relation between ideas and form, philosophy and style, that has to be reflected in how we approach his writings. In truth his position in the field of English literature has always been a little tense. During the drawn-out debates which preceded the institutionalisation of English literature as a subject of academic study in its own right at Oxford in 1893, Pater wrote to the *Pall Mall Gazette*,

> I should [. . .] be no advocate for any plan of introducing English literature in the course of university studies which seemed likely to throw into the background that study of classical literature which has proved so effective for the maintenance of what is excellent in our own. (L 69)

His natural aversion to reform surely contributed to this circumspection. It may also have deeper roots in a reaction against Matthew Arnold's identification of institutionalised English literature with 'right reason' and 'authority' and with the means to correct the 'injurious' want of these in contemporary society (Arnold 1869: x). Enlisting the arts as part of a crusade for moral improvement was not Pater's way. In a heated discussion on reform in the Brasenose common room, he ventured, 'At present the undergraduate is a child of nature; he grows up like a wild rose in a country lane; you want to turn him into a turnip, rob him of all grace, and plant him out in rows' (qtd Gosse 1894: 270).[9] In Pater's letter to the *Pall Mall Gazette* though his ostensible concern is not Arnold or the bland mass-production of undergraduates, but that English literature should be properly understood as part of 'an organic unity' with other subjects including study of the Classics, philosophy and European literature (L 69). In short, he feared a too narrow disciplinarity because he believed in the benefits of a wide education that understands and situates English literature as inextricably linked to other literatures, social sciences and philosophies.

It is piquant, then, that for decades discussion of Pater's work was largely confined to the very English faculties whose existence he wished to prevent. Today, happily, this narrow disciplinary and social conservatism is long gone. Such recent works as Lene Østermark-Johansen's *Walter Pater and the Language of Sculpture* (2011), *Victorian Aesthetic Conditions: Pater Across the Arts* edited by Elicia Clements and Lesley Higgins (2010), Stefano Evangelista's *British Aestheticism and Ancient Greece: Hellenism, Reception, Gods in Exile* (2009), Gowan Dawson's *Darwin, Literature and Victorian Respectability* (2007), and Laurel Brake's *Print in Transition 1850–1910: Studies in Media and Book History* (2001) all recover the inherently interdisciplinary writer that Pater understood himself to be.[10] These studies also indicate, again happily, that more than a century after his death interest in Pater is burgeoning. Properly understood, this shy Victorian makes an important contribution to the formation of twentieth-century conceptions of self-identity.

Focus and Argument

The present study takes Pater on his own interdisciplinary terms: focusing on how philosophical ideas and literary style interact in his works, as he attempts to explore what it means to be an individual in the late nineteenth century. Against the critical consensus, it argues that Pater's conception of the individual is at the centre of his aesthetic. Though threatened at every turn – by evolutionary theory, the 'death of God', empirical philosophy, and the pressures of society – the individual is never reduced to irrelevance. Indeed, I contend that the animating questions of Pater's writing are not primarily aesthetic ones but, rather, what does it mean to be an individual? In what does one's identity as a unique, feeling, being inhere? And, only then, what does art mean to the individual and how does it heighten our awareness of ourselves as distinct from the forces that conspire against our individuality?

Methodologically, I conjoin three aspects: close readings, the wider intellectual culture, and biography. *Pace* the much-touted 'death of the author', I believe that in order to understand the Paterian individual, one must look carefully at Pater as an individual, or at least look at the individual that he and his contemporaries understood him to be. Pater lived his life in the shadows, certainly, but there is something compelling about a life seen so dimly; a life many of whose details have slipped through the cracks of recorded discourse to be lost in what Pater called 'endless history' (PP 11). This may be why there have been few attempts at his biography, and none since Denis Donogue's brief *Walter Pater: Lover of Strange Souls* (1995). Still, Gerald Monsman has argued, Pater's writings are 'a mirror in which Pater causes his own image, inscribed within the textual apparatus, to turn back upon the image of his hero and his hero's age – which then, once again, turns back upon the author's life' (1980: 7). Hence I interweave biography with literary criticism, conceiving a full exploration of the Paterian individual as symbiotic with a study of Pater himself. As the great dramas of Pater's life were played out only in the theatre of his imagination and it is this unrecorded emotional life that vividly informed his writings, at times I shall bridge these using his own form, the imaginary portrait. Simultaneously, this book traces how Pater engages with and contributes to the intellectual currents of his age. Principally, it considers his responses in four areas: the new field of psychology and the empiricist philosophy from which it emerged; the religious scepticism beginning quietly to permeate Oxford life, the cult of sensuality, and Darwinian evolution. Here, culture and personality cast light on each other. The contradictions of Paterian individualism involve his contradictions, and its hesitations are his own. Similarly, his reconception of philosophical thought as inherently inconclusive and subjective is grounded in his troubled conception of the late-Romantic individual, understood in the context of a dynamic culture coming to terms with itself in modernity.

Walter Pater: Individualism and Aesthetic Philosophy thus aims to redefine Pater's relation to the history of philosophical thought. The research for this project began, in 2005, with a conviction that Pater was deeply influenced by the history of philosophy and that he was a philosophical writer. Whilst I stand by the former view, up to a point, I have come to reconceive the latter and would now maintain that Pater is in fact a *post-philosophical* writer. As we shall see, many of Pater's focal concerns do indeed stem from philosophical discourse; but he is more radical than I had initially supposed. His early student reading in the dominant traditions of modern Western philosophy, empiricism and transcendental Idealism directs the questions the mature Pater asks about the nature of the personal self and the relationship between self and world. However, he finds himself in the position of revising those systems of thought in the light of the very latest challenges and issues that confronted the individual in his day. He feels compelled to abandon impersonal forms of systematised philosophical discourse and seek a new idiom in which to discuss what it means to be human in the late nineteenth century: an idiom with space within it for perspectival and temporal relativism, since it understands that things can only be known under conditions – meaning there is no longer any place for abstract generalisations, metaphysical knowledge, and the systematisation of experience. Specifically, I see Paterian individualism as integral to the immediate post-Darwinian, pre-decadent world: caught in the transition between high-Victorianism and early modernism, amidst the liberal debates and university reforms that followed Mill's *On Liberty* (1859) and Arnold's vision, in *Culture and Anarchy* (1869), that culture might fit the space where religion once was; all this in the shadow of Darwinism, and as the aesthetic of 'art for art's sake' began to shape the contemporary arts in England. Here, Pater seeks to find a solution at the vanishing point of 'literature' and 'philosophy', in the dynamics between the individual and art.

If Pater is sometimes misconceived, one reason is a neglect of the full scope of his oeuvre. The present study is one of very few to be based on a detailed study of Pater's incomplete and unpublished manuscripts. Lodged in the Houghton Library at Harvard University, these key if fragmentary works show a little of Pater's unguarded face. Their often unpunctuated sentences, scribbled out lines, ellipses, and careful notation of synonyms not only give an insight into his composition methods, but (at least as importantly) suggest half-finished ideas which only appear in his published writings in more refined and reserved hints. In part, Pater's inability to complete these works was due to his ongoing struggle to write.[11] Gosse recalls,

> I have known writers of every degree, but never one to whom the act of composition was such a travail and an agony as it was to Pater . . . In his earlier years the labour of lifting the sentences was so terrific that any one with less fortitude would have entirely abandoned the effort. (262)

As uncensored reflections, the manuscripts are singularly useful in understanding the evolution of Pater's philosophical thought. It is no coincidence that these ambitious essays are Pater's most ostensibly speculative, philosophical works. Unfinished and abandoned by him, they illustrate a creative and intellectual failure: he raises questions which ultimately he was unable to adequately resolve. Importantly too, the manuscripts include some of his most philosophical writings: 'The History of Philosophy' (c. 1880[12]), for example, is his attempt to emulate the histories of philosophy which he had read in his student days, and also probably drew on notes from undergraduate lectures he delivered in the 1870s. 'The Aesthetic Life' (c. 1893) is his aborted attempt to fuse aesthetics with ethics and thus answer widespread and cutting criticism of *The Renaissance*.[13] Meanwhile, Pater's troubled relationship with Christianity is illuminated by his manuscript on 'Art and Religion' (c. 1886–8).[14]

Like the fluctuating self of which he writes in his Conclusion to *The Renaissance*, Pater's thought is 'constantly re-forming itself on the stream' (R 151); the radical young 'W. H. Pater' who wrote 'Poems by William Morris' in 1868 is not 'that dear old pussycat Walter Pater' who wrote *Plato and Platonism* in 1893 (Toynbee 21). The nature of Pater's shifting ideas and self-presentation has been critically divisive. Richmond Crinkley and Michael Levy conceive a distinct schism between Pater's work up to the early 1880s and the phase that began with *Marius the Epicurean* (1885) (1970: 137; 1985: 9ff). Much other criticism implicitly assumes this idea, tending relatedly to concentrate on *The Renaissance* by which Pater's name was (ambivalently) made. In contrast to that dichotomous schema, William Shuter proposes that Paterian thought is 'an incessant reshuffling': he revises and refines and redefines his ideas again and again (1997: 123ff). I agree with Shuter, and it is in this spirit that *Walter Pater: Individualism and Aesthetic Philosophy* approaches Pater's writings. His unceasing dialogue with himself cuts across any notion of a firm distinction between 'early' and 'late' Pater. A further merit is to broaden the critical focus to include what are often seen as the peripheries of his oeuvre; such as the posthumously published *Greek Studies* (1895) and *Miscellaneous Studies* (1895) and his last published book *Plato and Platonism* (1893), acclaimed by critics at the time but largely overlooked since. In a field where the vast majority of critical pieces on Pater are short journal articles or book chapters, the understandable impulse is to focus on the one book of Pater's that is widely read and the impact of which was definitive. Yet, like one of Pater's consummate aesthetic moments, *The Renaissance* is an intense sensation which quickly passes. It is, to be sure, a central point of reference:

Pater and those he influenced were in constant dialogue with the concept of the individual, the aesthetics and the ethics expressed there. But his lesser known or neglected subsequent works are no less vital, not least because they elucidate and rewrite the polemical and often compressed and allusive comments of *The Renaissance*.

Structure

The following chapters seek to track Pater's late-Romantic individual from the inside out: from the formation of self in Chapter 2 to ethical being in (or rather absence from) the social world in Chapter 9.

Chapter 2, 'Empiricism and the Imperilled Self', discusses how Pater comes to terms with the relationship between self and world set out by David Hume's *Treatise of Human Nature* (1739–40) and John Locke's *An Essay Concerning Human Understanding* (1690). Taking up the critical consensus that Pater was some sort of empiricist, it seeks to look at his most significant engagements with empiricist philosophy. It traces how Pater presents these works of empirical philosophy and their late nineteenth-century manifestations in psychology and natural science, in the Conclusion to *The Renaissance*, 'The History of Philosophy' (c.1880) and 'The Child in the House' (1878). In considering these works I argue that Pater was captivated by empiricism but ultimately disaffected by its dissolution of the individual into a posteriori sensations strung together on the continuous consciousness. In other words, I suggest that Pater was not at heart an empiricist at all.

Chapter 3, 'Subjectivity and Imagination: from Hume to Kant via Berkeley', argues that subjectivity answers Pater's call for 'unity with ourselves' (R 146). Subjectivity and creativity become the immutable, distinguishing elements of the Paterian individual. The problem is of how exactly subjectivity and creativity might be defined. This chapter considers how Pater explores the Lockean or Humean idea of the individual as a passive receptacle for experiences, the individual, contrariwise, as the Berkeleyan solipsistic creator of experiences, and the individual as a Kantian participator in the creation of experiences.

Chapter 4, 'Metaphysics: Pater's Failed Attempt at Atheism', revises the oft-perpetuated view that Pater rejected God and metaphysics in his early writings, arguing that he is never able to commit himself to the materialist view he entertains in Conclusion to *The Renaissance*. It focuses on how Pater uses light as a metaphor in 'Diaphaneitè' (1864) and 'Winckelmann' (1867, 1873) to represent the animating and individuating quality in each individual. It suggests that whilst light begins as a symbol of Hellenistic intellect, Pater is unable to give up the idea of a metaphysical quality animating the individual and, in consequence, the metaphor of light becomes irreducibly ambiguous. This chapter traces Pater's ostensible return to the Church in the latter part of his life and suggests that though he violently rejects Hellenistic light in 'Apollo in Picardy', he is never fully reconciled to faith or to its implications for his individualism.

Chapter 5, 'Sense and Sensuality: Caught between Venus and Dionysus', argues that the vexed issue of sensuality marks Pater's departure from the ideas of established philosophical discourse: he cannot accept Hume's presentation of sensual experience as simply a means to convey information about the world. Pater's exploration of sensuality is, rather, an attempt to come to terms with the emotional dimensions of sensuality, particularly touch. Furthermore, this section suggests that Paterian sensuality is more complicated than we might at first think, and considers its destructive potential.

Chapter 6, 'Pater's Copernican Revolution: the Desiring, Dying Body' develops this focus on sensuality in order to argue that Pater recentres his individualism on the physical experience of the body. In Pater's works a sense of one's self is necessarily embodied: 'I' is inextricably linked to its experience of touching, physical exertion, and the pains of growing old and dying. As it considers Pater's presentation of the body, this chapter develops and challenges the thought-provoking work on the desiring Paterian body by Jacques Kalip, Stefano Evangelista, and others, arguing that the it is not the young, desired, perfect male body that really stands at the centre of Paterian individualism, but the flawed, restrained, fragile body of the aesthetic spectator.

Chapter 7, 'Evolution and the "Species": the Individual in Deep Time', argues that deep time is the most vivid challenge posed to the flawed and fragile human subject in Pater's writings. It explores Pater's knowledge of, and belief in, Darwinian science, Spencer's social Darwinism, and Thompson's theory of entropy. It suggests though that Pater's attitude toward Darwinism is complex and inconsistent. He is able to accept Darwin's theory of evolution in the abstract, though it must be on his own aestheticist terms, but he is unable to accept the idea that the individual is one of a 'species'.

Chapter 8, 'The Moment and the Aesthetic Imagination', argues that the much discussed Paterian 'moment' must by understood as response to Pater's ultimate inability to reconcile himself to Darwinian idea of the individual as merely one of a species in deep time. It suggests that whilst he seems to accept evolutionary theory, the 'moment' draws on Romantic visions of the epiphanic or aleatory moment in order to recover the significance of personal experience. Moreover, though the Paterian moment has long been discussed as a single type, there are at least two modes of Paterian moment which I define here as the 'sensual moment' and the 'aesthetic moment'.

Chapter 9, 'Ethics, Society and the Aesthetic Individual', discusses how Pater attempts to develop an ethics from his conception of the individual. More precisely it addresses the two-fold ethical problem created by Pater's vision of a life lived for the 'moment': how can one live only for beauty whilst leading a moral life and how might the individualist expand his sympathies to society in general. This problem vexed Pater for years and become ever-more pressing in his last decade when he tried to reconcile ethics and aesthetics in *Marius the Epicurean* (1885) and 'The Aesthetic Life' (c. 1893). Critics including Regenia Gagnier, in 'The Law of Progress and the Ironies of Individualism in the Nineteenth Century' (2000b), and Matthew Potolsky, in 'Literary Communism: Pater and the Politics of Community', believe that he succeeded in so doing. I do not. This chapter suggests that whilst Pater led a quiet and kind life himself, he is ultimately unable to conceive of how the beautiful sensation of human sympathy might translate into ethical actions.

In one sense, these chapters are conceived as a series of studies in contradictoriness or disunity in Pater's ideas. He is in constant battle with the 'dramatic contrasts' (R 148) that define the individual, including sensual pleasure and pernicious craving for sensuality, the body beautiful and its inevitable decay, continuous time and the discrete moment. These are not only just his contradictions; they are the contradictions of his culture and his peers as the lived life of the modern individual comes into conflict with Faith and Romanticism. Yet at the same time these chapters are also a series of enquiries into the unifying principles that endeavour to transcend such contrasts. Pater suggests that philosophy is to offer 'unity in variety, to discover *cosmos* – an order that shall satisfy one's reasonable soul – below and within apparent chaos' (PP 35). He looks to assuage the chaos of being through desire, metaphysics, continuity of consciousness, ethical action, aesthetic creativity, and subjective experience. Just like his own self, such unity and order though proves 'elusive inscrutable mistakable'.

Notes

1. This is perhaps an indication that Pater read *The World as Will and Idea* (*Die Welt als Wille und Vorstellung*; 1819) by Arthur Schopenhauer which characterises a world of post-Kantian noumena and phenomena, in which

the former – the Will – is constantly striving, and at odds with itself. Within this vision, the metaphysical 'Will' (capitalised) manifests itself into the 'will' of the individual. Schopenhauer was the first philosopher to take music seriously, as well as being a very literary writer who was taken up by Thomas Hardy and George Gissing following the first translation of *The World as Will and Idea* in 1883, it would be surprising if Pater had not read Schopenhauer. I am aware though of no substantial evidence that he did.

2. On 7 September 1894 James wrote to Arthur Symons to decline his invitation to contribute to a volume in memory of Pater because he felt unable to adopt the appropriate tone for this eulogy: 'uttered in the real spirit of criticism, there might be a single line that wd. be a false note in a collection of the kind you mention – & yet that line might be the very one to which one wd. hold most' (1999: 433–4, n. 1).

3. For further discussion of late nineteenth-century Romanticism see Catherine Maxwell's *Second Sight: The Visionary Imagination in Late Victorian Literature* (2008), Kenneth Daley's *The Rescue of Romanticism: Walter Pater and John Ruskin* (2001), and *The Last Romantics* by Graham Hough (1947).

4. Patrick Bridgwater outlines the striking personal and intellectual parallels between Pater and Nietzsche, suggesting that 'It was because some of [Nietzsche's] areas of concern were, or sounded, familiar to English readers from writers such as Pater and Wilde, that Nietzsche found such ready acceptance in advanced intellectual circles at the turn of the century' (1999: 240–1). Yet tantalisingly, there is no evidence one way or the other as to whether Pater actually read Nietzsche or knew of his work.

5. Though the novel was published under her pen name 'Vernon Lee', Pater always wrote to 'Violet Paget'. *Euphorion* was dedicated to Pater: 'In appreciation of that which, in expounding the beautiful things of the past, he has added to the beautiful things of the present.'

6. Evidence of Pater's ability to read German comes from several sources. Billie Andrew Inman suggests that in the long vacation of 1860 'Pater was probably learning to read German and possibly reading Goethe' (1981a: 9). Ingram Bywater recalls that Pater knew enough German to read Hegel's *Phenomenology of Spirit* (1807; *Phänomenologie des Geistes*) in the Long Vacation of 1862 (Bywater 1917: 79). Pater's library borrowings during his undergraduate years include many philosophical works in German (Inman 1981a: 9ff.). This seems to disprove Gosse's assertion that 'He was no linguist, and French was the only language in which he could even make his wants understood. Although so much in Germany in his youth, he could speak no German' (256). One possible way to reconcile these contrary assertions is that Pater's shyness might have prevented him from *speaking* languages with which he was more than competent on paper.

7. He gestures toward this with his perennial assertions and questions about the nature of philosophy. For example, see *The Renaissance* (148; 152; 153), *Marius the Epicurean* (II, 220) and *Plato and Platonism* (21).

8. 'Giordano Bruno' was originally intended to be part of Pater's abandoned novel *Gaston de Latour* (1888–9). The above citation refers to Gerald Monsman's revised edition of the latter text.

9. In a comparable though unrelated passage, Friedrich Nietzsche wrote in 1889 that 'our universities, *despite* themselves, are really greenhouses for this sort of stunting of spiritual instincts' (1997b, 45; Nietzsche's italics).

10. I have written about the turn toward interdisciplinary criticism of Pater at greater length in 'Recent Scholarship on Walter Pater: "Antithetical Scholar of Understanding's End"'(2008). Since then, the works noted above have further expanded and enriched Pater studies for a new era of literary criticism which has fully assimilated the insights offered by – for example – queer theory, and is thus able to develop a more wide-ranging interdisciplinary critique.

11. Although extensive consideration of style falls beyond the scope of this enquiry, it should be noted that these manuscripts could make a significant contribution to our understanding of Pater's techniques of composition. Recently, Lesley Higgins has discussed 'The Aesthetic Life' in her article 'Walter Pater: Painting in the Nineteenth Century,' and in his revised edition of *Gaston de Latour* (1888; 1995), Gerald Monsman uses Pater's manuscript notes to piece together this controversial, revised, ultimately unfinished work. Given that Pater's manuscripts have never been available in print, where necessary these are quoted at some length here with the aim of providing greater context.

12. Billie Andrew Inman suggests 1880 as the most likely date: 'Since *Cardinal Newman* is referred to in ['The History of Philosophy'], it must have been written after 1879, but it does not seem to have been written much later' (1981a: xl).

13. For examples see Billie Andrew Inman's quotation and explanation of William Wolfe Capes's November 1873 sermon against Paterian ethics (1981a: 327–9) and John Wordsworth's infamous letter of rebuke to Pater, his former tutor and colleague at Brasenose (Seiler 1980: 61–3).

14. Drawing on the criticism of Lawrence Evans (ed. *Letters of Walter Pater*) William Shuter gives a convincing account of the likely dates for 'Art and Religion':

> The first page contains a criticism of Amiel, which Pater would not have ventured before 1886. On 23 December 1885, Pater wrote to Mary Ward that he was still reading her translation of Amiel's Journal and still forming his judgment of Amiel's religious position [L 64]. The emphasis on the religious significance of Montaigne's skepticism recalls a similar stress in chapters 4 and 5 of *Gaston de Latour* first published in 1888. I would therefore assign 'Art and Religion' to the period 1886–1888. (Shuter 1997: 131 n. 9)

Chapter 2

Empiricism and the Imperilled Self

If sensation is knowledge, being is change. Things are not but become.
Lewis Campbell's note from his edition of *The Theaetetus of Plato*
(36 n.)[1]

February 1861 found Walter Pater bent over a volume of Hume's *Philosophical Works,* making notes on little squares of paper in the gloom of his college library. He was a third year undergraduate, and Hume was part of a self-directed programme of reading that ranged far beyond the requirements of his degree in Literae Humaniores. His contemporary and friend Ingram Bywater recalled that Pater 'devoured all the serious literature of the period: Carlyle, Ruskin, Browning, J. S. Mill, and also our older writers, Berkeley and Hume' (1917: 79). Those 'older writers' of philosophy feature particularly prominently in Pater's library records inspired in part by his young tutor, the polymath, William Wolfe Capes. This was a time of increasing introspection and self-questioning in Oxford philosophy, as the natural sciences began to encroach on the domain of the moral sciences. A generation later, in December 1897, Bertrand Russell would declare that 'Philosophy, by the slow victories of its own offspring, has been forced to forgo, one by one, its high pretensions. Intellectual difficulties, for the most part, have been acquired by Science' (1999: 80). This realisation was just beginning to dawn in the early 1860s, as an iconoclast like Pater was well aware.

Alongside transcendental Idealism, empirical philosophy was a significant part of Pater's early reading. The books he borrowed as an undergraduate from The Queen's College Library included Hobbes' *Leviathan,*[2] Hume's *Philosophical Works*, and the *Works* of George Berkeley, Francis Bacon and John Locke.[3] These were fundamental in forming Pater's ideas on the individual. Throughout his career, he implicitly and explicitly engages with the idea that the individual is, as Hume believed, just 'a bundle or collection of different perceptions'

(1964: I. iv, 239). Yet if Pater's concern with the relation between the individual and the world begins with empiricism, he is a reluctant empiricist at best. Even in the 1860s and 1870s, when for the educated classes in Britain empiricism seemed to pattern the world, Pater is unnerved by the implications of sceptical empiricism for a sense of coherent self-identity. For others, 'the metaphysical discussions that raged during the enlightenment were resolved, for the time being at least, into an empirical consensus' (Russell 2005: 654); but Pater is never this complacent. He grapples with empiricist conceptions of self-formation, admiring their modest assertion of the authority of the senses, yet never fully satisfied with the thoroughgoing materialism with which Hume takes empiricism to its logical conclusion.

Peter Garratt describes Hume's presence in the nineteenth century as that of a ghost, prone 'to a deep ambivalence, to an existence neither fully acknowledged not wholly assimilated' (2010: 43). The same might be said of empiricism more broadly: it haunts some of the nineteenth century's most significant intellectual developments: associationism, positivism, the inductive method in science, common sense psychology, and, via Kant, transcendental Idealism. As British philosophy focused on the development of empirical principles to practical ends and to answer social questions, the sceptical questions posed by empiricism's founding thinkers lingered on, unanswered. As Pater commented, Berkeley's 'main point has never really been answered'; his idealism 'has still no philosophical antidote' (HP 22).[4] Locke was far from popular in nineteenth-century intellectual circles: derided as 'a sensualist, a materialist, a sceptic, an atheist, and a utilitarian', with his reputation 'more often a matter of opinion than of study and knowledge' (Aarsleff 1971: 392; 395).

Pater's own interest in early empiricism is rooted in his ongoing concern with how the individual can have knowledge of the world. His conception of the individual evolves out of the empirical assertion, presented by Locke and reiterated by Hume, that the individual, is a 'white paper, void of all characters' onto which are written the multifarious, ephemeral sensations of the world (Locke II. i §2, 109); 'The mind is a kind of theatre, where several perceptions successively make their appearance; pass, repass, glide away, and mingle in an infinite variety of postures and situations' (Hume I. iv, 239–40). This idea of personal identity as a posteriori, therefore without Original Sin, and formed from the sensations of our experience in the world, fulfils Pater's excited desire for self-renewal and new sensation: for it presents a world in which experience comprises new sensation after new sensation, given to a blank and unsullied self. Indeed, F. C. McGrath has suggested that

'Pater's career can be seen as a lifelong attempt to provide through an emphasis on the senses a corrective to the excessive rationalism that dominated Western culture from medieval Christianity through the eighteenth century' (1986: 55). I would not put it quite so strongly; as the next chapter illustrates, Pater was captivated by the rationalist theories of transcendental Idealism, and though he is sceptical about the veracity of rationalist enquiry his scepticism is not a rejection of metaphysics. But it is true to a degree that he sought 'a corrective' to rationalist excesses, and here empiricism offers him an alternative model for philosophical thought, rooted in the senses. At the same time Pater's writings suggest an unquellable anxiety regarding the empirical foundations of self-identity. His anxiety about empiricism is catalysed by his nagging Romantic vision of the individual. In his unpublished, incomplete essay, 'The Aesthetic Life' (c. 1893), he writes: 'the empirical philosophy of our day, carrying us so far into space and time seemingly infinite has, in inverse proportion, narrowed the spiritual, the imaginative horizon' (AL 2). In this brief characterisation 'the empirical philosophy of our day' seems to indicate a broad conception of empiricism, including the scientific advances that grew out of an empirical ethos and methodologies. Perhaps he also has in mind Matthew Arnold's not uncritical view that 'The bent of our time is towards science, towards knowing things as they are' (1867a: 16).

Like Hume and those others who, like himself, were influenced by empiricist philosophy in the nineteenth century – George Eliot, John Ruskin, George Henry Lewes, and Herbert Spencer amongst them – Pater believed that 'the proper starting point for all inquiry had to be the analysis of consciousness' (Garratt 2010: 43). Yet he differs from most of his contemporaries in going back to Hume's principles, for he believed Hume not to be a ghost at all but a corporeal force. Pater follows Thomas Reid's strongest objection to Hume, that he '"converted all qualities of matter into sensations," committing an error found in virtually all modern philosophies of mind, which after Descartes, saw consciousness as a series of simple ideas' (Garratt 2010: 48–9). If Hume 'had initiated a crisis of rational knowledge in *A Treatise of Human Nature* (1739–40) that the nineteenth century still regarded as unanswerable' (Garratt 2010: 43), few writers in his day grappled as seriously with the fundamental principles of Hume's epistemology as Pater. However, it is questionable how far Pater wanted to subscribe to empiricism. Whilst he engages with the tenets of empirical works such as Hume's *Treatise*, Locke's *Essay Concerning Human Understanding* (1690), and George Berkeley's *Of the Principles of Human Knowledge* (1710) and *An Essay Towards a New Theory of Vision* (1709), he simply cannot give himself up to an empiricist conception of identity.

Hume's Empiricism in *The Renaissance*

Hume's empiricism both defines and unsettles Pater's conception of the individual. Pater often avoided, or felt unable to write directly on his most compelling influences[5] and mentions Hume by name in his published works but a few times. In the Conclusion to *The Renaissance* (1868, 1873), though, he vividly evokes the potentially devastating implications of Humean empiricism for the conception of an individuated self. The Conclusion may be divided into three parts: the first deals with contemporary science, the second with sceptical philosophy, and the third sets out Pater's constructive thesis.[6] The negative thesis of Hume's *Treatise* and his legacy in the natural sciences feature prominently in the first and second of these parts, as Pater attempts to envisage the emotional, as well as intellectual, implications of Hume's 'characteristic modern scepticism' (HP 4).

To some extent Hume's assertion that reality is shifting and ephemeral and his rejection of metaphysics fulfil Pater's ideal of philosophy, stated pages earlier in his essay on 'Winckelmann' (1867, 1873): 'Philosophy serves culture, not by the fancied gift of absolute or transcendental knowledge, but by suggesting questions which help one to detect the passion, and strangeness, and dramatic contrasts of life' (R 148). It is this sensitivity to the fluctuating world, following the rejection of immutable metaphysical truths, that Pater is most drawn to in empiricism. In 'Coleridge' (1866, 1889), identifying empiricism with 'modern thought' per se (A 66), he writes,

> The philosophical conception of the relative has been developed in modern times through the influence of the sciences of observation. Those sciences reveal types of life evanescing into each other by inexpressible refinements of change ... It is the truth of these relations that experience gives us, not the truth of eternal outlines ascertained once and for all, but a world of fine gradations and subtly linked conditions, shifting intricately as we ourselves change ... (A 67–8)

This thesis follows empiricism and empirical science in rejecting a priori knowledge and asserting that all personal knowledge, feelings, and the individual's sense of self-identity are drawn from a posteriori experience in the world (1964 Introduction: 3–8). Pater is captivated by the idea that ephemeral sensations are the roots of all knowledge, and its consequence that 'knowledge' and self-identity are unstable and shifting.

Thus he opens his Conclusion to *The Renaissance* in sympathy with a Humean and scientific rejection of immutable truths: 'To regard all things and principles of things as inconsistent modes of fashions has more and more become the tendency of modern thought' (R 150). Hume's empiricism offers Pater a welcome theoretical corollary to contemporary scientific definitions of the physical world. Still, Pater distances himself from both Hume and science here with his use of the impersonal tense. Of course, as critics including George Levine (2000: 7ff) and Billie Andrew Inman (1981b: 12ff) have shown, Pater was greatly interested in science. Giving *Macmillan's Magazine* as an example, which published all of Pater's books and many of his later articles, Gowan Dawson notes that Pater would have been very much aware of scientific advances: the scientists Balfour Stewart, Alexander Bain, William Kingdon Clifford, Thomas Henry Huxley, and John Tyndall all published articles there, alongside Pater, in the 1860s and 1870s (2005: 40). It is possible to make the stronger claim that Pater never even doubted the veracity of modern science.[7] His various engagements with Darwinian evolution and William Thomson's Second Law of Thermodynamics, which will be discussed in Chapter 7, illustrate his belief and interest in scientific ideas. What is intriguing and often forgotten though is the way in which the Conclusion frames itself as an illustration of 'the tendency of modern thought'. That one sentence puts a barrier up between Pater's heartfelt beliefs and the veracity of empiricism and the natural sciences.

As the Conclusion continues, the narrative's critical distance collapses. It becomes immersed in the 'inconsistent' and ephemeral world it describes, with Pater's own prose becoming the 'perpetual motion' of the physical world; its foci and fleeting images rapidly changing (R 150):

> Our physical life is a perpetual motion of them – the passage of blood, the waste and repairing of the lenses of the eye, the modification of the tissues of the brain under every ray of light and sound – processes which science reduces to simpler and more elementary forces. Like the elements of which we are composed, the action of these forces extends beyond us: it rust iron and ripens corn. (R 150)

The kaleidoscope of relativity is insistent here. It utterly defines the individual and existence in the world, so that the reader loses the rather quaint sense that relativity is an aesthetic principle to take up or discard at will. At first Pater's tone is one of wilful enthusiasm for the ephemeral world in its infinite variety:

> Let us begin with that which is without – our physical life. Fix upon it in one of its more exquisite intervals, the moment, for instance, of delicious recoil

from the flood of water in summer heat. What is the whole physical life in that moment but a combination of natural elements to which science gives their names? (R 150)

There is no order, only the disorder of fluctuating reality, in which one has no sooner apprehended something than it has changed forever. These images come to a climax with the evocation of the ephemeral nature of the individual: 'birth and gesture and death and the springing of violets from the grave are but a few out of ten thousand resultant combinations' (R 150).

Humean empiricism and science emerges as an ambivalent position: on one hand, encouraging acute attention to the minutiae of the seen world as it constantly changes and, on the other, undermining the fabric of personal identity so that the individual might become a mere 'bundle or collection of different perceptions' (1964: I. iv, 239). As the narrative focus of the Conclusion shifts from external fluctuation to 'the inward world of thought and feeling' (R 151) it becomes clear that the most vexing question that Pater has inherited from Hume is: if I cannot depend on continuous consciousness to give coherence to my empirical impressions then 'what am *I*?' If the individual has knowledge only of what he observes, then it is not possible to have knowledge of one's self because, as Hume explains:

> I never can catch *myself* at any time without a perception, and never can observe anything but the perception. When my perceptions are removed for any time, as by sound sleep, so long I am insensible of myself, and may truly be said not to exist. (1964: I. iv, 239)

Hume contends that if we accept Locke's a posteriori self, then it follows logically that 'there is in truth no such demonstrable unity as a "person", merely *pointilliste* impressions of continuity; dots on a page which we might be disposed to join up' (Porter 330). Since this is the case, 'Personal identity [is] thus necessarily contingent and wreathed in doubt' (Porter: 330). Hume describes the individual as

> nothing but a bundle or collection of different perceptions, which succeed each other with inconceivable rapidity, and are in a perpetual flux and move- ment. Our eyes cannot turn in their sockets without varying our perceptions. Our thought is still more variable than our sight; and all our other senses and faculties contribute to this change; nor is there any single power of the soul, which remains unalterably the same, perhaps for one moment. The mind is a kind of theatre, where several perceptions successively make their appear- ance; pass, re-pass, glide away, and mingle in an infinite variety of postures and situations. (1964: I. iv, 239–40)

Thoroughgoing empiricism, Hume believes, cannot assume causality – that concept which binds the whole of the known world together – to be an eternal, indubitable link between the impressions of the individuated self. Of course, if all knowledge is gained by observation of the world, necessary causality is an inductive principle which has no place. Hume argues that although we habitually connect discrete ideas via causal principles, such a construct may at any time be defied by reality (1964: I. iii, 76ff). Thus the phenomena of the world have no necessary causal relation to each other; they are not unified by any metaphysical essence and only their appearance in sequence makes us imagine causal necessity.

Once the self is understood to be but a succession of discrete and ephemeral data, it becomes a very precarious 'thing' indeed. Pater is acutely aware that the possibility of any stable individual identity is left wreathed in doubt. The question of what 'I' is in an empiricist conception of being, and Hume's answer to this, are the basis of the Conclusion as it turns to focus on the individual. The exhilarated pace that defined the opening of the Conclusion continues unabated, conveying a sense of excitement and anticipation as it insists: 'This at least of flame-like our life has, that it is but the fusion, renewed from moment to moment, of forces parting sooner or later on their ways' (R 150). The flame, one of Pater's recurrent tropes, here symbolises Hume's idea that self is but a temporary concurrence of forces; it recalls Heraclitus' view that the individual is like fire; changing constantly but identifiable as the same substance until it burns away (Heraclitus 2003: 15).

The flame at first conjures the metaphorical link between fire and creativity that describes the ideal conditions in which artists 'catch light and heat from each other's thoughts' in Pater's Preface to *The Renaissance* (xxxiii). Yet the flame in the Conclusion also threatens to consume and destroy the individual, and it is this destructive potential that is foregrounded as Pater intensifies his focus on the individual: 'Or if we begin with the inward world of thought and feeling, the whirlpool is still more rapid, the flame more eager and devouring' (R 151). Pater's narrative frantically anticipates William James' famous metaphor, figuring consciousness as 'the race in the mid-stream' and a 'whirlpool [. . .] still more rapid' or a 'drift' (R 151). Alluding to Hume's critique of causality, he imagines the individual without the continuity given by causal links: 'the cohesive force [of selfhood] seems suspended like some trick of magic' (R 151). The accumulation of perceptions can no longer be taken for granted as the building blocks for self-identity:

> . . . colour, odour, texture – in the mind of the observer. And if we continue to dwell in thought on this world, not of objects in the solidity with which

language invests them, but of impressions, unstable, flickering, inconsistent, which burn and are extinguished with our consciousness of them . . . (R 151)

The fragmentation of Pater's narrative illustrates Hume's point that there are no a priori substances to give coherence to the random sense data encountered by the individual in the world (1964: I. iv, 239). Pater lacks Hume's rational narrative voice in presenting this state. Confronted by this 'bundle or collection of different perceptions' his narrative stutters, almost unable to move beyond mere apprehension of the deluge of phenomena to any constructive thesis. The narrative pace and the culmination of images, which had been exhilarating as it evoked the external physical world, becomes terrifying as it evokes the internal self as a random collection of ephemeral impressions. It is the spectre of the self as a Humean 'bundle' that makes the creation of unity one of Pater's most consistent concerns. From his early identification of 'the problem of unity with ourselves' to his late assertion of 'the unity of the thing with itself' (R 146; MS 51), he is perennially attempting to assuage Hume's negative thesis that 'I' is but a 'bundle or collection' of phenomena.

Yet unity here proves elusive. As the list of impressions in the Conclusion to *The Renaissance* gathers pace, the narrative almost seems to have lost control, buried beneath a deluge of discrete impression after discrete impression, from which one can no longer construct a coherent sense of self. The phenomena of the world that seemed at first to offer exhilarating sensations are now figured as a physical threat as Pater describes how 'experience seems to bury us . . . pressing upon us with a sharp and importunate reality, calling us out of ourselves in a thousand forms of action' (R 151). The effect is to overwhelm and imperil the individual with the very phenomena that had, in Hume's *Treatise*, made individuality possible. The climax is Pater's summation of the individual under these conditions:

> To such a tremulous wisp constantly re-forming itself on the stream, to a single sharp impression, with a sense in it, a relic more or less fleeting, of such moments gone by, what is real in our lives fines itself down. (R 151)

Echoing Hume's view that self-identity is founded only on perceptions which 'successively make their appearance; pass, re-pass, glide away, and mingle in an infinite variety of postures and situations', Pater characterises an unstable identity in which even memory ('a relic') is ephemeral and the space between objectivity and subjectivity is no longer clear.

Looking at Pater's Conclusion to *The Renaissance*, one can understand why Angela Leighton would conclude that 'Pater's own accounts of the self explicitly reject notions of autonomy or essential value' (2002: 18). The Conclusion embodies the heightened, lived reality of Hume's 'bundle' of self so vividly that it takes over his narrative. Still, the way in which Pater entertains the Humean, scientific self is essential to grasping its precise significance in his aesthetics. The negative imagery and loss of narrative control, and the framing of these visions as 'the tendency of modern thought' in the Conclusion suggest that Pater could not, ultimately, come to terms with Hume's vision of the individual.

Hume and Scepticism in 'The History of Philosophy'

In striking contrast to the Conclusion of *The Renaissance*, Pater's unpublished manuscript on 'The History of Philosophy' (c.1880) is a reasoned contextual discussion of Humean scepticism. What exactly Pater had in mind when he wrote this is uncertain: perhaps it was conceived as a lecture but possibly also as a larger essay on the history of philosophy. He had read several German histories of philosophy as an undergraduate[8] and readily accepted that philosophy should be understood historically. His view of the history of philosophy is typically idiosyncratic, with scepticism at its centre: 'It is one of the functions of the historian of philosophy to note and estimate the successive contributions to this scepticism, some of the chief of which may occur to the general reader . . .' (HP 5). Whatever his broader scheme for the piece though, this manuscript effectively shows how Pater quells the threat that empiricism had posed to the individual in *The Renaissance*.

Pater's discussion gives a history of sceptical thought, from Heraclitus and Zeno through to Hume, Berkeley and Kant, via Descartes. As it does so it sets up a schism between a '"golden age"' in which people were unconscious of metaphysical questions and modern philosophy which is dominated by speculative philosophy (HP 1):

> Could they have anticipated the history of thought as it had really been, few perhaps would have wished to change for themselves or others, that unconscious state, so natural, so harmonious with itself, and it must be added so simple in its faith, for the endless pathway of that conscious speculation, of which, whatever sense it may give one of mental superiority and a sort of intellectual high-breeding, the results have been in the main negative. (HP 2)[9]

Having established this distinction between ancient and modern thought, Pater quickly asserts the inevitability of speculative philosophy:

... it is however certain that the instinctive curiosity in which Plato sees an enthusiasm, a kind of divine prompting, would have impelled a certain number of minds here or there, the adventurers of the inward world, to pass the ↑f.m.m. [blank], in speculations as to what might lie, so to speak, on the other side of them. (HP 2)

In Pater's view, scepticism is also defined by the schism between ancient and modern. As one would expect, he argues for the necessity of scepticism:

And in this adventurous quest [for understanding], this way of discipline, in which the mind gains at least a kind of masterful knowledge of its own bearings and capacities, the first step is always an act of scepticism. For philosophy begins only when, under one of many possible guides [. . .] we enter into a sort of secondary consciousness, in which the common sense of the every-day becomes the subject of a dispassionate criticism. (HP 3)

Having sketched Zeno's ancient scepticism, Pater introduces Hume as the quintessential modern contrast: 'Conversely, in the characteristic modern scepticism, as typified by Hume, by his peculiar theory of causation, [10] the appeal lies from the notions of the understanding to the corrective authority of the experience of the senses' (HP 4). He reiterates the importance of Hume in the history of sceptical philosophy: 'the corrective experience of the senses, as exemplified most clearly ↑by in Hume' (HP 5).

By historicising Humean scepticism, 'The History of Philosophy' attempts to pacify its power to vanquish the individual. To a large extent this works. Pater's evocation of Hume is measured and explanatory. It is an academic assessment which shies from the imaginative engagement with Humean ideas that carries the Conclusion from the realms of the academy and into a distopian vision. Hume's negative thesis remains uppermost in Pater's conception of his philosophy. However, Pater focuses away from the effects on the individual and instead on the benefits to epistemology, by remarking how Hume shows 'the supposed inherent judgements of the understanding' to be false, leading men towards 'the corrective authority of the experience of the senses' (HP 4). He reiterates this sentiment in his later manuscript, 'The Aesthetic Life':

In so confused a world, so confused as to the ↑origin final final issue ↑tendency of things, it might well seem to be ↑the part of reason, ↑and the last word of sincere theory about them, to hold to ↑by that concerning which doubt has standing no ground to ↑place, the ↑world domain of sense. (AL 6)

Kant writes that Hume's scepticism awakened him from his 'dogmatic slumber' (2004: 2). Perhaps the same might be said of Hume's effect on

Pater, as it is evoked in 'The History of Philosophy'. Humean scepticism clears away all assumptions about innate knowledge and becomes integral to 'the extension of the positive knowledge of experience' that Pater sees in empiricism (HP 13) – even though the form of understanding he pursues will ultimately lead him away from the tenets of empiricism.

'The History of Philosophy' shows the limitations of Pater's sympathy with Humean empiricism and science:

> This growth of physical science has indeed involved an ever-narrowing limitation of its aim, to what is relative, temporal, apparent only, as it speaks with more and more detail and fulness of the circumstances of our visible life, less and less of anything really ranging beyond it; with such a wide scope of knowledge, yet never a step beyond the ↑f.m.m [blank] that. (HP 7)

Pater hints here at his impatience with the self-imposed material limitations of empiricism and science. He wistfully expands this further on the following page:

> To cool intellectual expectation, to repress the instinctive ambition of the mind towards a knowledge transcending its merely temporal experience, to limit its curiosity to the provable or the merely practical aim has become the conscious aim of enquiry, which under the name of philosophy seemed to Plato to promise nothing less than a likeness to God. (HP 8)

Empiricism is invigorating and renewing, giving the individual the vital energy to create art. However, it is also terrifying, with its destruction of all certainty, even the certainty of one's own mind. Pater cannot live for long with such uncertainty. He must look beyond Humean scepticism for some means to create unity within the individual.

Locke's Empiricism and 'The Child in the House'

On a small square of paper, of the kind on which Pater tended to make his notes, there survives a short note to himself: 'Child in the House: voilà, the germinating, original, source, specimen, of all my *imaginative* work' (qtd Evans xxix; Pater's italics). He may be referring to the way that this short story marks a shift in his conception of the imaginary portrait, away from biography to fiction. He would of course go onto develop the coming of age imaginary portrait in *Marius the Epicurian* (1885), *Gaston de Latour* (1888–9), and 'Emerald Uthwart' (1892, MS 1892), with varying degrees of success. Pater's triumphant assertion that he has found 'the germinating, original, source, specimen, of all my *imaginative* work' may though have another less obvious meaning.

Given the way that 'The Child in the House' (1878, IP 1887) focuses on the formation of the individual, his note may also refer to the way it locates tensions in Locke's conception of continuous consciousness as the basis of personal identity.

As Pater presents the child's Lockean evolution of self-identity in the story, he begins to question the stability of continuous consciousness, and to question what else – if not continuous consciousness – could be the basis of self-identity. Though Locke had been associated with 'The Sensualist School', it was not primarily as a sensualist that Pater read his work, but as a philosophical thinker addressing the foundations of personal identity. The very fact that Pater centres this enquiry on Lockean conception of personal identity is interesting. By the final quarter of the century, Oxford had rescinded its ban on teaching Locke,[11] and H. R. Fox Bourne's *Life of John Locke* (1876) and Leslie Stephen's *History of English Thought in the Eighteenth Century* (also 1876) brought Locke back into public consciousness whilst attempting to revise the negative perception of him that had pervaded nineteenth-century philosophy. Pater's almost contemporaneous use of Locke's philosophy in 'The Child in the House' indicates that he was his attuned to shifts in intellectual fashions and even sought to participate in these. Moreover, Locke's renewed reputation came at a time when Pater was looking away from the potentially destructive implications of Hume's sceptical empiricism, prioritised by his Conclusion to *The Renaissance,* to think more broadly and constructively about how self-identity could be formed empirically.

'The Child in the House' self-consciously engages with the conception of self-identity which Locke outlined in *An Essay Concerning Human Understanding* (1690). It centres on Florian Deleal, whose memories of his childhood home are reawakened after a chance meeting. Through Florian's fragment of memory from that time Pater narrativises Locke's conception of how the accumulation of experience in the world builds into a coherent self-identity. As I have noted, Locke's founding principle is that there are no innate ideas, and knowledge is acquired by receptivity to, or observation of, the external world alone:

> Let us then suppose the mind to be, as we say, white paper, void of all characters, without any ideas; how comes it to be furnished? [. . .] To this I answer in one word, from *experience*: in that, all our knowledge is founded; and from that it ultimately derives itself. (1997: II. i §2, 109; Locke's italics)

With another metaphor, Locke describes the cause of obscurity in simple ideas:

> if the organs or faculties of perception, like wax over-hardened with cold, will not receive the impression of the seal, from the usual impulse wont to imprint

it; or, like wax of a temper too soft, will not hold it well when well imprinted
. . . (1997: II. xxix §3, 327)

Pater overtly draws on the famous imagery of these passages, explaining at the outset of his imaginary portrait that the experiences of early
childhood 'figure themselves on the white paper, the smooth wax of our
ingenious souls' (IP 6). Positioned at the beginning of the narrative his
Lockean imagery seems to suggest assent to Locke's conception that the
individual is born as an empty vessel to be filled by experiences, whilst
creating an expectation that Florian will illustrate this conception of
self-formation. Locke's conception has obvious attractions for Pater:
born as a blank, we are without Original Sin and are free to create and
recreate ourselves as we wish.

So it seems at first. Pater's creation of the young child, Florian, enables
him to explore Locke's conception of how identity is formed. After all,
childhood is 'the time,' Locke tells us, when we are 'most susceptible to
lasting Impressions' (II. xxxiii §8, 356) and through the accumulation of
these impressions, the individual personality is formed:

> Children [. . .] are surrounded with a world of new things, which, by a con-
> stant solicitation of their senses, draw the mind constantly to them, forward
> to take notice of new and apt to be delighted with the variety of changing
> objects. (Locke II. i §8, 112)

Florian epitomises this vision of how curiosity and acute observation
form personality whilst Pater's narrative gently guides the reader toward
an empirical conception of the relationship between experience, place,
and identity. He describes for instance:

> that little white room with the window across which the heavy blossoms
> could beat so peevishly in the wind, with just that particular catch or throb,
> such a sense of teasing in it, on gusty mornings: and the early habitation
> thus gradually becomes a sort of material shrine or sanctuary of sentiment; a
> system of visible symbolism interweaves itself through all our thoughts and
> passions; and, irresistibly, little shapes, voices, accidents – the angle at which
> the sun in the morning fell on the pillow – become parts of the great chain
> wherewith we are bound. (IP 6)

Pater uses this first-person collective 'we' as a device to universalise
Florian's story so that it becomes the story of how each one of us
acquired self-identity through experience. Here he suggests the significance of even such fleeting experiences in the 'interweav[ing]' of the
individual, from seemingly small, discrete impressions into the 'great
chain' of one's self. The conception of self-identity as formed by an
organic, constructive process is reiterated by Pater's metaphors of the

'process of brain-building by which we are, each one of us, what we are' and, again, by the image of organic growth in 'the gradual expansion of the soul' (IP 4).

On the basis of these metaphors of development Pater suggests Locke's view that continuous consciousness is the basis of personal identity. Locke explains that the 'white paper' self acquires experiences which the mind strings together in the continuous consciousness:

> For since consciousness always accompanies thinking, and 'tis that that makes everyone to be what he calls *self*; and thereby distinguishes himself from all other thinking things; in this alone consists *personal identity* [. . .] and as far as this consciousness can be extended backwards to any past action or thought, so far reaches the identity of that *person*; it is the same self [. . .] with this present one that now reflects on it . . . (II. xxvii §9, 302)

'The Child in the House' takes on this idea that personal identity is founded on continuous reflective thought, first echoing Locke's spatial metaphor as he figures Florian's experience of a 'mental journey' and 'the great chain wherewith we are bound' (IP 6; 4). The metaphor of linearity is reiterated by framing images of Florian: the story opens with the image of Florian as an adult walking along a road and closes with Florian the child embarking along his 'favourite country road' (IP 17).

Questioning Lockean Empiricism

And yet, even as Pater establishes Lockean empiricism as the philosophical foundation of Florian's identity, his narrative cannot accept the Lockean conception of the individual, any more than it could accept the Humean individual. It is telling that he is selective in his reading of Locke: the prime example is that, whilst Locke believes personal identity to be formed in relation to society (II. xxvii §§7–15, 317–23), Pater wholly ignores this facet by sketching Florian solely in relation to his house and the stranger he meets on the road.[12] More subtly, Pater questions Locke's idea of continuous consciousness by gesturing to psychology to undermine the centrality of consciousness, and by structuring his narrative so as to question the continuity of consciousness.

Pater complicates Locke's conception of consciousness from the very start of the narrative. When the adult Florian's memories are evoked by his encounter with a man from his childhood home, Pater describes:

> a dream of that place came to Florian, a dream which did for him the office of *the finer sort of memory*, bringing its object to mind with great clearness,

yet, as sometimes happens in dreams, raised a little above itself and above ordinary retrospect. (IP 3; my italics)

The ambiguous mention of 'the finer sort of memory' complicates the figurative tropes that have established Locke's continuous consciousness as the guiding philosophical perspective of the story. Florian had not remembered his childhood home until this moment. His sudden recollection of it, catalysed by an unexpected association of ideas, anticipates Proust's 'involuntary memory' and, like Proustian memory, it opens the possibility that the key to one's identity might lie not in continuous *consciousness* but rather in the *un*consciousness, where it may or may not ever be recovered. With this Pater looks beyond Locke to the field of psychology that was emerging from empirical philosophy in the 1870s to become, by the close of the nineteenth century, empiricism's strongest legacy. Florian's memories, and therefore perhaps his identity, Pater teasingly suggests, may be located not in the conscious memories of Locke's continuous consciousness but rather in the unconscious mind.

Pater had cultivated an interest in psychology since at least the late 1860s. Indications of this may be traced in *The Renaissance*, which draws on current vocabulary and debates in the psychology of aesthetics (Small 1978: 81ff) and anticipates Freud with its 'portrait of the psyche in a state of wilful undress' (Meisal 2001: 759); and also in 'Coleridge' (1866, 1880), where Pater is interested in 'Coleridge's capacity for testing and tracing the involutions of his own consciousness' (Beaumont 2011: 5). Whilst it is true that, in 'The Child in the House', 'Pater's particular tropes of construction and dwelling places suggest a sympathy with the contemporary science of consciousness' (Moran 2007: 295), it would be misleading to overestimate this sympathy and see contemporary psychology as the inspiration for these particular tropes; as discussed above, they are taken directly from Locke. Rather, it is the way that Pater suggests a dialogue between Lockean empiricism and psychology that is interesting. One of the roots of Pater's interest in psychology is his understanding that it posed serious questions for the philosophies which had been the cornerstone of his intellectual life since he was an undergraduate. Psychology threatened not only the scope but the foundation of moral philosophy by taking the motivation for action out of the sphere of the human consciousness (Hext 2012: 699). Here, however, Pater suggests his hope that 'the finer sort of memory' might compensate for the inadequacies of continuous consciousness; quite apart from imperilling philosophy, psychology saves individual identity from its flaws. As the Proustian echo suggests, Pater conceives 'the finer sort of memory' as an aesthetic experience, with greater clarity and intensity than ordinary experience. The aestheticisation of memory accords with Matthew Beaumont's persuasive revision of discussions linking Pater to psychology.[13] Beaumont argues that Pater was more of a psychagogue – a necromancer who mediates between the living and the dead, in order to expand our spiritual knowledge of ourselves – than a psychologist: 'Psychagogy, for Pater, is a dialogue with the dead that enables, not only a deeper understanding of the consciousnesses that animated the past, but a deeper self-knowledge. It is an imaginary psychology' (2011: 11). The link here between psychology and imagination is pertinent. Pater is not, for himself, greatly interested in the science of psychology as such: rather, it is the imaginative possibilities suggested by the idea of an unconscious that captivate him. In addition to the opportunity for Pater to himself become a psychagogue through his imaginative portraiture, his linking imagination to psychology suggests that imagination eludes the continuous consciousness: it is unconscious, and thus cannot be accounted for by Lockean empiricism.

Pater's narrative structure problematises the reliability of Locke's continuous consciousness in a different way: by calling attention to the flaws in continuity between the past, present and future self. Whilst Pater's Lockean metaphors buttress the continuity between Florian the adult and his childhood self, the construction of the narrative around Florian's flashback arrests the narrative trajectory at the outset by fragmenting Florian the adult and Florian the child. The abrupt end of the story acts to intensify this fragmentation: Florian's 'process of brain-building' is halted when he leaves his first home at the end of the story, 'driven quickly away, far into the rural distance, so fondly speculated on, of that favourite country-road' (IP 17). This ending, on the road, subverts the image of the road as a symbol of progression by suggesting instead that Florian is an eternal wanderer on an unidentified, unlocated, indeterminate country road. Pater gave some thought to his ending. In the cover note to his manuscript, sent to George Grove, editor of *Macmillan's Magazine*, on 17 April 1878, he clarifies: 'It is not, as you might perhaps fancy, the first part of a work of fiction, but is meant to be complete in itself . . .' (L 30). With his decision not to frame the memory by returning to Florian's adult self, Pater advised Grove, '[I] mean readers, as they might do on seeing a portrait, to begin speculating: what became of him?' (L 30). Florian the child embarks on an unknown future, which is not linked back to his adult self who began the narrative. This reflects the culture-defining spirit of arrested progression emerging in the late 1870s as Victorian Progress met with *fin de siècle* sensibility.

Pater's Rejection of Constructive Empiricism

Despite the fact that the empiricisms of Hume and Locke had by the 1870s been superseded by more contemporary empirical ideas such as Comte, it is these two founding fathers above all who remain Pater's interlocutors as he thinks through the implications of the empirical self.[14] His early, formative reading of their works and his desire always to go back to fundamental ideas and issues means that they haunt Pater more vividly than they haunted the rest of the nineteenth century. It is when Pater is closest to Hume and Locke that stable self-identity is at its most precarious. In the Conclusion to *The Renaissance* the individual is engulfed by sense-data, and in 'The Child in the House' the fragmentation of continuous consciousness leaves an open question over the foundation of personal identity. Yet it is not because of this that Pater is not an empiricist. Ultimately, it is his rejection of empiricism's constructive thesis that indicates his disaffection from empirical philosophy.

Hume had argued that the individual can reinstate a sense of order amidst the fluctuating phenomena of reality and quell the passions by forming habits through 'custom and repetition' (1964: II. iii, 133). When Pater's calm and reassuring narrative emerges from the Humean flux in the later paragraphs of the Conclusion, however, it disdains such a resolution, wondering whether '[in] a sense it might even be said that our failure is to form habits' (R 152). This dismissal of Hume's resolution echoes Pater's earlier derision in 'Coleridge' (A 103) of people who become 'phlegmatic servants of routine', and his analogy between routine and mediocrity in 'Winckelmann': 'Winckelmann was saved from mediocrity, which, breaking through no bounds, moves ever in a bloodless routine, and misses its one chance in the life of the spirit and the intellect' (R 120). Again, later, in 'Giordano Bruno', he reflects: '– indolent habit! What would this mean in the intellectual life, but just that sort of dead judgements which are most opposed to the essential Spirit, because the mind, the eye, were no longer really at work in them?' (GL 76). In the Conclusion to *The Renaissance*, Pater's brief rejection of Hume's solution to uncertainty is followed in the next sentence by a no less brusque dismissal of Hume's most famous nineteenth-century successor, August Comte: 'What we have to do is to be for ever curiously testing new opinions and courting new impressions, never acquiescing in a facile orthodoxy, of Comte, or of Hegel, or of our own' (R 152–3). Pater's view that habit, customs, and system stifle individuality and intellectual life suggests a perverse desire for the very flux which in the first part of the Conclusion had been an object of fear. This paradox raises the question – especially in *The Renaissance*, where the fear of flux and the rejection of habit are closely juxtaposed – of how one can proceed. In other words, what constructive thesis would satisfy Pater's longing for some resolution to the flux and stable personal identity, whilst still allowing the thrill and fluidity of ephemeral sensations in an ever-shifting world?

If Hume's sceptical stance does not make Pater feel disillusioned with life (Inman 1981b: 20), the reason is not because he finds any comfort in it, or because he follows Hume's resolution, but because he never really believes it. Indeed Pater rarely embraced the theories of others, preferring to weave threads from them into a tapestry of his own idiosyncratic design. So Pater never quite allows the relative spirit to define the individual. He comes close in the Conclusion, when breathless excitement teeters on the brink of a loss of control. And he is certainly excited by the dynamism which relativity offers to the individual, with the opportunity to constantly invent one's self. However, Pater cannot give up autonomy and essential values, because these are integral to his aesthetic vision. Influenced as they were by Pater's sceptical turns, it would be the literary modernists a generation later for whom 'the outline of character almost disappears, all characters begin to look much alike, it is difficult to find any positive, authentic core of being that could be called the self' (Longbaum 1970: 170). We should be careful not to retroactively impress modernism's appropriation of Pater's writings onto our interpretation of Pater himself. If sometimes 'the difference between self and not self is lost' (Leighton 2002: 18), then for Pater this is but for a moment. He would not, does not, and cannot give up the idea of the individual, because the individual as subject and creator is at the centre of his aesthetic. Without a unified and at least semi-stable self, the opening question of Pater's *Renaissance* would be meaningless: 'What is this song or picture, this engaging personality presented in life or in a book, to *me*?' (R ixxx; Pater's italics). The question is what exactly defines individuality, if not continuous consciousness or habit.

On a personal level, one can only wonder how Pater reconciled his intellectual rejection of Humean 'custom and repetition' with his own unerring routines. Day after day, year after year and decade after decade he carefully ordered his life in Oxford by writing in the morning, reading in the afternoon and socialising and writing letters in the evening. So Pater was a man of habit himself. As in other cases it seems that his theory expresses an ideal that he could not himself fulfil; perhaps through natural caution, or the modesty that judged such daring to be beyond his powers as he believed himself to be, in his own words, a mere 'workman' (L 59). In practical terms at least he assumed Hume's solution; in his other life – the more vivid imaginative life – he cannot. The un-Romantic view of Hume and Locke, that creative genius is not born to us but generated subsequently and perfected with practice, is not a thesis that Pater is willing to follow. However, the rejection of habit as a principle of unity through which to form self-identity leaves him with a problem: what then is the unifying principle of the individuated *I*?

Notes

1. The fact that Pater read this edition of Plato in a formative period of his life, 1863, is significant: 'Pater's ideas on perception and the flux could have been clarified and crystallised by Campbell's clear, concise expression' (Inman 1981a: 43).

2. Later in his career Pater wrote notes on Hobbes' philosophy, which suggest he thought of him 'as the father of Locke and Hume and the anticipator of Darwin (in regard to the struggle for existence)' (Inman 1981a: 14). But it seems that Pater never went beyond the process of trying to situate Hobbes intellectually. His very rough, scribbled ideas are far less complete than many of his other manuscripts; they seem to me to be functional aides memoires on *Leviathan* (1642–51) rather than more organised essay-notes on Hobbes' significance.

3. I do not want to dwell at length on Pater's library borrowings. Suffice it to say that Pater went back to several key empiricist works as he put together the essays that comprise *The Renaissance*: for instance, he borrowed Hume's *Essays* and Bacon's *Works*. But he borrowed from various libraries and we do not have his library records from all of those, nor do we know what he read from these collected works. Hence such information can only offer an indication of his interests. Billie Andrew Inman's *Walter Pater's Reading: A Bibliography of his Library Borrowings and Literary References, 1858–1873* (1981a) gives a comprehensive and compelling account.

4. Berkeley's main point, made primarily in *A Treatise Concerning the Principles of Human Knowledge* (1710), is that once we accept Locke's proposition that experience is irreducibly subjective, the objective reality of this experience cannot be proved. There are only *ideas*, of whose objective materiality we cannot have unmediated experience.

5. Goethe would be another example: instead of writing on Goethe, Pater writes on Winckelmann, whom he characterises as his precursor (R 123–5). Similarly, Pater's interest in Sir Thomas Browne, about whom he wrote an eponymous, little read essay, revolves around his participation in the intellectual currents that would culminate in Humean scepticism (A 159).

6. Billie Andrew Inman has argued that Hume's sceptical argument in the *Treatise* is a 'less pervasive' influence on the scepticism of Pater's Conclusion to *The Renaissance* than is Gottlieb Fichte (1981b: 16). As Inman argues, 'it is easy to conclude that Pater made his first step in the philosophical search toward scepticism, while reading Fichte' (16) because his library records show that he read *The Vocation of Man* (*Die Bestimmung des Menschen*;

1800) first and because of certain resemblances between its account of scepticism and the second and third paragraphs of the Conclusion (R 16–17). Pater did read and was influenced by Fichte: as noted in the Introduction and discussed in the next chapter, he presented a paper on Fichte's conception of the Ideal Scholar to the Old Mortality Society in 1864 and, having read *The Vocation*, perhaps it contributed to his thoughts. In everything Pater writes there are threads from a multiplicity of sources, woven into a fabric that is uniquely his. With this in mind resemblances between Pater's scepticism and that of Fichte are perhaps better explained by the fact that Fichte, like Kant, was himself strongly influenced by Hume.

7. On Pater's reading in the sciences see particularly Inman, who discusses Pater's intertextualisation of scientific ideas in the Conclusion to *The Renaissance* (1981b: 12ff); and Gowan Dawson, who discusses scientific discourse in both *Marius the Epicurean* (1885) and the periodical press (2005: 38ff)

8. For example, see Billie Andrew Inman's discussion of Pater's reading of Schleiermacher's *Geschichte der Philosophie* (*History of Philosophy*; 1839) and Eduard Zeller's *Philosophie der Griechen* (*Greek Philosophy*; 1844–6): (1981a: 23; 64).

9. Pater uses the shorthand 'f.m.m.' in several places in his manuscripts. Despite my best efforts, I have been unable to identify what this stands for. In general terms, as the context suggests, it denotes a passing 'behind the veil', into a metaphysical realm.

10. Hume's theory of causation is explained best in his *Treatise* (1964: I. iii, 76ff).

11. For a full account of Locke's fall from grace and partial habilitation in the nineteenth century see Aarsleff, 395ff.

12. Similarly Pater draws inspiration from Schiller's *The Aesthetic Education of Man* (*Über die ästhetische Erziehung des Menschen*; 1793) but conceives the individual in isolation from society, narrowing Schiller's social aesthetic vision to a purely personal, solipsistic endeavour (Hext 2010: 285ff).

13. Such as Maureen Moran's 'Walter Pater's House Beautiful and the Psychology of Self-Culture' (2007) and Perry Meisal's 'Psychoanalysis and Aestheticism' (2001: 57 ff), both also cited above.

14. Pater was not wholly uninterested in Comte, one of most prominent nineteenth-century inheritors of empiricism, despite his dismissal of Comte's systematisation (R 152). Jonathan Loesberg notes that 'Pater had sympathy for Comte's "Religion of Humanity", since it bore resemblances to the humanism he admired in figures *The Renaissance* addresses' (Loesberg 1991: 52). Still, this sympathy was very limited and does not in my opinion add up to any substantive affirmation of Comte's constructive thesis.

Chapter 3

Subjectivity and Imagination: From Hume to Kant via Berkeley

Ours is no longer the age described by Carlyle, 'destitute of faith, yet terrified at scepticism.' It is an age clamorous for faith, and only dissatisfied with scepticism when scepticism is a resting-place instead of a starting point, a result instead of a preliminary caution.

G. H. Lewes, *Problems of Life and Mind* (1874: I, 1)

At just after nine o'clock on a Saturday evening, in July 1864, Pater delivered his second paper to the Old Mortality Society. Provocatively directed to his close friend Charles Shadwell who had nominated him for the Society, it was an audacious attempt to define a rare type of individual, one who 'crosses rather than follows the main current of the world's life' (D 154). It was called 'Diaphaneitè'. As well as being deeply personal, this essay shows Pater trying to work through what it means to be a subjective individual. Though unpublished until after his death when Shadwell himself included it in *Miscellaneous Studies* (1895),[1] it is crucial to understanding the evolution of Pater's individualism because it envisages – albeit as 'a collection of notes rather than a sustained argument' (Varty 205) – subjectivity as the centre of the individual. The vision of subjectivity and creativity suggested in 'Diaphaneitè' would be superseded in *The Renaissance*. Still, this early work's identification of subjective experience as that which defines the individual is the first step in Pater's internal dialogue on the nature of subjectivity that would continue throughout his career.

The fact that Pater chose to explore the relationship between individualism and subjectivity in an essay given to the Old Mortality Society suggests that his conception of subjectivity is defined by a serious engagement with philosophical ideas about selfhood. This society, founded in 1856 by a small group of Balliol students, was largely defined by the intellectual culture of Balliol: socially liberal and radical, with a distrust of mysticism, and a strong interest in German Idealism influenced both by the ever more prevalent influences of Benjamin Jowett[2] and Thomas

Carlyle.[3] When Pater was elected to the Society at the end of 1862 he was a relative outsider, an undistinguished undergraduate from The Queen's College; whereas by mid-1864 he was beginning to be thought of as a coming man, having been elected to a Probationary Fellowship in Classics at Brasenose on 5 February of that year. Membership of Old Mortality was an essential part of his invention of himself in this period, imperfect though this invention was. After reading assiduously on the history of modern philosophy Pater now wanted to develop his own philosophical ideas, especially on transcendental Idealism. Furthermore, he thought of himself – or wanted to think of himself – as being in the vanguard of philosophy at Oxford.

From 'Diaphaneitè' to *The Renaissance*, and in other later works, Pater's works effectively try out different philosophical forms of subjectivity. Entertaining successively the ideas of Hume, Berkeley and Kant, he seeks to establish a mode of subjective experience that could satisfy his desire to combine openness to sensuality with a creative or even spiritual principle. In 'Diaphaneitè' Pater proposes a Humean form of subjectivity in which the individual attains a singular quality of receptivity to the experiences of the world. Yet even when Pater is most interested in Humean empiricism, in the 1860s and 1870s, he does not fully accept that this can adequately account for the creative, imaginative individual. 'Diaphaneitè' thus sees him trying out ideas to ascertain what empirical epistemology can offer the creative subject, when adopted as an aesthetic principle. As discussed above, whilst intellectually he admires the modest assertion of the senses that is fundamental to empiricism, its rejection of metaphysics frustrates the Romantic in him. Pater has a very real, if often implicit, fear that a thorough-going materialism would demystify experience in the world, and particularly imaginative experience. This is nowhere more directly stated than in 'The History of Philosophy':

> Experience has largely justified the prominence of physical science, perfected its processes, shaken off ↓[unreadable] ↑confusing embarrassing interests, won for it fresh and fresh [sic] fields of enterprise, sometimes from the domain of the moral sciences now defined as its rival. This growth of physical science has indeed involved an ever-narrowing limitation of its aim, to what is relative, temporal, apparent only, as it speaks with more and more detail and fulness of the circumstances of our visible life, less and less of anything really ranging beyond it; with such a wide scope of knowledge, yet never a step beyond the ↑f.m.m [blank] that.' (HP 7)

Pater reiterates his concerns regarding the limits of empiricism in 'The Aesthetic Life' (c. 1893), commenting that 'the empirical philosophy of our day, carrying us so far into space and time seemingly infinite, has, in inverse proportion, narrowed the spiritual, the imaginative horizon'

(AL 2). These criticisms imply that the very expansion of scientific knowledge might be at the expense of 'the spiritual, the imaginative horizon'. Pater's comments in 'The Aesthetic Life' recall 'Literature and Science' (1882) by Matthew Arnold, which ends with the following plea:

> while we shall all have to acquaint ourselves with the great results reached by modern science, and to give ourselves as much training in its disciplines as we can conveniently carry, yet the majority of men will always require humane letters; and so much the more, as they have the more and the greater results of science to relate to the need in man for conduct, and to the need in him for beauty. (230)

Like Arnold, Pater addresses the claim of late nineteenth-century science to have 'embodied an almost ideal way of knowing' (George Levine 2000: 11). Pater is acutely aware that science based on the empirical model of knowledge defines the epistemological paradigm of late nineteenth-century Britain. Yet his dissatisfaction with this paradigm presents a challenge to any suggestion that he is a materialist. For, as these passages imply, he believes that there is something beyond 'what is relative, temporal, apparent only'. Pater's idea of 'the spiritual, the imaginative horizon' may sound hesitating, but for him this is immutable. To identify spirituality with imagination indicates a mode of thinking that cannot for long remain bounded by empiricist epistemology alone.

Even while Pater was drawing on Hume and Locke to characterise the subjectivity of the diaphanous man, he was simultaneously reading the founding works of German Idealism. For example, in 1861, in between borrowing the collected works of Hume and Bacon, he borrowed Kant's *Kritik der reinen Vernunft* (*Critique of Pure Reason*; 1781) and *Kritik der praktischen Vernunft* (*Critique of Practical Reason*; 1788).[4] This juxtaposition of empiricism and transcendental Idealism in his reading indicates the dialogue that would emerge in Pater's work as he considers subjectivity. The idealist pole here is not confined to Kant. Against a Humean account of consciousness that aligns subjectivity and creativity with receptivity to external experience, empiricist George Berkeley offers a vision of subjective Idealism that would help shape Pater's aesthetic, albeit ambivalently. Faced with Hume and Berkeley, the one who writes off the a priori subject and the other who dismisses the external world, Pater ultimately takes a middle course through Kantian transcendental Idealism: adopting Kant's conception of epistemology as comprising phenomena from the world fused by the imagination and the categories of the understanding.

Humean Subjectivity in 'Diaphaneitè'

Pater's essay on 'Diaphaneitè' specifically shows his determination not to give in to criticism. Months earlier, on 20 February 1864, his first essay for Old Mortality on Fichte's Ideal Scholar attracted severe criticism from conservative member S. R. Brooke. At the following meeting of the Old Mortals on Saturday, 27 February Brooke decried its 'selfish principles' and summed Pater's essay up as 'one of the most infidel productions it has ever been our pain to listen to' (qtd Monsman 1970: 371):

> Pater is said to [be the] best philosopher in Oxford, yet if what Pater affirms is to be understood intelligibly we can only say that Oxford is a very unfortunate place, and the philosophers must be very deluded people . . . Pater seldom makes what may be considered a really original remark.
>
> (qtd Monsman 1970: 380)[5]

Pater's essay on 'Diaphaneitè' suggests that his ideas had already moved on to a more original, constructive thesis since that first essay on Fichte. 'Diaphaneitè' is indebted to Humean empiricism for its conception of the individual as a transparent receptacle for experiences. This transparency becomes a trope in the essay, reappearing as 'the clear crystal nature' (D 153) and 'truthfulness of temper, [and] that receptivity' (D 156). In effect, subjectivity in 'Diaphaneitè' is a passive willingness to experience a variety of sensations. The transparency of diaphaneitè links it to glass, through which, like the Humean self, 'perceptions successively make their appearance; pass, re-pass, glide away, and mingle in an infinite variety of postures and situations' (1964: I. iv, 239–40), and having done so are gone forever, leaving no trace. What is distinctive about Pater is that he develops the diaphanous quality inherent in Humean epistemology into an ethical imperative. Traced to its ancient Greek roots, 'diaphaneitè' means '[you shall] become transparent!' or 'shine through!'[6] Assuming the form of a second person plural imperative verb, diaphaneitè is a command to the reader and it may be read as Pater's aesthetic manifesto (Brake and Small 258 n.).

As presented in 'Diaphaneitè', the individual has little power to define the world: 'It is just this sort of entire transparency of nature that lets through all that is really life-giving in the established order of things' (D 156). That last phrase – 'the established order of things' – hints at the powerlessness of the individual against a seemingly implacable status quo. Still, the individual may reclaim some agency through his subjective interpretations of and responses to this order. The very willingness of the diaphanous type to let all experiences pass through himself indicates, for Pater, a character whose self-valuation derives from within, not from how the world is:

> the spirit that sees external circumstances as they are, its own power and tendencies as they are, and realises the given conditions of its life, not disquieted by the desire for change [. . .] The character we mean to indicate achieves this perfect life by a happy gift of nature, without any struggle at all. (D 155)

Here Pater makes receptivity into a quality of perception rather than the very essence of perception, as it is in empiricism. He takes the edge off empirical epistemology by representing receptivity as a principle of aesthetic creation. With this, he makes what had been a fundamental aspect of how experience is possible for Locke and Hume into a quality of experience. In this respect he is following Charles Baudelaire, who writes in 'The Painter of Modern Life' ('Le peintre de la vie moderne'; 1863):

> Thus, the lover of universal life enters into the crowd as though it were an immense reservoir of electrical energy. Or we might liken him to a mirror as vast as the crowd itself; or to a kaleidoscope gifted with consciousness, responding to each one of its movements and reproducing the multiplicity of its life and the flickering grace of all elements of life. (2006: 10)

Baudelaire's flaneur anticipates Pater's diaphanous type, with the 'kaleidoscope' and 'multiplicity' of the personal perception mirroring the 'relative spirit' of the Paterian individual. They differ in that Baudelaire looks to a modernity in which epistemological issues no longer matter: the shifting ephemeral world energises his flaneur for its own sake. Pater can never be just a flaneur: he is unable to turn his back on the epistemological questions posed by Hume, despite wanting very much at times to do so.

In 'Diaphaneitè' the diaphanous individual is distinct from the artist; indeed, Pater sets the diaphanous type in contrast to 'The saint, the artist, even the speculative thinker' (D 154). In this essay it is important to Pater to preserve the diaphanous individual as a quality of being rather than of action. Some years later though, the diaphanous quality becomes embodied by Wordsworth in Pater's companion essays, 'Coleridge' (1866, 1880) and 'Wordsworth' (1874, 1889). Pater believes that Wordsworth's greatest gift as a poet is his understanding 'that in all creative work the larger part [is] given passively, to the recipient mind' with 'An intuitive consciousness of the expression of natural things, which weighs, listens, penetrates' (A 41; 43). Through Wordsworth's clear crystal diaphanous mind, Pater suggests, the ever-shifting, ephemeral, relative world presents itself unimpeded by metaphysical pretensions. This sensibility is essential to aesthetic creativity because it closely connects art to the sensuous and fluctuating world. It is thus Wordsworth's 'relative spirit' (A 66; 103) that gives his poetry a living connection to the true conditions of life in its infinite variety. For this is the reality of a world in which 'nothing is, or can be rightly known, except relatively and under conditions' (A 66).

Berkeley's Idealism in the Conclusion to *The Renaissance*

As noted in Chapter 2, Pater's fascination with George Berkeley's subjective idealism rests in part on his view that Berkeley's 'main point has never really been answered'; his idealist question mark over whether the world as perceived by the individual corresponds to an external reality 'has still no real philosophical ↑antidote [blank]' (HP 22). Perhaps, though, Pater's interest has a more particular motivation. After all, Berkeley's subjective idealism promises the individual a creative power to imagine the whole world into being.

In his *Essay Towards a New Theory of Vision* (1709), which Pater identifies as a primary work of modern sceptical philosophy (HP 3–5), and *A Treatise Concerning the Principles of Human Knowledge* (1710), Berkeley took Lockean empiricism to its inevitable conclusion. He argued that to be is to be perceived (*esse est percipi*). In other words, if, according to Lockean empiricism, the individual has no evidence of the material world except that provided by the senses, so there is no evidence of mind-independent matter: 'all those bodies which compose the mighty frame of the world, have not any subsistence without a mind; [. . .] their being is to be perceived or known' (1999: §6, 23). Berkeley thus rejects the subject-object relationship of the Lockean self and the materialism of the Hobbesian self, positing instead the subject-subject relationship of the self and an immaterial world which exists only when it is perceived. This central argument is premised on Berkeley's belief that material objects always exist in the mind of God who makes them appear in the minds of men (1999: §§7–15, 5–10). Without God, 'what we take to be material objects would have a jerky life, suddenly leaping into being when we look at them' (Russell 2006: 589).

The seriousness of Pater's response to Berkeley is interesting in the context of intellectual culture in the late nineteenth-century. Unlike Hume and Locke, Berkeley had become a marginal figure by the 1860s, and the questions of solipsism 'had already begun to look relatively passé to the mid-Victorians . . . one finds such debates consigned largely to footnotes or appendices, marginalized by the thrust of more consciously modern arguments' (Garratt 30). Despite G. H. Lewes' detailed consideration of

Berkeley in his *History of Philosophy* (1853: IV, 4–32), there was little broader resurgence of interest in Berkeley during Pater's lifetime.[7] His earnest consideration of Berkeley's solipsism is indicative not of his following a trend, but of precipitating one, and again illustrates the way that he went back to the founding works of modern philosophy to consider them on their own terms. Whilst Pater was involved in new modes of thinking, and was well read in contemporary thought, he did not slavishly follow trends. Bearing in mind the status of Berkeleyan idealism in his day one might even see a protest in Pater's claims that 'Berkeley's main point has never really been answered' and that his idealism 'has still no philosophical antidote'. This implicit dig at those who cast Berkeley aside also bespeaks Pater's own preoccupation with the immutable question of whether the world exists beyond the subjective mind.

It is true that Pater's thought seems sometimes to develop by 'drifting, as it were, toward impressionism on the one hand, positivism on the other, though intimately related through long traditions of German post-Kantianism and of British empirical thought' (George Levine 2000: 15). Still it should be added that Berkeleyan solipsism is a perennial and significant interlude in this drift. Solipsism prompts Pater to question the tenets of his subjective criticism. Among the tumultuous evocations of 'the tendency of modern thought' in the Conclusion to *The Renaissance* (R 150), Pater first takes up Berkeley's theory that the essence of an object lies in its being perceived:

> . . . if we continue to dwell in thought on this world, not of objects in the solidity with which language invests them, but of impressions, unstable, flickering, inconsistent, which burn and are extinguished with our consciousness of them, [the world] contracts still further: the whole scope of observation is dwarfed into the narrow chamber of the individual mind. (R 151)

The most significant difference here from Berkeleyan idealism is that, as the passage above suggests, Pater surreptitiously removes God from his version. He dares to think what for Berkeley was unthinkable, that the immaterial world hangs on the consciousness of the individual perceiving it. Pater's evocation of solipsism embodies the point that without God as deus ex machina, material objects have only a 'jerky life': 'unstable, flickering, inconsistent'. The phenomena that threatened to engulf the Humean self earlier in the passage are cut down to size by the solipsistic self, which holds the power to create and destroy the phenomena of the world. Yet the power that this might offer to the autonomous, secular imagination is undermined by Pater's imagery, evoking the mind of the idealist as an isolated and claustrophobic space. For he continues: 'Every one of those impressions is the impression of the individual in his isolation, each mind keeping as a solitary prisoner its own dream of a world' (R 151). The increasing sense of deprivation and loneliness here provides a halting counterpoint to liberation and expansiveness of the diaphanous individual.

Rereading the idealism episode in the Conclusion to *The Renaissance* alongside the most famous assertion of the Preface of that work casts each in a new light. The Conclusion's vision of 'the individual in his isolation' emerges as no more than the negative manifestation of Pater's subjectivism in the opening pages of the Preface:

> To see the object as in itself it really is, has been justly said to be the aim of all true criticism whatever; and in aesthetic criticism the first step towards seeing one's object as it really is, is to know one's own impression as it really is . . . (xxix)

Here, as is often remarked, Pater is primarily modifying Matthew Arnold's conception of criticism in 'The Function of Criticism at the Present Time' (1865): '"the main effort, for now many years, has been a critical effort; the endeavour, in all branches of knowledge, theology, philosophy, history, art, science, to see the object as in itself it really is"' (1865: 1).[8] At the same time he engages with Berkeley's central thesis, that to be is to be perceived. Pater thus sets up a distinction between art as it exists objectively and one's impression of art, in order to suggest that the impression is all that really exists. This claim to subjectivity is fairly innocuous as it appears in the Preface; it can be understood narrowly as a corrective to Arnold's critical position and a justification for Pater's impressionistic aesthetic. However, between the Preface and the Conclusion this subjectivity gets out of hand and becomes monstrous: taking what had been an aesthetic principle in the Preface and entertaining the implications of expanding this into an entire epistemology. As Pater writes in his Conclusion, 'Every one of those impressions is the impression of the individual in his isolation, each mind keeping as a solitary prisoner its own dream of a world' (R 151). Repetition of the word 'impression' from the Preface ('to know one's own impression as it really is') foregrounds the essential phenomenological problem of Pater's subjective criticism: how to conceive the relationship between self and world once you have asserted the individual as a subjective critic. In other words, how can the outside world be incontrovertible when one has asserted that knowledge is no more than to 'know one's own impression'? Indeed, once Pater has insisted that art as it appears to the individual is but an impression, how is it possible to ascertain that an objectively real world precedes our impressions at all?

Considering the place of Berkeleyan idealism in the Conclusion to

The Renaissance, Perry Meisal suggests that Pater evokes it 'in order to deny it' (1981: 115). If we are each in 'our own dream of a world,' Meisal asks, 'where is the "without" from which forces are supposedly to pass through?' (114). However it is mistaken to suppose that Pater has constructed the Conclusion as a single unified philosophical position, which is consistent between his exposition of the material world (the '"without"')[9] in the Conclusion's opening section and Berkeleyan idealism in the second section. Jonathan Loesberg identifies similar flaws in Pater's subjective idealism:

> critics have wondered how this solipsism can coexist with the firmly asserted empirical vision of the external world in the first paragraph. If no real voice ever reaches us, how can we know that the outer world is in flux? Moreover, what in empiricism allows the division between outer and inner here? And can solipsism ultimately even coexist with the deindividuating view of the self implicit in empiricism's definition of it as a bundle of sensations?' (1991: 21)

To an extent Loesberg and Meisal are correct to call attention to the fact that Pater's idealism does not stand up to philosophical scrutiny. Yet this fails to capture the spirit of Pater's subjective idealism, whose main significance in his work is by no means as a strictly worked through philosophical concept. As noted earlier, Pater's ideas are irreducibly inconsistent and shifting; his idealism is no exception.

The significance of idealism for Pater is its imaginative power. More widely, Pater finds idealism compelling because it positions imagination at the centre of the world: both for good, in granting creative and cognitive power to the individual, and for ill, because the world then precariously hangs on the individual consciousness. To gain a clearer sense of the spirit in which Pater considers subjective idealism it is necessary to look beyond the Conclusion to *The Renaissance*. For instance, in his essay on 'Wordsworth' (1874, 1889) he again characterises subjective idealism as a personal rather than a God-ordained creative power, describing Wordsworth's fantasy of solipsism:

> the actual world would, as it were, dissolve and detach itself, flake by flake, and he himself seemed to be the creator, and when he would the destroyer, of the world in which he lived – that old isolating thought of many a brain-sick mystic of ancient and modern times. (A 55)

Here Pater is ambivalent about the power of the imagination to create 'its own dream of a world' (R 151). He effectively distances his narrative voice from solipsism by both making this Wordsworth's fantasy and, in the final clause, by dismissing solipsism unconditionally. Yet the rhythm and alliteration of the first part of the sentence positively savour the power of such a solipsistic fantasy, whilst the pauses given by Pater's commas give the reader a sense of control over the world of his or her solipsistic creation.

In 'The History of Philosophy' (c. 1880) Pater again teases himself and his reader with the implications of placing the individual into the gap where God had been, to become the creator and destroyer of the world. Putting the individual at the centre of the universe would be the ultimate triumph over the uncertainties that haunt Pater's writings. Yet he both wants and fears the implications of this power, as the passage from 'Wordsworth' suggests, and he is unable to resolve this ambivalence in the way that he characterises subjective idealism:

> objects which have seemed to [the individual] to be in reality its own creations to make and unmake and how wildly in each of us it struggles against any degree of suppression as if the being of the whole world hung upon its continuance. It would seem to be the one object in the whole sum of things of which we have a really intimate knowledge. (HP 23–4)

In notable contrast to the Conclusion of *The Renaissance*, here subjective idealism becomes a wilful, desperate response against 'suppression'. Perhaps it is a power grasped 'wildly' out of fear of its fragility. This reverses the power balance in the relationship between the individual and world, so that now it is not the continuous consciousness of the individual that is fragile but the world itself. At the same time there is a suggestion in Pater's repetition of 'seem' and 'seemed' that the world hangs on a continuance of the individual's conceit that he or she is its creator, rather than any real sense that the individual consciousness creates the world. Pater knows that the existence of the ordered world depends not on the metaphysics of idealism but on a belief in idealism: the only thing that saves the individual from feeling overwhelmed by the phenomena of the world.

Subjective idealism is sometimes a fantasy in which Pater indulges, at other times it is a wild fear, and at yet others a philosophical problem. Perhaps it was a fancy of Pater the shy outsider, wishing to extinguish a world with which he was too often at odds. After Pater's death, Arthur Symons wrote that

> He was quite content that his mind should keep as a solitary prisoner its own dream of the world; it was that prisoner's dream of the world that it was his whole business as a writer to remember to perpetuate. (2003: 98)

Inspired by Berkeley, it may be Pater's own fancy to muse that the solipsistic individual has the creative power to bring the world into being and the destructive power to extinguish it at will. Ultimately, though, Pater's belief in the external reality of the world never really wavers through his forays into subjective idealism: the sensations of the outside world are too insistent, 'calling us out of ourselves in a thousand forms of action' (R 151).

Kantian Idealism and Paterian Creativity

For Pater to present an essay on Fichte's Ideal Student was brave given the Old Mortality members' knowledge of German Idealism. Like his fellow member T. H. Green, Pater was introduced to German Idealism as an undergraduate via Benjamin Jowett.[10] Unlike Green and the British Idealists, though, he does not address the relationship between self and world as a metaphysician or as a systematising philosophical thinker. As noted in Chapter 1, like J. S. Mill and Newman, Pater was far more comfortable articulating 'Life-Philosophies' than abstract, universal ideas (Bruns 1975: 906–7). In consequence the sources of his philosophical ideas must be pieced together from intertexualised fragments and allusions, and he may seem at once a Berkeleyan solipsist (Symons 2003: 98; Meisal 1981: 114) and a sceptic-cum-postmodernist (Leighton 2002: 18). All told, Pater is both and neither. He will not give up 'the spiritual, the imaginative horizon' (AL 2) for a thoroughgoing empiricism and nor will he turn away from the 'relative spirit' (A 66; 103) to metaphysical philosophy. For this reason, he looks cautiously to Immanuel Kant's transcendental principles to reconstruct a Romantic vision of subjectivity and creativity in the wake of his rejection of constructive empiricism.

Pater's turn to transcendental Idealism positions him at the vanguard of a shifting philosophical culture in 1870s Britain. For, if the 1860s and early 1870s saw 'an empirical consensus' amongst British intellectuals in general (Russell 2005: 654), Jowett and Old Mortality were turning the tide in Oxford. Pater's Fellowship at Brasenose, made largely on the grounds of his knowledge of German philosophy (Wright I, 211) anticipated the turn back towards Idealism. Following T. H. Green's 305-page 'Introduction' to Hume's *Treatise*, published in 1874, transcendental Idealism regained adherents in academic philosophy, and these would only increase in the following decade. If Green's apocryphal declaration to 'Close your Mill, and your Spencer, and turn to Kant and Hegel', in 1876, was an ambitious statement of intent it was also a reflection on the increasing prominence of German Idealism in Oxford philosophy (qtd Garratt 45). This prominence would only increase as F. H. Bradley and Bernard Bosanquet directed British Idealism to address the social problems of their age.[11] It would be easy to overlook the significance of this Idealist intervention today, relatively short-lived as it was and out of step with an intellectual history of what Henry Sidgwick would call 'common sense' in the history of British ideas (1895: 145).[12]

So whereas Paterian scholarship more broadly has tended to focus specifically on Hegel's influence, Elizabeth Prettejohn is quite right to say that Pater's aesthetic is underpinned 'not casually but rigorously, by the German tradition of philosophical aesthetics that proceeded from Immanuel Kant's *Critique of Judgement*' (3). What should be stressed is that Pater was singularly influenced, like others in post-Kantian philosophy, by the central premise of Kant's philosophy: the distinction between noumenal and phenomenal worlds. The enduring significance of Kant to Pater's view of the world is not immediately obvious when he opens 'Prosper Mérimée' (1890) with a rare explicit reference to the philosopher. In characterising the intellectual mood at turn of the nineteenth century, he writes:

> In the mental world too a great outlook had lately been cut off. After Kant's criticism of mind, its pretensions to pass beyond the limits of individual experience seemed as dead as those of old French royalty. And Kant did but furnish its innermost theoretic force to a more general criticism, which had withdrawn from every department of action, underlying principles once thought eternal. A time of disillusion followed. (MS 1).

Here Pater accepts the importance and veracity of Kant's view that the rational mind cannot conceive the metaphysical foundations of our existence; it cannot, to use Kant's own terms, comprehend the world as it is in itself. Pater values Kant as a sceptic (HP 3ff) whose refusal of metaphysics refocused attention on the seen world, even though the short, bathetic final sentence in the quoted passage suggests some regret at this loss of metaphysical illusions.

More broadly, despite Pater's disdain for Kant's philosophical systematisation, he accepts the central ontological principle of his transcendental philosophy: that there is a distinction between the world as individuals experience it (the phenomenal world) and the world as it is in itself (the noumenal world). In his *Critique of Pure Reason* (1781), Kant asserts that intelligible experience is only possible when intuited phenomena from the world are conceptualised by the a priori Categories of the Understanding, within the individual mind. So the individual's intelligible experience of the world effectively comprises two elements: the a posteriori phenomena of Hume's empiricism, on one hand, and a priori Categories of Understanding and imagination, on the other. It is out of this fusion that intelligible experience is possible and 'I' comes into being. In his Preface to the second edition of the *Critique of Pure Reason*,

Kant characterises this philosophy as a Copernican Revolution: just as Copernicus proves that the sun is the scientific centre of the universe, so Kant 'proves' that the individual is the epistemological centre of the universe, giving shape to the random sense data that appear to it from the world (1929: 25). Kant's principle suggests to Pater a philosophical exposition of Baudelaire's belief, in 1863, that 'by "modernity" I mean the ephemeral, the fugitive, the contingent, the half of art whose other half is the eternal and the immutable' (2006: 12). This ontological dualism functions on three epistemic levels in Pater's work: first, it acts a priori to shape random sense data into intelligible experience, secondly, it merges with the diaphanous quality in artistic creativity and, thirdly, this active principle fuses with the art object to create aesthetic experience.

In 'The History of Philosophy' Pater implies a Kantian dualism between the a priori and a posteriori distinguishing, like Baudelaire, between 'the ephemeral, the fugitive, the contingent' and 'the eternal and the immutable'. Iterating this dualism in his own work, Pater describes the individuals of ancient Greece in 'full enjoyment of their receptive and active powers' (HP 1). This is expanded in 'Giordano Bruno' (1889):

> It would be a mistake, [Bruno] holds, to attribute to the human soul capacities merely passive or receptive. She, too, possesses initiatory powers as truly as the divine soul of the world, to which she responds with the free gift of a light and heat that seem her own. (GL 74–5)[13]

Echoing Kant, these extracts suggest that representative consciousness has two distinct facets: the 'passive or receptive' capacity that intuits phenomena from the world, and the 'initiatory powers' that are given by the individual, and which thus positions the individual at the creative centre of the universe. These 'initiatory powers' stand supremely above the deluge of empirical phenomena, with their self-possession ('her own') indicating an a priori origin. The metaphor of 'light and heat' in 'Giordano Bruno' recalls Pater's image for creative inspiration; elsewhere he describes an ideal in which artists and philosophers 'breathe a common air, and catch light and heat from each other's thoughts' (R xxxiii). Perhaps this quality is premised on 'the spiritual, the imaginative horizon', which empiricism, in Pater's view, denies. Or perhaps it is what Pater intriguingly evokes, in 'The History of Philosophy', as 'that other sort of knowledge' which 'must be attained, if at all, by purely intellectual intuition, by faith, or by conscience' (HP 7).

At an epistemic level, the Kantian dynamic between self and world inflects Pater's most explicit statements about how intelligible experience is possible. In 'The History of Philosophy', he characterises the significance of Kantian transcendental Idealism as follows:

Such as it has actually been in the course of men's thoughts is the idea of ↑nature or the cosmos, summed up so austerely in the dry terms of Kant. Gathering himself ↑together from that complex world and standing back as it were to gaze upon it the mind of man [. . .] may figure to himself as the master of nature and akin to its creator' (HP 18–19).

The first part of the second sentence here suggests an empirical episte-mology: the individual is more or less like Hume's 'bundle or collection of different perceptions' (1964: I. iv, 239) as he is pictured 'gather-ing himself together'. But the second part of this sentence seamlessly refigures the associationism that would follow from this premise for an empiricist. Instead the individual is conceived as a dynamic creator who brings order to the world. This dualism reappears in the Conclusion to *The Renaissance*, as Pater describes how intelligible experience is created out of 'the perpetual motion' of empirical elements and forces: 'That clear perceptual outline of face and limb is but an image of ours, under which we group them – a design in a web, the actual threads of which pass out beyond it' (R 150). This suggests that the individual creates experience from the threads of data that are presented, a poste-riori, by the world. In the act of perception we create a design without which there would be but a jumble of threads. These are necessary to the design but we find it impossible to make sense of them; we can only see what they all mean when the threads are arranged into a design and there must be a design or the threads of experience remain a meaningless confusion of phenomena. In Kant's terms, this jumble of threads is the random sense data and the design is the world as we experience it.

This dualism between 'capacities merely passive or receptive' and 'initiatory powers . . . truly divine' underlies Pater's conception of artistic creativity. Kant presents artistic creation as a fusion between sensations from the world and the a priori quality of genius. Pater's vision of genius involves the diaphanous quality, and we saw this in his assertion that 'in all creative work the larger part [is] given passively, to the recipient mind' (A 41). Considered in these terms, scattered empiri-cal terms like 'temperament' and 'taste' (A 98; R 156) may suggest an a posteriori explanation of artistic genius, in which its characteristics are acquired through experience, not brought to experience. Yet, for Pater as for Kant, 'Genius is the innate mental predisposition through which nature gives the rule to art' (Kant 1987: §46, 174). At the begin-ning of *The Renaissance* Pater strikes this keynote by quoting William Blake: '"The ages are all equal [. . .] but genius is always above its age"' (R xxxi). This brief suggestion is compounded elsewhere when Pater defines creative genius as an 'intense and individual power' and a 'quite unusual sensibility, really innate within [the individual]' (A 40; 44). The expression of such personal qualities is 'the central aesthetic formulation of *The Renaissance*' (Lyons 767ff). As Pater declares, 'expression [is] the purging away from the individual of what belonged only to him' (R 43). For this reason, it is defined against 'the mere accidents of a particular time and place' that are the very conditions of genius in empirical philosophy (R 43). This Romantic idea makes genius exempt from the fluctuations and ephemera so vividly evoked in the Conclusion as an innate and personal quality.

Pater's presentation of Dante Gabriel Rossetti in his eponymous essay (1889) offers an example of how a posteriori sensations and a priori creativity combine in the artistic genius. At the climax of his evocation of Rossetti, Pater writes:

> Spirit and matter, indeed, have been for the most part opposed, with a false contrast or antagonism by schoolmen, whose artificial creation those abstractions really are. In our actual concrete experience, the two trains of phenomena which the words *matter* and *spirit* do but roughly distinguish, play inextricably into each other . . . in the vehement and impassioned heat of his conceptions, the material and the spiritual are fused and blent: if the spiritual attains the definite visibility of a crystal, what is material loses its earthiness and impurity. (A 212; Pater's italics)

In Pater's view the diaphanous quality of Rossetti's language is essential to his poetry:

> he had this gift of transparency in language – the control of a style which did but obediently shift and shape itself to the mental motion, as a well trained hand can follow on the tracing paper the outline of the original drawing below it. (A 206)

Stressing the analogy between this transparency and the sensible world, he adds that there is 'a seal of reality' on Rossetti's expression of the world and 'a definiteness of sensible imagery' (A 206; A 207). Rossetti illustrates though that diaphaneitè alone is not sufficient for the creation of art. Rossetti's a priori, shaping imagination is also an important element in Pater's work: 'the very midst of profoundly mystic vision' (A 207).

Kantian Idealism and Subjective Criticism

Kant's transcendental Idealist distinction between noumena and phenomena is also at work in Pater's impressionistic criticism, behind the immediate influences of Dante Gabriel Rossetti and fellow Old Mortality member Swinburne. Swinburne wrote to John Morley in

April 1873, a couple of months after the publication of Pater's *Renaissance*,

> I admire and enjoy Pater's work so heartily that I am somewhat shy of saying how much, ever since on my telling him once at Oxford how highly Rossetti (D. G.) as well as myself estimated his first papers in the Fortnightly, he replied to the effect that he considered them as owing their inspiration entirely to the example of my own work in the same line . . . (qtd Inman 1981a: 161–2)

Swinburne's essay 'Notes on the Designs of the Old Masters at Florence', itself inspired by Baudelaire's 'Salon of 1859', was published in 1868, the same year that Pater began writing his Renaissance essays. Pater also owned Rossetti's aesthetic criticism in copies of *The Germ* (1850) and his *Collected Works* (1887), which included a precursor to Pater's imaginary portrait essays in Rossetti's influential fable about the artist Chiaro dell' Erma (124–31). Even so, Pater may well have overstated the influence of Swinburne and Rossetti to flatter these older, more accomplished critics.

Pater's 'cogitating spirit' (Lionel Johnson 364) meant that he was not content to simply follow Swinburne, no matter how à la mode that might have been in the late 1860s and early 1870s. For a start Pater developed an aesthetic theory to underpin Swinburnian impressionistic criticism, grounding this in the dualism of 'capacities merely passive or receptive' and 'initiatory power' (GL 74). He prepares us for this in his Preface to *The Renaissance*: 'in aesthetic criticism the first step towards seeing one's object as it really is, is to know one's one impression as it really is, to discriminate it, to realise it distinctly . . . ' (R xxix). As discussed above, Pater subverts Arnold's well-known dictum to assert that there exists no objective, intrinsic meaning in artistic works; the 'function of criticism' is therefore to express one's own subjective impression of an artwork. With this, Pater asserts himself at the vanguard of aesthetic criticism alongside Swinburne and Rossetti. At the same time, his subjectivism takes a more theoretical shape through Kantian idealism.

The same dualism of 'capacities merely passive or receptive' and 'initiatory power' which defines the Paterian artist also defines, for him, the aesthetic spectator. As Lane says, 'Pater attempted to incorporate the spectator's look into a dynamic model of criticism so that the object could be "realised" and not simply "seen"' (1994: 31). This mode of active spectatorship is stated right at the outset in the Preface to *The Renaissance*, in the sentence quoted in the preceding paragraph. This assertion that aesthetic value is not immanent in the work of art but 'realised' in the imagination of the subject is central in Pater's aesthetic.

As discussed in the previous chapter, it makes the subjective individual necessary to the creation of aesthetic experience. In so doing it also serves to consolidate the position of the individual at the centre of the universe. The perceiving individual becomes the over-arching principle of unity in art, and an active participant in the creation of art; in each exercise of this creative criticism he finds his existence confirmed. Perhaps then it is the 'initiatory power' – creativity, in other words – that saves the individual from being 'but a bundle or collection of different perceptions', as in Hume's conception (1964: I. iv, 239) and as Pater briefly and fearfully suggested in the Conclusion to *The Renaissance*.

To put this another way, in 'Winckelmann' Pater refers to 'the dramatic contrasts of life' (R 148). Here again, it is the dualism of the 'capacities merely passive or receptive' and 'initiatory powers' (GL 74) which places the individual at the centre of life's 'dramatic contrasts'. As the individual initiates and mediates the fusion of fleeting phenomena with the creative spirit, he stands at the very centre of the universe. It is thus that Pater's Kantian dualism seeks to resolve the dichotomy between self and world: or more precisely, between the transcendent a priori self and the a posteriori 'bundle' of perceptions. On one hand, the individual is created out of the ever-changing external world, whilst on the other hand he defines himself against this flux by his gift of creativity and subjectivity. The repeated suggestion of these qualities, woven into the fabric of *The Renaissance*, saves him from the ephemera of merely passive sensations.

It is also worth pondering the ways in which Pater did not follow Kant. A key case is his refusal to perform an anatomy of creativity, something which aligns Pater with the Romantics. Whereas Kant confidently set out to explain the workings of the mind, the Romantics modestly refrained, believing the mind to be unfathomable through reason alone. Relatedly, and radically, Romanticism relocates the essence of selfhood from the mind to the imagination. The mind had been central to Western conceptions of selfhood since Rene Descartes' assertion that 'cogito ergo sum', and was reconceived by Locke's 'continuous consciousness' as the core of the empirical self. Romanticism unceremoniously knocks the mind off its philosophical throne: imagination is king.

From an Idealist viewpoint, Romanticism represents a retreat and a refusal. Kant would identify with a model of transparency, given his conviction that the philosopher can see through man into the mechanics of the mind. By contrast, Pater's diaphaneitè does not at all take transparency that far. Instead he retreats to the awkwardly woolly Romantic position of suggesting that there is *something* beyond our comprehension, without being able to explain what exactly it is. Whether this 'certain mystical sense' is analogous to what Pater called 'that other sort of knowledge' (HP 12), and how creativity is linked to spirit, are questions to which we will turn in the next chapter.

Drawing as Pater did on such diverse philosophical schools, and struggling or at least shifting the balance of emphasis in his various efforts to integrate these and work out his own position, critical efforts to pin him down too rigidly are elusive and often mistaken. For example, while Leighton aptly says of Pater's characterisation of the individual as creative subject that 'outside conditions permeate the self, shining through it,' it does not follow that for him 'the difference between self and not self is lost' (2002: 18). This proto-postmodern vision of Pater is as faulty as the oft-perpetuated idea that Pater's flirtation with empiricism in the Conclusion to *The Renaissance* is 'irrefutable proof of his commitment to an empiricist conception of self' (Beaumont 5). Not so. Whilst Pater entertains the possibility of an empirical self, and even sees the possible dissolution of the unified individual through empiricism, this is devastating for him to contemplate, and hence he does not stick to an empirical idea of creativity for long. Catherine Maxwell has the balance right, noting very astutely of Pater that 'rather surprisingly, in a writer so much associated with sensory relations . . . there is also a distinct pull towards the visionary and the unseen' (2008: 71).

Finally, it is a curious irony that although Pater asserts subjectivity as a core aspect of individualism, his narratives tend to distance themselves from the personality of the subjective individual. For all that Pater focuses on the individual his gaze rarely, if ever, goes beyond the abstract, and this is never more clear than in his conception of the spirit. As if he cannot penetrate his own 'thick wall of personality' (R 151) to empathise with others such that he could imagine the personality of another, Pater does not really get beneath the skin of his characters. He even promised that there should be no personalities in *Marius* (Wright II, 80). Marius, Pater's most sustained protagonist, is a vessel of competing and evolving ideas that mark the space of years till his death. But a vessel or battleground is not necessarily a character, and perhaps this is why this novel is so divisive. In the case of Marius, as with the various figures on whom Pater focuses in his imaginary portraits, spiritual light animates creativity and gives life to the individual in unseen ways. Yet the very brightness of this aura has the effect of obfuscating the relationship between the nebulously metaphysical and the empirical spirit. Much as Pater foregrounds the individual, he can never convincingly draw individuals. The abstract idea was where he felt most at home.

Notes

1. Pater reuses ideas and even some sentences from 'Diaphaneitè' in 'Winckelmann' (1867, 1873). Anne Varty discusses this in 'The Crystal Man: A Study of "Diaphaneitè"' (210ff).
2. Transcendental idealist philosophy was at the centre of Jowett's reconception of Classics at Oxford: 'Jowett and his pupils were impregnating Balliol, and, through Balliol, the mind of Oxford and the nation, with German idealism' (Knickerbocker 126).
3. There was a large number of Scottish students at Balliol in this period: 'Down from Glasgow to Balliol had come the Snell Exhibitioners, students of Carlyle and German idealism, always older and more serious than their English counterparts' (Monsman 1970: 366). Over half a dozen Snell Exhibitioners became members of Old Mortality in the its early years, including its founder John Nichol.
4. To be clear, I am giving the titles first in German here because Pater borrowed the German editions.
5. Lesley Higgins notes that S. R. Brooke warned Gerard Hopkins against Pater 'as early as February 1864' and long before Hopkins and Pater met (1991: 78). It seems likely that Pater's first essay reading at the Old Mortality Society was the catalyst for this warning. Pater tutored Hopkins between 1866 and 1868.
6. Morito Uemura has persuasively traced the title 'Diaphaneitè' to its French roots, drawing attention to the appearance of 'diaphaneité' (note the acute accent) in Victor Hugo's *Les Misérables* (Hugo 27; 118–19) and *Les Travailleurs de la Mer*. In these contexts, the rough translation is the same as in the Greek: it refers to transparency, but unlike the Greek it is a noun. For example: '*et cette diaphaneité laissait voir l'ange*' ('a quality of transparency through which her saintly nature could be seen to shine'). Given his fluency in French and his particular admiration for Victor Hugo (A 37; A 38), it is quite possible that Pater was aware of this usage and even these particular contexts. There is evidence that Pater knew *Les Misérables* in several works, and he was familiar enough with *Les Travailleurs de la Mer* to refer to it in 'Winckelmann' (R 143). Having said this, the *imperative* of the Ancient Greek word is essential to Pater's meaning because it emphasises the element of personal endeavour that is essential to his conception of self-perfection.
7. As Frederick Copleston notes, Berkeley underwent a somewhat unexpected rehabilitation at the close of the nineteenth century (106). Echoing Pater's protest that 'Berkeley's main point has never really been answered', Huxley writes in 'Science and Morals' (1886) that 'the arguments used by Descartes and Berkeley to show that our certain knowledge does not extend beyond our states of consciousness, appear to me to be as impregnable now as they did when I first became acquainted with them some half-century ago' (131).
8. In this passage Arnold is actually quoting himself in 'On Translating Homer' (1861), but the later context is the best known and most relevant to the current discussion. In 'The Critic as Artist' (1891), following Pater's impressionistic criticism, Wilde is more explicit: 'Criticism really is, the

record of one's own soul . . . the primary aim of the critic is to see the object as in itself it really is not' (2001a: 237; 240).

9. The '"without"' – here meaning of course outside, not absent or lacking – quoted by Meisal occurs at the beginning of the Conclusion: 'Let us begin with that which is without – our physical life' (R 150).

10. Thomas Wright notes that Green and Pater were friends (I, 260), but there is no strong evidence for this. Circumstantial evidence must suffice. Pater and Green are linked first by their friendships with Benjamin Jowett, who tutored both of them at different times. In turn, in the late 1860s, they both tutored Gerard Manley Hopkins. Pater and Green were also members of the intimate and exclusive Old Mortality Society, whose members mostly studied at Balliol. Green joined in 1856 and Pater in 1863. The regulations of the Society stated that members remain members for life but, unfortunately, its records of attendees at its weekly meetings had petered out by the time Pater joined, so we will never know whether they attended the same meetings or exactly how well they were acquainted.

11. Works such as Bradley's *Ethical Studies* (1876), Green's *Prolegomena to Ethics* (1883) and Bosanquet's *The Philosophical Theory of the State* (1899) are examples of how these British neo-Idealists fused speculative philosophy with the social concerns that were prominent in their day, but which were more usually addressed using empirical-utilitarian principles.

12. Sidgwick's 1895 article 'The Philosophy of Common Sense', first published in *Mind*, addresses itself directly to Kantian Idealism (145ff) and it draws on Thomas Reid's epistemology of 'common sense'.

13. 'Giordano Bruno 'was published as an essay in the *Fortnightly Review* but it was also adapted by Pater in a chapter entitled 'The Lower Pantheism' for his unfinished novel *Gaston de Latour*. The quotation above and all others used here from Pater's essay/chapter are unchanged between the two versions. I am citing from Gerald Monsman's revised edition of *Gaston de Latour*.

Chapter 4

Metaphysics: Pater's Failed Attempt at Atheism

Oh! for a godlike aim through all these silent years.
                    Walter Pater, 'Oxford Life' (qtd Wright, I, 194)[1]

'The silence of those infinite spaces,' says Pascal, contemplating a starlight night, 'the silence of those infinite spaces terrifies me . . .'
                    Walter Pater, *The Renaissance* (27)

Dappled light on wet cobblestones and light drizzle in the air. Against the glare of a low sun an incongruent pair is silhouetted, wandering west along Brasenose Lane. One is relatively tall and big-boned, with a slight stoop; the other is short and delicate, and they are engaged in hushed but earnest conversation. At least, the taller man animatedly talks. The other, in deferential silence, stays close and listens, venturing to interrupt only occasionally. Their faint single shadow follows them between the walls of Lincoln and Exeter, and as they turn right onto the Turl, we lose them amongst the end-of-day bustle.

It was early evening on 30 May 1866, and perhaps it was later that night, in his room, as the rain returned, that Gerard Manley Hopkins recorded the episode in his diary: 'Pater talking two hours against Xtianity' (1959: 133). Not that this was particularly unusual. Nearly a month earlier he had described Pater as '"Bleak-faced Neology in cap and gown": no cap and gown but very bleak' (1959: 138). Benjamin Jowett had recommended Pater to tutor Hopkins – then a Balliol undergraduate – three years earlier, in the vain hope that this rather vocal dissident would counteract the influence of Cardinal Newman.[2] In truth, Hopkins and Pater were not so dissimilar and one may expect that each knew it; perhaps it was this that drew them to one another.[3] They were both young men in 1866 – twenty-one and twenty-six, respectively – and each had his own struggles with Christianity.

At that time the religious atmosphere of Oxford was tumultuous. The tensions brought by the Oxford Movement had faded, but new ones arose concerning the relationship between the Church and the University. The clerical hegemony that had long defined university life was in battle with the liberal Anglicanism contentiously expressed in *Essays and Reviews* in 1860 and the radical anti-clericalism of Algernon Swinburne. His 'Hymn to Proserpine' was published in 1866:

> Thou hast conquered, O pale Galilean; the world has grown grey from thy breath;
> We have drunken of things Lethean, and fed on the fullness of death. (1917: 24)

Swinburne was a founder member of the Old Mortality Society and Pater probably counted him as a friend, albeit an older and rather grand friend.[4] It is similarly vehement frustration that one hears in *The Renaissance* as Pater denounces God as 'a sort of mythical personage without us, with whom we can do warfare' and proclaims that metaphysical questions of beauty are 'as unprofitable as metaphysical questions elsewhere' (148; xxx). Such outbursts were fundamental to Rev. John Wordsworth's 'grieved' and 'pained' response to Pater's first book (61). For, in *The Renaissance*, Pater presents a violent antagonism between the 'mythical personage' of God and humanity in which God appears as a fantasy, self-destructively imagined into being to chain and imprison the individual. Perhaps the most telling passage here is the (in)famous climax of the Conclusion to *The Renaissance*. Speaking of the brief interval of a human life, Pater writes 'Some spend this interval in listlessness, some in high passions, the wisest, at least among "the children of this world," in art and song' (R 153). The unreferenced quotation in this sentence is taken from Luke 16: 1–10 in which Jesus negatively compares 'the children of this world', those who act without Christian morality for earthly benefit, with 'the children of Light', who are Christian (88). In Pater's reappropriation of this image 'the children of this world' lose their negative connotations. Indeed, he is addressing 'the children of this world': those who recognise as truth that which Jesus condemned: that life ends with death, and earthly pleasures are what we live for.

Pater's views on metaphysics, however, are less polemical and less easily fixed and formulated than he, or his later critics, would like to believe. Almost in spite of himself, he is steeped in Christian culture and its structures of thought. Doubters and would-be reformers notwithstanding, it is difficult to overestimate the pervasiveness of Anglicanism in all areas of academic life in Oxford during his lifetime. Although, to all intents and purposes, the prising apart of Church and University had begun with the University Reforms Act of 1854 and there had been sustained pressure from the government and liberals within the university for further reform, 'the spirit of the place remained the same' (V. H. H. Green 152).[5] That is to say, the university was in the grip of the clerics; most dons were ordained, and the overwhelming 'spirit of the place' was Anglican, re-emergent after the waning of the Oxford Movement. Although Pater himself was a non-clerical don – one of the new breed created by the first Reform Act – Anglicanism was the air that he breathed. Moreover, it was the air he had breathed since childhood, when his religious devotion convinced his Aunt Bessie that he would become a priest, and even as he took his BA he wrote with some certainty, 'I shall take orders in the spring, probably for a London curacy (Wright I, 91; L 2).[6]

After his painful disillusionment with religion 'he always privileged the concrete over the abstract' (Higgins 1991: 86). Or at least he tried. But his complex antipathy to God the Father and his apparent concentration on materialism is not analogous with *atheism*, which is quite different:

> he was never in his heart of hearts a confirmed atheist [. . .] he hung to religion, as it were, by a few fibres, just as – if we may borrow a simile from the countryside – the hawthorn trunks hang to the parent root-stocks after the hedge has been 'laid'. (Wright I, 204)

In his manuscript essay, 'The Aesthetic Life', he experiments with a more impartial view, suggesting 'We live (it is said daily) amid the wreck of religious theories of the unseen' (1). The parentheses and objective, impersonal tense doubly distance him from the anti-clerical views he had espoused in *The Renaissance* and in private. In middle-age he returned to the Church, as Oscar Wilde, Aubrey Beardsley and Swinburne would later. So Pater never could vanquish God, not really. The silence would be too much to bear. God lingers in Pater's conception of 'spirit', which is nowhere more evident than in his conception of the individual. And so, this chapter argues that Pater is unable ever to fully give up the Abrahamic conception of an individualised, divine, metaphysical soul. Even as he denounces the Church, the sense of some metaphysical realm is fundamental to his conceptions of creativity and individuality. In Pater's presentation of the individual the 'spirit' is insistent; sometimes taunting the reader with the suggestion of knowledge that cannot be possessed and, at others, consoling the reader with the possibility that the individual is not, after all, disinherited from the infinite. The Paterian individual is therefore nebulously underpinned by a metaphysical essence that he can neither define nor do without. As this chapter tracks its main vicissitudes we shall consider how Pater's figurative and often shifting language endows the individual with an innate metaphysical quality.

At times, echoes of Matthew Arnold, T. H. Green, John Henry Newman, Emanuel Swedenborg and others may be heard in Pater's voice as he speaks of the spirit. However, his thoughts are formed less in dialogue with other thinkers than in quiet meditation with himself. When, in a unique passage, mentioned in Chapter 1, he turns his full attention to this animating principle of the individual, he falters, describing 'the idea of the mind itself or of the ego or of personality or will[7] or of the soul or spirit of man as it is variously named' (HP 19).[8] In this rough, unpublished draft Pater is irreverent about the true nature of this variously named 'it'. Blurring these very different conceptions into one, he makes a mockery of the futile endeavour to distinguish between them. These distinctions, as he notes elsewhere, are 'hard to ascertain philosophically' (A 25). One cannot ignore the sense, sometimes, that he does not care to try. Terms like spirit and soul can slip into his prose, almost furtively, as if to paper over the cracks with cultural cliché. Yet this is not a true picture, all told. It does not mean that he is any less convinced by the existence of something divine that animates each individual and makes each unique. He keeps returning to 'the soul or spirit of man', ever preoccupied with the metaphysical notions which he disavows in the same breath.

Hellenistic Light in 'Diaphaneitè' and 'Winckelmann'

Pater's early essays explore ways to relocate the unique animating 'spirit' of the individual from heaven to humanity. In a world where God is but 'a mythical personage' and metaphysical questions are discarded, the status of hitherto metaphysical terms like *spirit* and *soul*, though, is necessarily ambiguous. Nietzsche would later write, 'I'm afraid we're not rid of God because we still believe in grammar . . .' (1997b: 21). Pater's early writings attempt to find a language with which to distinguish a secular, individuated spirit from a God-given soul. To this end, 'Diaphaneitè' and 'Winckelmann', in which Pater develops a number of ideas from the former essay, attempt to reappropriate the symbol of light from Christianity.[9] In these essays light becomes an important if ambivalent and inconsistent metaphor for the secular, animating principle of the Paterian individual.

Cassandra Laity has illustrated that light is a trope of decadent poetics, appearing in the works of Pater, Wilde and Swinburne, where it variously symbolises the intellect, male-male desire, creativity and spirit

(2009: 70–3). Whilst Laity follows Richard Dellamora's *Masculine Desire: The Sexual Politics of Victorian Aestheticism* (1990) in her focus on the erotic significance of light in Pater's works, light is also a shifting metaphor for the animating intellect of the individual. In this respect it draws on Matthew Arnold's discussion of 'sweetness and light' in *Culture and Anarchy* (1869: 89).[10] Arnold speaks more of sweetness than of light (89–103), but he suggests light as a symbol of Hellenistic intellect (89–90). Pater emboldens Arnold's faint identification between Hellenism and light in 'Winckelmann', conjuring Hellenistic philosophy as an illumination to the dark corners of the mind where superstition and mysticism might otherwise lurk: Hellenism is, in this essay, 'the principle pre-eminently of intellectual light' (R 122) and 'Hellenic culture is a sharp edge of light across the gloom' (R 131). In parentheses, Pater draws attention to the clarity and simplicity that define Hellenism in contrast both to the sensual excesses of modernity and the spiritual excesses of the middle ages: '(our modern culture may have more colour, the medieval spirit greater heat and profundity, but Hellenism is pre-eminent for light)' (R 122). In Pater's essay, Winckelmann himself embodies the qualities of Hellenistic intellect with his 'native affinity to the Hellenic spirit' strongly linked to the fact that he is 'still uninfected by any spiritual sickness, finding the end of all spiritual endeavour in the aspects of the human form, the continual stir and motion of a comely human life' (R 122; 117). With this, Pater attempts to replace metaphysics with the intellect as the animating principle of the individual.

Pater cannot for long pursue his revaluation of the individual solely on the intellectual terms offered by Hellenism. Catherine Maxwell argues that the transparent quality of the diaphanous man means that he exists 'on the borders of vision', in a liminal space between the material and spiritual worlds (2008: 74); he also exists, ultimately, on the borders of Hellenism and metaphysics. Pater's identification between light and Hellenism is unsustainable because he is ambivalent about the scope of reason on which Hellenism is founded. This ambivalence may be rooted in Arnoldian Hellenism. After all, Arnold links Hellenism with the function of criticism, writing that: 'The uppermost idea with Hellenism is to see things as they really are' (1869: 91). This link between Hellenism and the Arnoldian vision of literary criticism, which Pater famously revises in the first paragraph of *The Renaissance*,[11] reminds us that Pater's aesthetic is founded on principles of subjectivity and imagination that are ultimately at odds with the objective, rational self suggested by Arnoldian Hellenism. For Pater to pursue a strictly Hellenistic vision of the individual would be to relinquish the ineffable qualities that are fundamental to his broader vision of the late-Romantic individual: imagination and metaphysics. Pater also recognises that the faculty of reason is fragile: when Winckelmann dies at the hands of his lover[12] he is figured as Apollo, god of light and reason, crushed by Dionysus, god of sensual excess and passion, because in Pater's view of the individual, like that of Hume, reason is always slave to the passions. Pater knows well that there are more things in heaven and earth than are dreamt of in Hellenistic philosophy. Passion and desire are two of these things, and in Pater's writings they form two of his departure points from Hellenistic philosophy. I will return to these in Chapters 5 and 6; spirituality is another.

On the subject of spirit, Pater is often at odds with himself. He is uncertain of how to vanquish God when he wants to retain the nebulous spirituality and divinity which the Christian God had granted to the individual. His uncertainty is illustrated by the ambivalence of his symbol of light. Alongside and at odds with light as a symbol of reason, Pater presents light as a metaphor for a metaphysical quality within the individual. This is first suggested in 'Diaphaneitè', in which the diaphanous man is defined by 'a mind of taste lighted up by some spiritual ray within' (D 155). The compound image rests on an implicit distinction between the 'mind of taste' and the 'spiritual ray within' it. The mention of *taste*, first, evokes Edmund Burke's empirical aesthetic, in which the quality of taste is based on understanding and may be developed 'by extending our knowledge, by a steady attention to our object, and by frequent exercise' (Burke 25). Pater, though, transforms this empirical idea with the description of 'some spiritual ray'. Light, here, suggests itself as a symbol not of the rational mind but of an undefined, possibly metaphysical force. It illuminates the imagination and not the rational mind, anticipating the 'light and heat' metaphor for creativity in the Preface to *The Renaissance* (xxxiii) and suggesting that this creative light is distinct from the empirical mind. The integral relationship between spirit and imagination is refined later in the essay as Pater describes the 'pure white light that one might disentwine from the tumultuary richness in Goethe's nature' (D 158).

The adjective 'some' in this first description reiterates the unfathomable character of this light: it is not *the* spiritual ray but *some* undefined other. Here Pater is at the limits of any empirically defined epistemology, and his conception of 'spirit' is emblematised not so much by 'clear crystal' as by 'that hard gem' with its myriad of opaque, beautiful surfaces. He is a quintessential Romantic: aware of a spiritual dimension in our ordinary perceptions but believing this to be beyond the range of rational analysis. This is a nebulous force in Pater's visions of art and the individual; but a force, nonetheless. If he is, as he purports to be, liberating us from that 'sort of mythical personage without', he is unable to do it as a good Hellenist through the faculty of reason. His liberation emerges as a middle course that seeks to erase God but to retain the personal metaphysical quality of spirit. The light which had been the *ex*ternal light of Hellenic culture in general or bequeathed to the individual by God is now *in*ternalised, consolidated within the individual. To an extent, this is analogous to Winckelmann's triumph of 'finding the end of all endeavour in the aspects of the human form' (R 117). The difference is that whilst Winckelmann did this through the cultivation of reason, the 'spiritual ray' suggests an indefinable quality at the heart of the individual that cannot be reduced to reason or even personality or character. Paterian spirit assumes the qualities of light, becoming unbounded, unquantifiable, indivisible and immaterial. In marked contrast to the Romantics' placing of spirit in the heart, and the empiricists' and psychologists' location of 'spirit' in the brain, the Paterian spirit emanates from the general *within*. It diffuses through every part of the individual.

The internal quality of spirituality and imagination is expanded through the image of light, which grants the individual god-like divinity. In a passage in 'Winckelmann', Pater begins to describe an unnamed Greek statue with the image of 'pure light on its gleaming surfaces' (R 136). The evocation of light reflecting off the contours of the statue at first suggests an external source as in the light of Hellenic reason or the light of faith brought by Jesus. After skirting this form, though, Pater's eye returns to the image of light, which has shifted from surface reflection to a 'white light' – the hottest and strongest light that could be created in the late-nineteenth century – that emanates out from the 'unchanging characteristics' within the individual: 'That white light purged from the angry bloodlike stains of action and passion, reveals not only what is accidental in man but the tranquil godship in him as opposed to the restless accidents of life' (R 137). The dichotomy between the inner-life and the frenzied 'action and passion' in the outer-world evokes this internal 'white light' as pure, tranquil and eternal: borrowing the immutable element implicit from the Abrahamic soul in sharp contrast to the 'accidental' and 'restless accidents of life'. In this way, the Paterian individual is intricately linked with this 'supposed secondary, or still more remote meaning, – that diviner signification held in reserve, *in recessu divinius aliquid*' (R 23).[13] The analogy between 'white light' and creative genius reminds us of the slippage between spirituality and creativity. It also stresses the a priori nature of this spiritual-creative quality, building on the gestures of Pater's metaphor of light in order to depart from an ostensibly empirical materialism toward a metaphysical vision of an a priori quality at the centre of the individual.

Pater takes the 'tranquil godship' one step further by positing that the individual actually becomes a god. Quoting the neo-Platonist metaphysician Plotinus, he writes that 'we may see [. . .] ourself in splendour, filled with the light of intellect, or rather light itself, pure, buoyant, aerial, become – in truth, being – a god' (GL 78). With this, Pater's yearning for 'a god-like aim through all these silent years' finds its mark within the individual. This innate quality, symbolised by light, individualises truth and gives the individual power to create and to redeem himself. It imbues brief human life with divinity, making it intrinsically perfect. This autonomy renders Jesus or God the Father superfluous because the individual need not search for external forces to determine truth or ethics. Nietzsche would call this 'a revaluation of all values' (1982: 656), and though Pater taps too softly for Nietzsche's philosophical hammer, here too the individual emerges from the eternal taint of Original Sin in order to become an end in himself.

At the same time, Pater's prose attempts to find a new idiom through which to speak of the individual. He rejects the Biblical rhetoric that one often hears echoed in the 'prophetic mode' of Carlyle, Ruskin, and Arnold (Peterson 376). In the quotation above, the 'light of intellect' is revised in mid-sentence as though capturing those 'decisions and revisions which a minute will reverse'. It leaves *pure* light: the adjective for no definable quality, but itself the divine quality which exalts the individual to the status of a god. Human divinity is an antidote or at least an attempt at an antidote to the insecurities of a godless world. With this in mind I cannot agree with William Shuter's argument that 'It was when Pater's thinking was least conventional that his voice was most assured and when his thinking was most orthodox that it was least confident and assertive (1997: 40). Such a statement finds support in the Conclusion to *The Renaissance*, but it is too sweeping as an assessment of Pater's broader oeuvre. Thinking back to Nietzsche's belief that 'we're not rid of God because we still believe in grammar . . .', Pater's prose attempts to remake the grammar of the Bible, dissipating its declamatory tone and didacticism into those wondering, wandering sentences which seek to capture the uncertain, fallible individual hesitating in the wake of God's death, unable to make assertions without the assurance of God's word. Whilst Nietzsche sought to define the post-God world by assuming Biblical tones and allegories in *Thus Spoke Zarathustra* (*Also Sprach Zarathustra;* 1883–5), the 'death' of God leaves Pater insecure and unsure, and his stuttering ever-shifting prose reflects this even as it gestures towards the dawn of a new secular spirit.

Through Pater's imagery of light, this quality within the individual emerges to become fundamentally distinct from 'the idea of mind itself or of the <u>ego</u> or of the personality or will' with which it had been inter-changeable in 'The History of Philosophy' (c. 1880: 21). The images of light effectively suggest that this quality is intangible and ethereal, as ego and personality are not. These qualities make spirit resemble the Abrahamic soul, with the crucial distinction that by consolidating 'godship' within the individual alone Pater may, with a neat secular twist, dispense with God Almighty. However, the relationship between this spiritual light within the individual as '<u>ego</u>', 'personality', or 'will' is neb-ulous. In 'The Aesthetic Life', for example, Pater seems unable to decide as he writes that 'the higher life ~~life~~ of mind ~~and~~ or spirit will involve pref-erence' (AL 15). His crossing out indicates an unresolved notion of the distinctions between the finite mind and the infinite, metaphysical soul. His sentence reconsiders the rash 'and' which grants them co-existence, and his replacement 'or' is a withdrawal of confidence: a declaration of uncertainty as to whether mind and soul are different substances after all.

Pater's prose reaches beyond itself for a conception of the self that cannot be encapsulated in words, only evoked in the imagination. Light becomes an ever-shifting metaphor with its variously incompatible sug-gestions of Hellenic reason, spirit, divinity and creativity. It locates the confused nature of the animating quality at the heart of the individual at the same time as it illustrates Pater's inability to give up the idea of an innate quality to define the individual. What we find in each concep-tion, though, is not after all so different from the Abrahamic soul of Christianity. Each account evokes an internal quality that exalts the individual above the merely material Humean 'bundle or collection of different perceptions' (1964: I. iv, 239). The spiritual light conceived in 'Diaphaneitè', 'Winckelmann' and 'Giordano Bruno' grants the indi-vidual autonomy from God as an individuated external force, whilst retaining an individuated and potentially metaphysical and quality at the centre of self-identity.

Pantheism and Creativity

In Chapter 3 I noted the confluence of Pater's interest in German Idealism with that of fellow Old Mortality member T. H. Green. Again, with his conception of 'the tranquil godship', Pater recalls Green's pantheistic belief that there 'is the presence in us of God' (1874: 131). Pater sketches an intimate relationship between the individuated spirit, pantheism and creativity that quickly departs though from Green.

Pater's nebulous conception of 'some' individuated spirit expands into what he variously calls 'world-spirit' and 'spirit of life' (A 56; GS 95). This is founded on Pater's idea that the central forces of the world, which Christianity places in the hands of God the Father, pulse through the creative individual and the world. Operating through the imaginative individual, the spirit promises to give order to the individual's 'unstable, flickering, inconsistent' impressions of the universe, in order to provide the 'unity in variety' Pater seeks (R 151; PP 35):

> To enforce a reasonable unity and order, to impress some larger likeness of reason, as one knows it in one's self, upon the chaotic infinitude of the impressions that reach us from every side, is what philosophy as such proposes. (PP 21)

The imagination comes to take the place of 'the larger likeness of reason': imagination impresses unity onto 'the chaotic infinitude of impressions' in Pater's aesthetic vision. For one often credited with identifying the disunity of modernity, Pater is surprisingly preoccupied with unity; and the idea of a pantheistic spirit offers him the possibility of creating 'an energetic unity or identity [which] makes itself visible amid abounding variety' (A 79).

Pater first fastens onto the idea of a unifying spirit brought into being through the imagination in 'Wordsworth' (1874, 1889):

> the network of man and nature was seen to be pervaded by a common, universal life: a new, bold thought lifted him above the furrow, above the green turf of the Westmoreland churchyard, to a world altogether different in its vagueness and vastness, and the narrow glen was full of the brooding power of the one universal spirit. (A 56)

The humanistic dimension of pantheistic unity is particularly striking in this passage with the 'common, universal life' perhaps characterising spirit as a universal sympathy between individuals. Pater develops this quality in his later essay, 'Giordano Bruno' (1889) to indicate that sympathy between individuals offers redemption from a godless world:

> The ghastly spectacle of the endless material universe – infinite dust, in truth, starry as it may look to our terrestrial eyes – that prospect from which the mind of Pascal recoiled so painfully, induced in Bruno only the delightful consciousness of an ever-widening kinship and sympathy, since every one of these infinite worlds must have its sympathetic inhabitants. (GL 78)

The 'ever-widening kinship and sympathy' presents itself as a humanistic consolation to the silence of a godless universe. It suggests that pantheism, as a metaphor for the energy of sympathy that surpasses individuals, relocates forgiveness and understanding from a God Almighty who might be reached by prayer alone, to other individuals.

Pater's evocation of pantheism in 'Wordsworth' is energised by a strong identification between himself and Wordsworth, and his depiction of the poet's 'inward', 'quiet', apparently 'monotonous' life self-consciously reflects his own (A 44).[14] Still, the concerns here are more Paterian than Wordsworthian. As with each new clause the narrative ascends to 'the one universal spirit', it also moves beyond Wordsworth's pantheism and into that of Pater. The 'one universal spirit' promises to assuage the random and discrete phenomena that characterise the world depicted in the Conclusion to *The Renaissance*. Both its singularity and its universality give a sense of unity in diversity, achieved on terms that gesture beyond the material world to 'the spiritual, the imaginative horizon' that he felt had been narrowed by empirical philosophy (AL 2). The importance of the imagination is implicit in the passage from 'Wordsworth': the pantheistic vision evoked by Pater brought into being by Wordsworth's imagination (and Pater's). Echoing this imaginative pantheism, in 'Shakespeare's English Kings' (1889) for example, Pater writes that lyric poetry has a 'unity of impression' that is at the crux of 'artistic perfection' (A 203): 'all the various expressions of the conflict of character and circumstance falling at last into the compass of a single melody, or musical theme' (A 203). The unifying quality of music here recalls Pythagoras' theory of *musica universalis* or 'the music of the spheres'.[15]

Pater's aestheticised version of pantheism is central in his reconception of the relationship between spirit and matter. Through the imagination spirit and matter become two interpenetrated aspects of being, as Pater argues for an end to the 'false contrast or antagonism' of them (A 212). His conception of 'spirit' would change dramatically over the course of his career but he is consistent in his endeavour to understand spirit and matter as two aspects of one substance. Aligning himself with pantheism he writes in 1875 of

> some spirit of life, akin to that which makes its energies felt within ourselves [. . .] Such a philosophy is a systematised form of that sort of poetry (we may study it, for instance, either in Shelley or in Wordsworth), which also has its fancies of a spirit of the earth, or of the sky, – a personal intelligence abiding in them, the existence of which is assumed in every suggestion such poetry makes to us of a sympathy between the ways and aspects of outward nature and the moods of men. (GS 95–6)

Pater's suggestion that matter and spirit are two aspects of a single fundamental substance alludes to the Christian belief that body and soul will be reconciled in Heaven in order to radically relocate this reconciliation to the present time, in the material world. Or Pater's pantheistic ideas can also be seen as a humanistic return to the time before the Fall and Original Sin when body and spirit were in harmony. The inter-penetration of spirit and matter is analogous to Pater's more famous reconception of the relationship between form and content in art, out-lined most clearly in 'The School of Giorgione' (1877: 1888): in all arts, except for music, he notes, 'it is possible to distinguish the matter, and the understanding can always make this distinction, yet it is the constant effort of art to obliterate it' (R 86). Angela Leighton argues that form is to 'obliterate' content in art (2007: 84ff), but I would suggest that it is the *distinction* between form and content that is obliterated, and not the content itself in Pater's vision. This interpretation makes more sense in the context of the essay, 'The School of Giorgione', in which Pater suggests that 'in their union or identity, [they] present one single effect to the "imaginative reason"'; 'they inhere in and completely saturate each other'; 'the perfect identification of matter and form' (R 88; 88; 90). This is a fusion of the equally significant elements of art, privileging neither, only redressing the balance after the over-emphasis on content at the expense of beautiful form in prose.[16] This interpretation reveals a strong analogy between the dynamics of content and form, and those of spirit and matter.

The figure of Dante Gabriel Rossetti individualises and epitomises the fusion of spirit and matter. Pater presents him as an artist in whom 'the material and spiritual are fused and blent': 'In our actual concrete experience, the two trains of phenomena which the words *matter* and *spirit* do but roughly distinguish, play inextricably into each other' (A 212; Pater's italics). The interplay of matter and spirit are reflected in Rossetti's ability to fuse form and matter in his poetry and it echoes his significance as an exemplar of balanced receptivity and creativity. In this fusion, 'if the spiritual attains the definite visibility of a crystal, what is material loses its earthiness and impurity' (A 212). Pater's meta-phor draws on the fact that at extreme reductions of temperature gases become liquids and are eventually crystallised into solids. In the same way, his spirit crystallises so that it becomes something tangible; some-thing that we may commend to the understanding. Despite the figurative contradiction it proposes to Pater's accompanying image of creative heat and light, the spirit as crystal suggests its beauty and preciousness, and a little of its ethereal nature. The transferral of qualities on each side, spiritual to material and material to spiritual, means that we may now perceive the spirit, which could not be perceived before, as a crystal.

The metaphysical connotations of Pater's pantheism need no proof because his assertion of subjectivity renders objective truth virtually irrelevant. As the passage from Wordsworth indicated, he is more interested in how the belief in pantheism recentres the imagination from God to concrete sensual experience. As he writes of Bruno,

> His pantheistic belief that the Spirit of God is in all things, was not inconsistent with, might even encourage, a keen and restless eye for the dramatic details of life and character however minute, for humanity in all its visible attractiveness, since there, too, in truth, divinity lurks. (GL 75)

In the first part of the statement pantheism presents itself as an encouragement to artistic vision, the truth value of which is irrelevant. The narrative's view has shifted by the end of the sentence in order to qualify this ambivalence with its final assertion that, indeed, 'in truth, divinity lurks'. So the sentence moves from scepticism to affirmation and as a result pantheistic spirit is transformed from a myth created by the individual to a true divinity inherent in the creative individual. Pater presents *Venus de Melos* (300–100 BC) as the positive embodiment of this quality, as a work conceived with the 'keen and restless eye' of a pantheist creator, because in the apprehension of the statue:

> The mind begins and ends with the finite image, yet loses no part of the spiritual motive. This motive is not lightly and loosely attached to the sensuous form, as its meaning to an allegory, but saturates and is identical with it. (R 132)

Pater defines his ideas against the Christian view that spirit transcends the image or that the image points beyond itself to a metaphysical otherworld. In his conception of the 'spiritual motive', this exalts art so that spectatorship is itself a spiritual experience, not premised on an after-life or gesturing to a spirit elsewhere in time, but an immanent, immediate experience of the spiritual through aesthetic subjectivity, simply for that moment's sake.

Pater's characterisation of pantheism links his desire for 'a godlike aim' with the creative imagination. The ontological status of pantheism in Pater's work is irreducibly ambiguous: whether 'spirit' inheres in matter in any objective sense or whether it is but the product of the imaginative individual is unclear. In the context of Pater's broader view of the subjective mind though, this question is marginalised. The decentring of objective criticism in the Preface to *The Renaissance* in favour of the subjective mind is problematic for the subjective idealism it might ultimately unleash.[17] Still it makes the ontological status of pantheism unimportant: whether pantheistic spirit is in the imagination or inherent in the external world, it is all the same. Like all reality, it is founded only on the unsteady ground of the subjective mind, where it reinstates spirituality to materiality and assuages the fragmentation of modernity. Moreover, Paterian creativity seeks to liberate the individual from God, as it later would liberate Stephen Dedalus. There is an implicit elitism whereby this divine Abrahamic soul is refounded in creativity. Steven Lukes argues that Romantic individualism 'especially as applied to the artist' led in one direction to 'the purest egoism and social nihilism' (18). It is unclear as to whether Pater is suggesting that spirit is peculiar to imaginative geniuses or whether ordinary, uncreative people are also 'lighted up by some spiritual ray within'. If Pater's fusion of spirit and creativity implies the former though, the others become but part of the herd in 'collective life' (D 157).

The Christian Soul in Pater's Later Essays

When with dark mischievous humour Pater declared that he would seek to be ordained in 1862 it was because he thought it the most wonderful game to become a priest who did not believe. He would be an enemy within. Thirty-two years later, shortly before his death, he was again thinking of taking holy orders. This time it was without irony.

Pater's return to the Church has variously perplexed and disappointed critics, who wish to claim him, as others have wished to claim him, as a champion of the atheist cause. Yet, his return to the comfort of the Church does not create a schism in his thought. It should be seen more as an evolution that brings him, not from atheism to faith, but from one kind of agnosticism to another. As respective emblems of the secular quality and the God-defined quality in one's self, Pater's use of the terms 'spirit' and 'soul' indicate that his religious evolution is fuzzy. Like a vestige of Christianity, the Abrahamic soul is never fully removed from Pater's writings. It is noted in *The Renaissance* as 'a wonderful outpour-ing of soul'; '[t]he beating of the soul against its bars' (R 5; R 122), where its perennial appearances indicate Pater's inability to dispense with the ideology of Christianity.

In 1894 he muses in an aside in 'Pascal' that 'the doubts never die, they are only just kept down in a perpetual *agonia*' (MS 61). The fun-damental shift in his religious life around the early 1880s was perhaps Pater's realisation that he needed belief. As Thomas Wright records, one friend asked '"What [. . .] was your object in writing *Marius*?" "To show," replied Pater, "the necessity of religion"' (II, 87). By the mid-1880s, Christianity offers Pater one of the very things he rejected as a young man: reassurance. He resolves an uncertain self into the certain-ties of religious faith. In a sense, the nature of this uncertain self will become clearer as we proceed, looking to the pressures that threaten to dissolve the individual in the following chapters, and leave him teetering always on the brink of his own dissolution. In his later works, Pater sees in Christianity most of what he wanted to see imbued in the pagan world: beauty, mystery and compassion, but gifted with God-ordained certainty. Armed with such certainty Pater subverts his metaphor of light, suggesting his ultimate disavowal of pagan spirituality. It is in this context that we should understand the dynamics between the individual and Christianity in 'Pascal', 'Style' (1889), Pater's Introduction to Charles Shadwell's edition of Dante's *Purgatorio* (1892), and his ultimate renunciation of the pagan spirit in 'Apollo in Picardy' (1893).

God does not have a substantive presence in the world of Pater's words. Pater only explores God insofar as God affects one's sense of one's own individualism and aesthetics. He presents Christianity through the individual, drawing out its humanism and the sense of hope it gives. This absolute centrality of the individual and of kindness, compassion, and love between individuals is a constant even though the fabric of the world is gradually reconceived. Pater admires the compassion of Dante's Christianity, with its 'assurance that [. . .] "boundless grace / Hath arms of such a large embrace, / That they will straight admit / Whatever turns to It"' (xxi). And 'the breadth of Dante's theological horizon'; his 'cosmopolitan genius' (xxiii), offers Pater a way in which to reconcile his pagan aesthetic with Christianity.[18] In this way, Pater reformulates the humanism of his pantheistic vision of 'an ever-widening kinship'. Christianity redefines the individual, so that he exists in a perpetual state of hopefulness:

> An age of faith, if such ever there were, our age certainly is not; an age of love, all its pity and self-pity notwithstanding, who shall say? – in its religious scepticism, however, especially as compared with the last century in its religious scepticism, an age of hope, we may safely call it, of a development of religious hope or religious hopefulness. (Pater 1892: xx)

Faith defines the individual, here, not by the absence or presence of God, but by that state of mind that is crucial to Pater: a sort of unfulfilled but undenied sense of the possible.

Christian belief gives validation to Pater's faith that there is some metaphysical, mysterious dimension to the individual. Mrs Humphry Ward recalls that later in life 'he became more endlessly interested in [Christianity] and haunted by the "something" in it which he thought inexplicable' (121). In a theological conversation between herself and Pater, he remarked, 'You think it's all plain. But I can't. There are such mysterious things. Take that saying, "Come ye up to me, all ye that are weary and heavy laden." There is a mystery in it – something supernatural' (122). The allure of the supernatural was great. The word 'strange' – repeated again and again in his essays – is suggestive of at least this much.

Christianity underpinned the inexplicable with faith. In 'Style', God appears as a deus ex machina to justify the inexplicable soul, pulled out in the essay's final moments to concretise a subtler shift that we see when soul and mind come to define two different aspects of literature:

> By mind, the literary artist reaches us through static and objective indications of design in his work, legible to all. By soul, he reaches us, somewhat capriciously perhaps, one and not another, through vagrant sympathy and a kind of immediate contact. (A 25)

Here, the definiteness of the distinction between mind and soul is in striking contrast to Pater's uncertain consideration of 'the idea of the mind itself or of the <u>ego</u> or of personality or will or of the soul or spirit of man as it is variously named' in 'The History of Philosophy'. In 'Style', the soul has vanquished spirit to reign alone over Pater's aesthetic and it gives him confidence to assert that the difference between the 'essentially finite' mind and the infinite soul is 'real enough practically' (A 25).

Pater's friends tended to stress his aesthetic reasons – the melody and whiff of the bells and smells – for his attendance at the churches of St Aloysius and St Barnabas in Oxford. However, we see that the Church affects Pater's aesthetic as much as Pater's aesthetic defines his religiosity. The distinction, Pater argues, in an attempt to resolve this indeterminacy on his own terms, is made apparent by its expression in art:

> By mind, the literary artist reaches us through the static and objective indications of design in his work, legible to all. By soul, he reaches us, somewhat capriciously perhaps, one and not another, through vagrant sympathy and a kind of immediate contact. (A 25)

Again, Pater draws Christianity as a supremely humanistic religion as the soul is cast as a medium through which to attain 'sympathy' and 'contact'. The Paterian soul emerges as a creative force catalysed by 'the glory of God' (A 38). A sense of God's glory is a prerequisite of 'great art' to the extent that the essential quality of great literature is personified as soul: 'The way in which the theological interests sometimes avail themselves of language is perhaps the best illustration of the force I mean to indicate generally in literature, by the word soul' (25). In this way, soul and, with it orthodox Almighty God, usurp spirit and the secular sentiment it represented. There is a sense in which, perhaps, Pater has settled with an orthodox conception of God-given *soul*. His later revisions illustrate a loss of that youthful confidence, and this defines his later period. Individualism and creativity are now underpinned by God. Perhaps it is the tired, tacit acceptance of one who no longer has the energy to pursue the uncapturable.

The Rejection of Light in 'Apollo in Picardy'

Just how far Pater has moved from his early vision of spiritual light is only really clear in 'Apollo in Picardy', written and published in 1893. This short story centres on the encounter between the mysterious Apollyon and an ascetic academic and monk called Prior Saint-Jean, in medieval France. Having charmed the Prior and his companion Hyacinth, Apollyon mysteriously unbalances the Prior's mind, undermining his ability to finish his book on mathematics, before wreaking violent havoc on the quiet town and on the Prior's life. Apollyon acts as a shocking subversion of Pater's early symbol of Hellenic light. Emphasising the obvious link between Apollyon and Apollo, the story picks up on the language used to evoke Hellenic light in 'Winckelmann' and 'Diaphaneitè' – for instance, 'that astounding white light!' (MS 140) – and subverts its significance as a symbol for rational knowledge or spirit into a symbol of irrationality and violence. Pater suggests in his introductory comments:

> [Apollo] presented a strange example of a cold and very reasonable spirit disturbed suddenly, thrown off its balance, as by a violent beam, a blaze of new light, revealing, as it glanced here and there, a hundred truths unguessed as before, yet a curse, as it turned out, to its receiver, in dividing hopelessly against itself the well-ordered kingdom of his thought. (MS 122)

The formerly truth-revealing quality of light certainly emerges in the story as 'violent' and 'a curse' to the hitherto rational Prior. Pater evokes goes on to evoke light frequently as a metaphor for irrationality and evil, as when Prior Saint-Jean imagines his cell 'alight, alight softly' sees outside 'a low circlet of soundless flame, waving, licking daintily up the black sky . . . "It is hell-fire!" he said' (MS 125), or when he figures the anguish caused by Apollyon as 'lightning flashes; flashes of blindness one might rather call them' (MS 141). Apollyon initially appears to epitomise innocence, charming his companions and magically attracting animals and birds to his side (MS 134). However, his callous murders of these animals and of the innocent boy Hyacinth show that his powers work both for good and evil (MS 144).

Under the mysterious influence of Apollyon, Prior Saint-Jean experiences profound truths: 'matters no longer to be reasoned upon and understood, but to be seen rather, to be looked at and heard' (MS 140). The cruel irony is that this 'beam of insight' (MS 140) negates his ability to rationalise and communicate his thoughts. The threat that it poses to 'the well-ordered kingdom of thought' is at one level the threat of homoerotic desires awakened in the Prior by Apollyon[19] but it is also the threat of paganism – of the rejection of the Christian God – to the religious status quo. In 1873 this was Pater's hope; in 1893 it is his fear. In 'Apollo in Picardy' Prior Saint-Jean is overcome with a destructive 'white light':

> – that astounding white light! – rising steadily in the cup, the mental receptacle, till it overflowed, and he lay faint and drowning in it. [There was] no way of escape from the baffling strokes, the lightning flashes; flashes of blindness one might rather call them. (MS 141)

This is a thorough subversion of the symbol of light presented in 'Diaphaneitè' and 'Winckelmann'. The 'white light' that, in those essays, promised a 'tranquil godship' (D 154) in the individual, here, becomes an intrusive and destructive force, which recalls Dante's blindness in the face of Heaven's brilliant bright light. Only Prior Saint-Jean's blindness is not temporary. It annihilates his ability to think and does so with such violence that it threatens to annihilate him. In the story's final paragraph, Pater briefly describes how, after the disappearance of Apollyon, the Prior lost his wits and later died suddenly in an asylum (MS 145–6). His mind has become, one might say, the '"madhouse cell"', from which Pater once believed pagan art could deliver the individual (R 23).

Once one accepts that Pater never really gives up metaphysics though, his return to the Church no longer seems radical. On the contrary, it is almost inevitable. Pater was never a thorough-going materialist. He enjoys 'the elusive inscrutable mistakable self' (HP 23) too much to have it subjected to a full exposition. Fundamentally distinct from temperament, personality or mind, it holds the promise that the individual is somehow greater than the powers of reason or empirical investigation could ever determine. In the silence of those infinite voids it gives Pater comfort to know that the value of the post-Romantic individual is confirmed by his imagination. The intimate relationship between creativity and spirit runs throughout Pater's writings, from pagan to Christian. The mystery on which this is founded is not assuaged by music or by any other aesthetic experience; it is impenetrable and incomprehensible. In Pater's writings, the nebulous space of spirit is located always just beyond the comprehensible. His narrative reflects the way that it evades our comprehension and exists, in so far as it exists at all, as something felt. He strives toward it almost as if to find the limitations of expression. In this way, the abstract comes to haunt the concrete and Pater pushes the limits of what can be explored by rational thought alone.

The 'spirit or soul' denotes an issue rather than a concept for Pater, and one that is absolutely necessary to his aesthetic. His writings explore its vistas, wandering between secularism, pantheism and Christianity, infusing the material world with grandeur and seeking to affirm that there is divinity within the individual. This is where 'analysis leaves off' (R 152) as Pater looks beyond the rational and empirical horizons offered by modern philosophy to assert the absolute necessity of 'that other sort of knowledge' (HP 12).

Notes

1. Wright quotes from an unpublished poem by Pater dated 27 March 1860.
2. Pater did not actually begin to tutor Hopkins till 1866, perhaps due to the warning against Pater issued to Hopkins by S. R. Brooke, as discussed in Chapter 2.
3. Matthew Kaylor discusses the possibility that their mutual sympathy centres on homoeroticism (2006: 207ff). He is quite right to be cautious in introducing this idea because this speculation rests on shaky foundations.
4. Just how well Pater and Swinburne knew each other is contested. It is likely that they first met through the Old Mortality Society in the early 1860s. Edmund Gosse writes that 'the poet [Swinburne] was not an unfrequent visitor in those years [c. 1870] to Pater's college rooms. To all young Oxford, then, the name of Mr. Swinburne was an enchantment . . .' (254). However, Swinburne himself told Thomas Wright years later that 'he never met Pater, to speak to him, more than twice – once in London and once at Oxford, and that even then only a few words passed' (Wright I, xv).
5. The various turns in the relationship between Oxford University and the Church in the mid-nineteenth century are detailed by V. H. H. Green in *A Short History of Oxford University* (143ff).
6. In fact, Pater attempted to take holy orders in the autumn of 1862, after completing his degree, regardless of the fact that he had no Christian faith. His former friend John Rainier McQueen notified the Bishop of London that Pater had no faith and consequently his ordination was blocked. Michael Levey gives a full account of this episode in *The Case of Walter Pater* (91).
7. This is perhaps an indication that Pater read Arthur Schopenhauer's *The World as Will and Idea* (*Die Welt als Wille und Vorstellung*; 1819). Schopenhauer characterises a world of post-Kantian noumena and phenomena, in which the former – the Will – is constantly striving, and at odds with itself. Within this vision, the 'Will' (capitalised) manifests itself into the 'will' of the individual. Since Schopenhauer was the first philosopher

to take music seriously, as well as being a very literary writer, and given Pater's extensive reading of other German transcendental idealists, it would be surprising if he did not read Schopenhauer – but there is no concrete evidence.

8. Pater's ambivalence regarding these terms is also apparent in 'The Aesthetic Life', where he notes that 'the higher life of mind ~~and~~ or spirit will involve preference' (AL 15), as discussed below.

9. Jesus brings truth and faith to alleviate darkness in the hearts of His people in the Gospel of John (8: 12, 113) and, again, in William Holman Hunt's *Light of the World* (1853–4).

10. *Culture and Anarchy* was one of few books that Pater owned personally. He had a first edition, signed 'Walter H. Pater' (Inman 1981a: 341).

11. ' "To see the object as in itself it really is," has justly been said to be the aim of all true criticism whatever; and in aesthetic criticism to first step towards seeing one's object as it really is, is to know one's impression as it really is . . .' (R xxix; Arnold 1865: 1). Pater quotes Arnold for the express purpose of highlighting the space between the *disinterestedness* of Arnold's view and his own subjective, relative aesthetic. I discuss this passage more fully in Chapter 3.

12. Pater glosses this: 'One morning [Arcangeli] entered Winckelmann's rooms, under pretence of taking leave [. . .] a cord was thrown round his neck' (R 126). As Alex Potts has explained, Winckelmann's homoerotic relationships were by this time well known and recent studies of Pater have discussed at length his aesthetic minoritising discourse in 'Winckelmann'. For further reference, see Dellamora's chapter on 'Arnold, Winckelmann, and Pater', especially page 114. Pater's quotation later in the essay of Samuel 14: 43 may allude back to Winckelmann's death to intimate the unutterable: '*I did but taste a little honey with the end of the rod that was in mine hand, and lo! I must die*' (R 142). This phallic allusion certainly has the arch humour of a man who would have joined the Church without belief. Oscar Wilde, of course, alludes to this, making the homoerotic metaphor more obvious in 'Hélas!': '. . . lo! with a little rod / I did but touch the honey of romance – / And must I lose a soul's inheritance?' (449).

13. The Latin is translated as 'some divine quality in the depths' (Phillips 162 n.).

14. In full, the passage from 'Wordsworth' is strikingly similar to Denis Donoghue's comments on Pater in his biography: 'There are weeks or even months in which he seems to have taken literally his favourite motif of evanescence and drifted away. We assume that he is still alive, but the evidence for his breathing is meagre [. . .] he has been teaching, tutoring a few students, or spending the Long Vacation in France or Italy [. . .] By comparison to his contemporaries he seems hardly to have lived' (23–4).

15. This metaphor is touched on again when Pater discusses Pythagoras' vision of cosmos through numbers in *Plato and Platonism* (35).

16. Pater's desire to invigorate the status of prose is closely related to a more general sense that poetry was unable to express the modern condition and frustration at the apparent limitations of poetic form. Pater felt that prose was the art form of emerging modernity. He advised the student Oscar Wilde to give up poetry for prose, and with less success he later wrote to

Arthur Symons: 'You know I give a high place to the literature of prose as a fine art, and therefore hope you won't think me brutal in saying that the admirable qualities of your verse are those also of imaginative prose [. . .] I should say, make prose your principal *metier* [sic]' (L 80).

17. See discussion in Chapter 3.

18. The intellectual relationship between Pater and Dante deserves more attention and from a scholar better versed in Dante than I. Suffice to say here that the spirit of Dante hovers in the background of Pater's early writings – 'Diaphaneitè' and *The Renaissance* – but acquires a new significance in this very frank, personal Introduction to Charles Shadwell's translation of *Purgatorio*. Like Shadwell, Pater was a member of the Oxford Dante Society. He was elected in December 1890.

19. The Prior's first sight of Apollyon is evoked with a homoerotic description of his sleeping body (MS 127). This could be linked to Pater's earlier works, 'A Study of Dionysus' (1876) and 'Denys L'Auxerrois' (1887), which tell similar stories of the sensual, homoerotic god reappearing in a later age to unsettle the well-ordered lives of a small town.

Chapter 5

Sense and Sensuality: Caught between Venus and Dionysus

And haply when the tragic clouds of night
Were slowly wrapping round thee, in the cold
Of which men always die, a sense renewed
Of the things sweet to touch and breath and sight
                    Michael Field, 'Walter Pater: A Poetic Tribute'

Walter Pater carefully satiated his desire for innocuous sensations. He kept a bowl of rose petals on his desk and fresh orange peel on his window sill to create exquisite aromas (Bussell 285). Once, at a luncheon party, he was playfully asked: if he were to be a fish what kind of fish he would be. To this he replied, 'a carp' (qtd Seiler 1987: 105). In this dry parody of his popular image Pater would be, no doubt, an ornamental carp with luminescent silvery multi-colours to make him a fish of vivid beauty. He would exist to experience pure, unreflective, superficial sensations, aware only of himself and his immediate surroundings. Not only was he painfully conscious that his aesthetic followers conceived him as such, there was an element to Pater that wished to be this complete and unreserved aesthete. Yet it was not to be. Despite his quiet enjoyment of heightened sensations, his famous affirmations of sensual experience and the appropriation of his ideas by a generation of undergraduates, in Pater's broader aesthetic philosophy sensation has ambivalent status: it is not so much a creed as a problem. And so this chapter explores the underlying dangers of 'the things sweet to touch and breath and sight' in Pater's writings. It suggests that he is intensely concerned with the way sensuality may enslave the passions of the individual and it argues that, ultimately, art offers him a meta-sensuality played out in the theatre of the imagination to control the danger of sensuality enacted on real flesh.

There is but little precedent for such trouble in Pater's formative influences. He begins, as we have seen, from an empirical philosophy in which sensations are understood primarily as that which conveys knowledge of the world. Sensuality is not for its own sake; it is a 'corrective authority' to vanquish superstitions (HP 4). Still, sensation proves far more problematic for Pater than it ever was for Locke or Hume. After all, their conception of sensation is founded on a stable relationship between sensation and the individual. In comparison to Pater, Hume was naïve about sensations. In his *Treatise*, he argued that moral judgements are formed through impressions and ideas, and subject to the faculty of reason: sensations as far as Hume considers them will be judged as good or bad according to the feeling of pleasure or pain that they evoke (1964: II. iii, 178–83). Meanwhile Kant's aesthetic theory, outlined in the *Critique of Judgement* (*Kritik der Urtheilskraft*; 1790) crucially asserts that pure aesthetic judgement is *disinterested* from the ordinary whims and earthy desires of the subject (Kant 1987: 44–53). It is precisely because aesthetic judgement transcends personal attachments that, Kant argues, it has a claim to universality (1987: 53–4). So whilst Pater looks to Kant's conception of the individual as a creator, he presses this founding idea of Kantian aesthetics with his insistent belief that sensuousness may be an end in itself. Pater marginalises the role of sensation as a vessel for knowledge and puts into question the extent to which it bears any straightforward relation to reason and ethics. In the Conclusion to *The Renaissance*, he grasps for Epicurus more in hope than expectation of a salvation from the potential excess and decadence that sensuality for its own sake might unleash. Epicurus' prudent vision that the intellect teaches moderation so that pleasure is maintained at its sustainable height (1994: 33) is glimpsed as Pater declares that 'to maintain this ecstasy is success in life' (152). Yet Pater realises that the emergence of sensuality as a problem is distinctly modern, and its resolution will not be found in the history of philosophy.

Pater attempts to negotiate the tensions between the cerebral conception of sensation in which he was philosophically grounded and the allure of sensuality that had emerged in 1860s aestheticism and the periodical press. He is captivated by the ambivalent thrill of sensations to mind and body, and in this of course he is reflecting a spirit of the age. The potential for sensuality to become all-consuming arises from the very heart of Gautier's vision of *art pour l'art*[1] which allows sensation to span out from empirical knowledge, disinterested aesthetic judgement and the yoke of reason, so as to evoke pleasure for its own indiscriminate sake. In irreducible contrast to the Kantian aesthetics that influenced it, aestheticism promotes a necessarily *interested* aesthetic, involving the passions in a tautology of desire, sensation and pleasure, such that connections with integrity and judgement are loosened irreversibly.

Pater would also have been aware that sensation was causing a stir in broader literary culture with the phenomenon of 'Sensation Mania'

(Wise 1866: 266) in 1860s fiction. Writing in the next but one edition of the *Westminster Review*, after Pater's first essay was published there in January 1866, J. R. Wise called sensation fiction 'a virus [. . .] spreading in all directions' (270). Meanwhile, Pater's Oxford colleague, the Professor of Ecclesiastical History and philosopher, H. L. Mansel[2] infamously weighed into the debate in the *Quarterly Review* in 1863:

> Excitement, and excitement alone, seems to be the great end at which [sensation novels] aim – an end which must be accomplished at any cost by some means or other, *si possis, recte; si non, quocumque modo*. And as excitement, even when harmless in kind, cannot be continually produced without becoming morbid in degree, works of this class manifest themselves as belonging, some more, some less, but all to some extent, to the morbid phenomena of literature – indications of a wide-spread corruption, of which they are in part both the effect and the cause; called into existence to supply the cravings of a diseased appetite, and contributing themselves to foster the disease, and to stimulate the want which they supply. (45)

Mansel might have been writing of the Conclusion to *The Renaissance* with its own 'morbid' incitement 'to burn always with this hard, gem-like flame' (R 152). Indeed, the moral panic over the priority of intense and gratuitous sensuality in sensation fiction anticipates the panic that would follow the publication of Pater's *Renaissance*. Given Pater's professional interest in periodicals and his quiet enjoyment of escapist novels and plays, 'sensation mania' and the criticism it attracted may have shaped his conception of sensuality for its own sake, which was first outlined of course in the anonymous 'Poems by William Morris', published in the *Westminster Review* in October 1868.

Giving up Kantian disinterestedness as a lost cause, Pater undermines the distinctions between the sensations of art and sensations enacted on the body. The sensations created by art become indistinguishable from those created by other stimuli, and each becomes indistinguishable from the individual's emotions or passions. Thus in *The Renaissance* the sensations of art, nature and personality become one as Pater describes 'any stirring of the senses, strange dyes, strange colours, and curious odours, or the work of the artist's hands, of the face of one's friend' and 'the picture, the landscape, the engaging personality in life or in a book, produces this special impression of beauty or pleasure' (R 152; xxx). As aesthetic and physical sensations merge, they give the lie to the idea that reality and the realm of art are separated like 'some tragic dividing forces on their ways' (R 152). In the Conclusion, Pater's narrative shifts almost seamlessly from 'any exquisite passion' to 'any stirring of the senses' to effectively equate the physical feeling of sensation with the emotional passion that it may excite

(R 152). Art for art's sake and sensation for sensation's sake become analogous.

Pater is haunted by *art pour l'art*: captivated and alarmed at once by the idea that sensation may be *for its own sake*, unleashed from reason and the simple conveyance of data. Ever mindful of this problem Pater wavers between an enthusiasm for sensual pleasure for its own sake and concern for its implications. On the one hand then he affirms our 'one desperate effort to see and touch' in the heady moments of the Conclusion to *The Renaissance* (152), whilst on the other he frets that such unbridled seeing and touching subjects us to 'the tyranny of the senses' (R 142). Pater softly treads the line between these antithetical visions of sensation, ever fearful that to submit to sensual pleasure would be – once and for all – to lose control.

The History of Sensuality in 'Poems by William Morris'

Pater's ideal of sensual experience is set out in 'Poems by William Morris', which was one of his first works.[3] Conceiving the significance of bodily sensation in terms of the broad scope of history, this essay illustrates Pater's early ideal of sensation as it indicates how he conceives the proliferation of discourses on sensation in the 1860s. It thus sets the scene for Pater's own intervention in the history of sensation.

In this review essay Pater presents sensuality in the historical frame that would become central to his conception of his aesthetic project in the 1860s and early 1870s. The history of sensual experience has moved, he suggests, successively from sensual freedom in Ancient Greece, to the repression of sensuality in the middle ages, sensual freedom in the Renaissance, then another period in which sensation was repressed, and so to the present day in which Pater anticipates a return of sensual freedom. Therefore, history is a series of dichotomies: a perpetual movement between epochs of uninhibited, acute sensual awareness and freedom, and periods when sensuality is repressed to be replaced by excess spirituality, or 'Reverie, illusion, delirium' (WM 302). This contrast between the sensual and the spiritual is symbolised for Pater by William Morris' poetic evolution from *The Defence of Guinevere* (1858) to his *Life and Death of Jason* (1867):

> the change of manner in the interval [between these works] is entire; it is almost a revolt. Here there is no delirium or illusion, no experience of mere soul while the body and bodily senses sleep or wake with convulsed intensity at the prompting of imaginative love; but rather the great primary passions under broad daylight as of the pagan Veronese. (305)

Pater also uses the metaphor of sleep and wakefulness to articulate the transition from repressed sensuality to sensual freedom; from sleep to wakefulness; from 'dreamlight' to 'daylight' (WM 305). Elsewhere, he figures this transition as a change from 'the cloister' to 'a later space of life . . . never anticipated' (WM 302). As Pater's images compound each other, uninhibited sensual awareness is identified with freedom and clarity in one's perceptions of the world and of one's self. The progression of history in these terms of sensuality-spirituality or thesis-antithesis anticipates the structure of *The Renaissance*, in which each essay centres on the drama of 'revolt' or renewal. As Richard Lyons has argued, 'Pater finds unity most often in moments of transition', concentrating on these 'beginning and endings' to suggest 'a continuing or dialectical process' (769–70). Lyons' alludes to Hegelian dialectic here but the stage of synthesis – essential to Hegelian dialectic – is absent in Pater's formulation. Pater's history of sensation is not a progressive dialectic, but instead a cyclical process of thesis-antithesis-thesis-antithesis, and so on, without hope of ultimate resolution.

'The Aesthetic Life' (c. 1893) illustrates that Pater continued to believe in this thesis-antithesis of history his later career. Looking back to the Ancient Greeks with nostalgia, and equating this historical period with the child's innocent pleasure in sensation, he writes:

> It was with the sensible world, with the unsophisticated presentations of eye and ear ~~man~~ man began, as ~~th~~ children begin still, so delightfully, so well-satisfied: and there was an intelligence ~~abo~~ in the eye and ear. ~~Little by little~~ Afterwards the queries of ~~pure~~ abstract reason ~~disturbed~~ came to disturb him: ~~distrusted~~ he distrusted, little by little, deserted that beyond or below it; substituted for it his ~~own~~ shadowy hypotheses concerning its origin, its issue and under-side, a visionary abstract vision of his own place of what he really saw: and now he might seem, at least, amid the ruins of so ~~many~~ much abstract and artificial ~~theories~~ theory, to have ~~compted~~ completed the circle, to stand again, again, in some respects, as like a little child, at the point when he set out, acquiescing in the sensible world as the ascertained utmost limit of his horizon. (6–7)

The way in which Pater deplores the baleful effects of 'abstract reason', 'shadowy hypothesis' and 'abstract and artificial theory' reiterates his more famous dichotomy between 'facile orthodoxy, of Comte, or of Hegel, or of our own' and the 'exquisite passion' to be found in 'courting new impressions' (R 152). Here Pater assents to the philosophical premises of empiricism, but does not expand on the epistemological and metaphysical issues that it involves. His point is essentially an aesthetic one: to turn attention to sensual experience as an end in itself. Pater imagines history as an ever-repeating cycle, as his own repetition of 'again,

again' suggests, which may still bring the civilisation back to a state of innocence. The individual may aspire to reach beyond the horizon of the sensual realm into abstract reason, but he is brought to earth again 'amid the ruins of so much abstract and artificial theory'. Pater's image of the child mocks the notion of progress, reducing man to an eternal child, but at the same time offering the opportunity to reignite a feeling of wonder at the sensible world. Moreover, childhood has an innocence which denies any sexual connotations of sensuality, thus effectively absolving the individual from any charge of immorality. 'There is always something lost in growing up', he reflects in *Plato and Platonism* (1893: 18). For Pater, growing up taints sensuality inexorably with assumed moral values; sensuality becomes inhibited forever after by the 'thou shalt not' of a world grown grey with the breath of excessive piety. It is one of the reasons why Pater's protagonists are men in that short span between adolescence and adulthood, and one of the reasons why he cannot condemn '"the children of this world"' (R 153).

Touch and Sensation

What though does Pater mean by sensation? Of all the senses that he evokes in 'Poems by William Morris', the experience of touch is the most vivid. Like Samuel Johnson's famous riposte to Berkeley when, by kicking a stone, he claimed to have refuted the non-existence of matter, Pater clings to the vivid experience of touching and being touched by the external world to constantly confirm its existence. Moreover, the appeal of touch is sensual as well as intellectual. The feeling of touch is created by physical contact with the body, and as such it is the most intimate of the senses. It may tantalise with its promise of erotic sensation.[4] Equally, it may be transitive, involving two bodies in the reciprocal experience of touching and being touched. This mutual experience of touch held singular attractions for Pater as the physical expression of friendship, love, and creation. As such, he identifies with the sympathy between Adam and God in Michelangelo's *Creation of Man* (c. 1511), as he anticipates the touch of their fingertips: 'he hardly has strength enough to lift his finger to touch the finger of the creator; yet a touch of the finger-tips will suffice' (R 48).

The focus of 'Poems by William Morris' is the individual's experience of being touched by water. Touch becomes the conduit for ideal sensual experience in the essay, as Pater notes 'the most lovely waking with the rain on one's face' (WM 305) and 'the touch of water as one swims, the salt taste of the sea [. . .] The sea touches are not less sharp and firm [than snow], surest of effect in the places where river and sea, salt and fresh waves conflict' (WM 306). Water here becomes defined by the subjective feeling it stimulates. Its intensity is imperative, dissolving the boundaries between sensation and emotion, and pleasure and pain, so that the sea, with its 'sharp and firm' touch and its 'salt taste', becomes a deeply intimate masochistic pleasure. It is so personal in fact that it cannot be expressed in terms that would allow it to enter into critical aesthetic discourse.

Touch may be Pater's ideal sensation because of this very fact: that it evokes sensations and emotions prior to the intellectual act of conceptualisation. Linda Dowling has argued in *The Vulgarization of Art: The Victorians and Aesthetic Democracy* that Paterian sensuousness in the late 1860s and early 1870s should be understood as 'a document of Victorian liberalism' written in the spirit created by Mill's *On Liberty* and the Second Reform Bill (1996: 79). The idea that aesthetic judgement is subjective and impressionistic, as asserted in the Preface of *The Renaissance*, means that the response of each individual is valid, and 'endows everyone with the freedom to find on an individual basis what was most pleasing and satisfying about the world' (1996: 82). For Dowling this individual freedom is inextricably linked to the idea that 'Pater's larger aim was to realize a dream of cultural politics: the social transformation of Victorian life through an enlarged and emboldened sensuousness – his own version of the liberal idea of aesthetic democracy' (1996: 77). I would take issue with Dowling's leap from Paterian individualism to the idea that he has some broader social programme in mind. Pater could not really envisage society and did not much care to try.[5] Yet the idea that sensation in Pater's writings can be understood as the assertion of freedom from forces of cultural authority is compelling, and Pater's prioritisation of touch in 'Poems by William Morris' adds a further dimension to this. In this essay the implications of prioritising touch are still more radical than Dowling suggests from looking at *The Renaissance*: the experience of touch is liberated from all aesthetic-intellectual discourses that might legislate the terms of its experience. The sensation of touch is irreducibly subjective and intimate precisely because it cannot be legislated by the critic or by popular taste. For Pater, the act of personally discerning sensations becomes an affirmation of one's right to personal judgement and, ultimately, consolidates the sense of one's self as an individuated subject. Accordingly, Pater notes the experience of sensation rather than its objective source, as in the example of the sea evoked by its 'salt taste' and 'sharp and firm' touches, and the 'mood of passion' and 'the exquisite passion' created by sensation (WM 311; R 152).

In 'Poems by William Morris', the images of raindrops give way to images of the sea, which are superseded by images of the turbulent sea and river and finally by 'the flood' (310; R 150). The volume and intensity of the water are ever-heightening: as if the flood cannot be contained within Morris' poetry, it seeps out beyond it; instead of being described by Morris, it comes in the end to define Morris. So, Pater writes of *The Earthly Paradise*, 'it is not less medicinal, not less gifted with virtues, because a few drops of it are without effect; it is water to bath and swim in' (309). He continues,

> *Atlanta's Race, The Man born to be King, The Story of Cupid and Psyche*, and in *The Doom of King Acrisium*, the episode of Danae and the shower of gold, have all in a pre-eminent degree what is characteristic of the whole book, the loveliness of things washed with fresh water. (WM 309)

Like the sea, Morris' poetry becomes an intense sensual experience, enfolding its reader into itself as it stings and caresses. The final image anticipates Botticelli's Venus rising from the sea in 'A Fragment on Sandro Botticelli' (1870),[6] or perhaps recalls the first baptism after which Morris' poetry – representative of modern literature – emerges as the Truth, the Way, the Life. The identification between art and nature dignifies the poem as an experience so intense that it transcends the emotional or spiritual and becomes a physical convulsion. Perhaps Morris' poetry even displaces the physical touch of water because it is more voluminous, suggesting that the exhilaration it evokes is identified with physical feeling. The effect of transferring the feeling of water into a metaphor for Morris' art is to narrow the division between art and nature. It cleanses literary art of the tawdry marketplace and releases it into unspoilt landscape.

The primacy of touch and its significance for the individual was important for Pater in the material production of *The Renaissance*. Printed on ribbed paper, bound in dark blue-green cloth binding with chocolate-coloured end papers and gold lettering on the back, the look and feel of *The Renaissance* was carefully defined by its exacting author who wished so much to give it, in his words, an 'artistic appearance' (BB 70). Arthur Symons recalled in his later Introduction to *The Renaissance* that 'it was from reading Pater's *Studies in the History of the Renaissance*, in its first edition on ribbed paper (I have the feel of it still in my fingers), that I realised that prose could be a fine art' (1919: xv). The material presence of Pater's *Renaissance* embodies the principle of Anders-streben which he outlines in 'The School of Giorgione' (1877, 1888):

> it is noticeable that, in its special mode of handing its given material, each art may be observed to pass into the condition of some other art, by what German critics term an *Anders-streben* – a partial alienation from its own

limitations, through which the arts are able, not indeed to supply the place of each other, but reciprocally to lend each other new forces. (R 85)

The material object of *The Renaissance* is a work of literature aspiring beyond its intellectual content to make sensual experience of touch integral. It embodies, as Pater does, the desire to transcend the intellectualisation of sensation.

Venus and Sensual Pleasure in *The Renaissance*

The Renaissance develops Pater's conception of sensual experience through the figure of Venus, goddess of love and sensual pleasure. Venus enters Pater's *Renaissance* as the herald of a cultural rebirth centred on sensuality. As such, rendered in Pater's prose, she comes to signify the return of sensual pleasure, liberal imagination and pride in the body: values which he wishes to play a role in contemporary Victorian Britain. Yet even as Venus expands Pater's conception of sensuality, she begins to rewrite the particular vision of it outlined in 'Poems by William Morris'; prioritising now not subjective aesthetic judgement as the centre of individualism, but erotic freedom.

Venus marks moments of transition throughout *The Renaissance*, leading up to the Conclusion. More specifically, her appearances herald the return of sensuality to the world in place of abstract spirituality, and must be understood in terms of the vision of history that Pater first outlined in 'Poems by William Morris'. She appears first as Tannhauser's Venus, in the first essay of *The Renaissance*, 'Two Early French Stories', where she embodies 'the medieval Renaissance':

> its antinomianism, its spirit of rebellion and revolt against the moral and religious ideas of the time. In their search after the pleasures of the senses and the imagination, in their care for beauty, in their worship of the body, people were impelled beyond the bounds of the Christian ideal; their love became sometimes a strange idolatry, a strange rival religion. It was the return of that ancient Venus, not dead, but only hidden for a time . . . (R 16)

Venus is identified here as the herald of sensuality, in defiance of an over-spiritual, prurient culture. Her presence brings sensuousness and beauty together with eros, to suggest their interpenetration and to foreshadow the difficulties of setting moral boundaries between them.

Pater's evocation of Botticelli's *Birth of Venus* (1485), which he probably saw in the Uffizi, develops the connection between Venus and eroticism. The painting emerges, in Pater's essay, out of discussions of Botticelli's earthy Madonnas, and once again it marks a turning away from the spiritual motives of those earlier paintings, towards the 'Greek temper' (R 38). In introducing the painting, Pater skirts over the body of Venus – 'a figure that reminds you of the faultless nude studies of Ingres' – before letting his eye dance around the canvas touching on the painting's 'strange draperies', its cold light, the 'emblematical figure of the wind', even 'the dainty lipped shell on which she sails' and 'the sea "showing its teeth"' (R 38–9). It is as though the spirit of Venus has saturated the canvas completely so that her pronounced sensuality is reflected in its muted pinks and blues and greens. However, even as Venus proclaims the primacy of physical sensation, there are disquieting inconsistencies in her character (Keefe 1987: 161). Tannhauser's portrayal of her as 'the whore-goddess' (R 16) comes to the fore in *The Birth of Venus* and whilst she appears as a new-born virgin rising from the sea (R 38), Botticelli's cold, mournful palette inspires Pater to meditate on the more sombre aspects of her figure. Thus he reflects, 'you might think that the sorrow in her face was at the thought of the whole long day of love yet to come' (R 38). Sensual pleasure, here, is finite and freighted with sorrow: '[w]hat is unmistakable is the sadness with which [Botticelli] has conceived the goddess of pleasure as the depository of a great power over the lives of men' (R 39). The sorrow resides partly in the transience of sensual pleasure, partly in the controlling power of sensual desire and with it, perhaps, fear of its effects. This note of discord is a new turn in the character of Venus, and she emerges as a potential threat to order. In mythology Venus is said to wear a girdle that gives love, sensuousness and beauty the quality of grace and restraint (Schiller 2006: 127ff). In Pater's retelling, though, it is unclear whether Venus has grace and restraint. Her muted, pernicious power over men makes her another of Pater's rather disquieting *femme fatales*. Like those confronted by Medusa, whom he also describes (R 67–8), Pater's gaze must be averted as he describes Botticelli's Venus for fear that all men who look on her are turned to stone.

Pater's aspiration to identify his own era with Ancient Greece and the Renaissance as an epoch of sensual freedom comes to the fore again in 'Winckelmann', where the *Venus de Melos* (300–100 BC) represents a visitation of compounded Ancient Greek and Renaissance sensibilities in the contemporary world. The *Venus de Melos* was excavated in 1820 in the Aegean island of Melos and taken to the Louvre where it was widely publicised. Pater taps into contemporary familiarity with the statue to posit it as a tangible symbol of Ancient values resurrected in the modern world. This is Venus' final appearance in *The Renaissance*, and it brings her presence into the nineteenth century. Within the text Venus marks a moment of cultural change to Renaissance sensibility, with a particular emphasis on the moment of arrival, while through the text she signals Pater's modification of his dichotomy between the sensual and the spiritual. He explains that in contemplation of Venus,

> The mind begins and ends with the finite image, yet loses no part of the spiritual motive. This motive is not lightly and loosely attached to the sensuous form, as its meaning to an allegory, but saturates and is identical with it. (R 132)

Venus suggests not the eradication of spirit with sensuality, but rather a pantheistic fusion of spirit and matter. As in Schiller's *Aesthetic Education of Man* (*Über die ästhetische Erziehung des Menschen*; 1793): 'The physical nature and moral sentiments, matter and mind, earth and heaven, melt together with a marvellous beauty' (Schiller 2006: 129). In this attempt to fuse the sensual and the spiritual in a new aesthetic, Venus also serves to further Pater's aestheticist ambitions for art. For the repeated archetypal images of the naked Venus foreground her femininity, dissociating the sensuality she brings from the artistic marketplace and reconnecting it with organic creation.

Overall, Venus, as she appears in Pater's *Renaissance*, has a three-fold resonance. In mythology, she signifies the dawn of Hellenistic sensibility. Painted by Botticelli, she heralds the return of Greek sensibility to medieval France, fifteenth-century Italy, and Renaissance Italy. Rendered in Pater's own evocative words these rediscoveries of Venus are a knowing attempt to herald sensual freedom in the nineteenth century. After 'Winckelmann' she does not reappear in *The Renaissance*. Her role as a herald has been fulfilled and she retreats, with the sensibility that she suggested now fully absorbed into the consciousness of the writer. Bringing back sensation to assuage an excess of spirit, she symbolises the transition from spiritualism to sensuality that had been outlined in 'Poems by William Morris'. But here a rumble of thunder jolts the bright light of Pater's new sensual day, for Venus has a darker side. The dangerous power she holds, and the taint of death that defines her in Botticelli's Venus, cast long shadows over the cultural rebirth she inaugurates.

The Conclusion, which immediately follows 'Winckelmann' in *The Renaissance*, exemplifies what is at stake when sensation becomes heightened:

> While all melts under our feet, we may well grasp at any exquisite passion, or any contribution to knowledge that seems by a lifted horizon to set the spirit free for a moment, or any stirring of the senses, strange dyes, strange colours, and curious odours, or the work of the artist's hands, or the face of one's friend. (R 153)

While Pater at first suggests a balance between the elements of intellect, passion and sensation in this extract, the final section threatens to eclipse intellect and passion as the prose expands the stirring of the senses on and on. In his own effort to attain the highest quality of each moment as it passes, Pater's narrative begins to lose itself to the seduction of the senses. The essential problem of sensation is how to moderate it; and this sentence portends Dionysian sensual excess, in which sensual pleasure overcomes all other intellectual and spiritual endeavours. Again, the sensations appear 'strange' and the repetition of this word is quite menacing: suggesting not only something unknowable, but substances whose mystery holds power over us.

As for Epicurus, the pleasures of sensation in Pater's Conclusion to *The Renaissance* are tightly bound to their transience: sensation exists in a brief moment, which cannot endure. Perhaps this is a symptom of its intensity, or perhaps Pater cannot envisage the full implications of expanding these 'consummate moments' (R 88) through all time. In either case this transience poses a serious problem for his idea of a cultural renaissance, which requires temporal endurance if it is not to be undermined, once more, by excessive spiritualism as in his view of the middle ages. Still the fast-burning flame of Pater's narrative, in the Conclusion, extinguishes itself before it must confront the implications of its own assertions. Unable even to maintain its own ecstasy, it intensifies to reach an unsustainable climax, after which it must cease to be.

Pater's Dionysus and the Subversion of Sensation

On 30 November 1878 Pater personally halted the publication of his second book, *Dionysus and Other Studies*, when he had a sudden change of heart. The reason, he told Alexander Macmillan, was his unhappiness with 'so many inadequacies' in the manuscript (BB 87). At every turn Pater was 'a constantly revising author' (Small 1991a: 36), never quite content that he had found *le mot juste* or the right sequence in which to arrange it. Such exactitude is often the reason for his deliberation in publication. However, Macmillan queried whether this was so in the case of his essays on Dionysus. He read the proofs himself and replied to Pater in unusually emphatic mode, 'Please don't! At lease wait a little till we have gone carefully over the proofs. There is no reason so far as I have seen for your apprehension. I think this will be a quite worthy successor of your *Renaissance*' (BB 88). If Pater replied to Macmillan's plea, there is no record. The clear sympathies between *Dionysus and Other Studies* and *The Renaissance* noted by Macmillan may be the very source of Pater's apprehension: an unwillingness to subject himself again to the censure of critics and the University that had greeted *The Renaissance* in 1873; criticism tartly summarised by George Eliot: 'Mr. Pater's book [. . .] seems to me quite poisonous in its false principles of criticism and false conceptions of life' (92). In the note sent by Pater with a cheque to cover the costs of the aborted publication he tells Macmillan, 'I am sorry to have given you so much trouble for nothing' (BB 89).[7]

The full humiliation of how Pater was perceived by some of his contemporaries in the late 1870s became evident in the year leading up to his decision to take *Dionysus and Other Studies* out of production, when W. H. Mallock published *The New Republic*: first as a series of sketches in *Belgravia* (June–December 1876) and then as a novel in 1877. Gosse plays down the impact of Mallock's parody of Pater as Mr Rose in his novel, suggesting that although Pater 'thought the portrait a little unscrupulous [. . .] he admired the cleverness and promise of the book, and it did not cause him to alter his mode of life or thought in the smallest degree' (258). But perhaps Mallock quickened Pater's realisation that in *Dionysus and Other Studies* he had written a far more subversive work than *The Renaissance*. Although the most inflammatory essays were published separately in journals,[8] it was quite another thing to bring them together in a book in which 'writing is translated from the ephemeral [sphere] of the periodical essay into the permanence of the book [. . .] The corporate institutional authorship of a work is obfuscated, and authorship is shifted into a context which foregrounds the individual' (Brake 1991: 45–6).[9] Whatever the impact of *The New Republic*, it is clear that 'what really did ruffle him, was the persistence with which the newspapers at this time began to attribute to him all sorts of "aesthetic" follies and extravagances' (Gosse 258). It is unlikely that the intense sensual extravagances and frenzied violence described in the essays on Dionysus would have done anything other than exacerbate this disapproving critique.

With hindsight then it is clear that Alexander Macmillan was correct. From an editorial point of view *Dionysus and Other Studies* was indeed an appropriate sequel to *The Renaissance*, expanding the exploration of sensuality heralded by and woven through that earlier collection. Dionysus comes to embody the obsessive and pernicious potential in sensual experience. In spite of the pervading spirit of Venus which defines *The Renaissance*, Dionysus – with whom Venus had an affair in Pausanias' telling of the Priapus myth – comes to brood over it, especially in the irreverent passages at its climactic Conclusion. The obsessive and destructive underside of sensation comes to the fore in what were to be the opening essays of the aborted collection, 'A Study of Dionysus' and 'The Bacchanals of Euripides', as they take up the momentum of the Conclusion and carry its principles to dangerous excess. Just as Venus incarnates the freely chosen erotic sensuality of touch in *The Renaissance*, Dionysus embodies the anxious, obsessive eroticism that may take hold of the individual in these later essays. Perhaps having reached some resolution to this issue in his own mind, Pater wrote to William Sharp in June 1888:

> imagination is a Divine gift, as was the Bacchic vine; but each can intoxicate the heedless, and so enslave where it should serve. Therefore, I do not say with you that X. Z. is great because of his magnificent imagination, but because of his magnificently controlled imagination. (L 85–6)

So it is in Pater's depictions of Dionysus, through whom he illustrates how the desire for sensation may become a self-destructive end in itself, unravelling the rational mind. In 1878 Pater was a writer intensely conscious of his literary reputation and unsure as to whether the hedonistic image he had acquired following *The Renaissance* was one he wanted to cultivate.

Pater's Dionysus is a bipolar god: both manically life affirming and darkly depressed and destructive, he is 'a dual god of both summer and winter' (IP 38). Summer always turns too soon to autumn and winter. The 'dark possibilities' (39) of Dionysus are implicit in the sensual experiences of his 'quainter side' (37) and such possibilities dominate Pater's depiction of Dionysian sensuality. In the climactic scene of 'The Bacchanals of Euripides', Dionysus' wild desire for sensations excites the passions of local townspeople who join him in an ever-intensifying ritual dance. As they become more and more inflamed by sensual experience, the 'wild dancing' of their Bacchic frenzy obliterates their individuality:

> the sympathies of mere numbers, as such, the random catching on fire of one here and another there, when people are collected together, generates as if by mere contact, some new and rapturous spirit, not traceable in the individual units of a multitude. Such *swarming* was the essence of that strange dance of the Bacchic women . . . (GS 53; Pater's italics)

This scene is the beginning of 'An odd sickness' (57) inflicted by Dionysus: 'a sort of madness, a madness which imitates the true *Thiasus*' where they become sensuous creatures, their bodies foregrounded and their minds unreflective (57). Echoing their loss of reason, Pater's narrative takes refuge in his favourite adjective, 'strange', as he wonders at 'the strange dance'. In their frenzy, the '*swarming*' women are dehumanised by their desire for sensations of 'a fine rain of water', 'a fount of wine', 'skimming the surface with their finger-tips' and, subverting the Biblical connotations, '[an] abundance of milk' and 'streams of honey' (69). In contrast to the cultural rebirth symbolised by Venus, here Pater follows Euripides (40–4) to describe how the women leave their families to engage in the Bacchic dance. Possessed by lust for sensation, they become symbolic of Dionysian hedonism, eschewing the organic regeneration of culture for the decadent, atemporal *now*.

Thus the Bacchic dance becomes a distortion of Pater's Conclusion to *The Renaissance*; an apocalyptic vision in which life spent 'in art and song' (R 153) undermines the possibility of the future. The suggestion that 'we will hardly have time to make theories' (R 152) is realised in this new and darker world to horrific effect. This dance is a parodied, frenzied art, overwhelming and eradicating the moderate and sustainable sensual experience central to Pater's Epicurean vision in the Conclusion to *The Renaissance*. The Bacchic women cannot 'maintain that ecstasy' (R 152) because it escalates out of control, to a climactic height where it transmutes into lust for the ultimate sensation: murder. Lost to the ecstasy of movement and madness, the women fling themselves into a 'grotesque scene' of murder, as they tear peacefully grazing calves limb from limb (71).

If these orgiastic scenes derive from Euripides, those in Pater's second retelling of the Dionysus myth, 'Denys l'Auxerrois' published in 1887, are of his own invention. The revolutionary 'assertion of individual freedom' led by Denys in Auxerre (50) reiterates the identification between sensuality and political liberalism which Dowling has found in *The Renaissance*, with Denys arriving in medieval Auxerre just as some cities are 'turning their narrow, feudal institutions into a free communistic life' (50). The emergence of the individual from the homogenising forces of society and its institutions again underlines Pater's concern to establish the possibility of free, autonomous individuality. However, the 'new spirit' brought by Denys does not actually liberate the citizens of Auxerre but takes them into a new form of slavery – enslavement to his persistent and insidious influence. 'It was,' as Pater explains, 'a period, as older men took note, of young men and their influence' and, at the height of Denys' influence, '[h]e was making the younger world mad' (52; 55). In effect, 'Denys at his stall was turning the grave, slow movement of politic heads into a wild social license' (53). With his calls for political freedom he stimulates a radical desire for sensual freedom that overtakes the call for political rights. Denys' 'freedom' marches become sordid scenes like the Bacchic dance, where the individuals of Auxerre become enslaved to their own dormant passions:

> The hot nights were noisy with swarming troops of dishevelled women and youths with red-stained limbs and faces, carrying their lighted torches over the vine-clad hills, or rushing down the streets, to the horror of timid watchers, towards the cool spaces by the river. A shrill music, a laughter at all things, was everywhere. And the new spirit repaired even to the church to take part in the novel offices of the Feast of Fools. Heads flung back in ecstasy – the morning sleep among the vines, when the fatigue of the night was over – dew-drenched garments – the serf lying at his ease at last . . . (53)

Intoxicated, heedless and enslaved to the sensation that might have liberated them, these 'swarming troops' recall the Bacchic women. Simultaneous images of the 'lighted torches' and the 'hot nights' remind us of Pater's ideal of creative 'light and heat' in *The Renaissance* (xxxiii), corrupting it into a signifier for the squandered passions of these dishevelled persons who do not create but only destroy. Allusions to the music and ecstasy that characterise the climactic finale of *The Renaissance* serve to compound this impression: as the melody becomes 'shrill' and the glorious irreverence of ephemeral ecstasy is grotesque in the lamplight, we see this 'Feast of Fools' glutted on sensual excess. If *The Renaissance* was Pater's nod to the liberal principles of The French Revolution, 'A Study of Dionysus', 'The Bacchanals of Euripides' and 'Denys L'Auxerrois' evoke The Terror.

Pater marginalises these political connotations in his earlier Dionysus, brushing such implications aside as he suggests that '[t]here were some who suspected Dionysus of a secret democratic interest; though indeed he was *liberator* only of men's hearts' (D 15 n.; Pater's italics). Pater's coy refusal to look beyond the individual and the private sphere to the broader implications of his liberal sensuality is a recurring characteristic of his writings. Residing in 'the narrow chamber of the individual mind' (R 151) he fears society; worse, he is unable to believe in it. Still the judgements of society haunt Pater's depiction of Dionysus, as he draws on the ambiguous sexuality attributed to him in mythology (GS 53; 59; 61). The sexual deviance of Dionysus confounds the dual drives of sex and death: transgressive erotic sensuality leads to self-destruction. When Pater considers with what difficulty painters have attempted to capture Dionysus he settles on a modern interpretation with strong personal resonances to develop this suggestion:

> in a *Bacchus* by a young Hebrew painter, in the exhibition of the Royal Academy of 1868, there was a complete and very fascinating realisation of such a motive; the god of the bitterness of wine, 'of things too sweet'; the sea-water of the Lesbian grape become somewhat brackish in the cup. (GS 37)

The 'young Hebrew painter' is of course Simeon Solomon: Pater's friend who twice painted Dionysus and who had been arrested for indecent exposure with the intention of sodomy in 1873 and 1874. The link between the two sensual, persecuted souls of Dionysus and Solomon slips into an analogy centred on Solomon's singularly 'complete' understanding of Dionysus and the reader's understanding that each was vilified by the mob that once praised him. Pater's uncharacteristically explicit evocation of transgressive desire between men is defined by its negativity. The 'Lesbian grape' figures a transgressive eroticism, which turns from sweetness to bitterness, suggesting that the inevitable and irreversible decay characteristic in the natural world nature also defines erotic love. Whilst the link to Solomon suggests that this decay arises from the social boundaries imposed on trangressive love, the destructive and obsessive passions evoked by Dionysian sensuality indicate some broader sense in which decay is implicit in erotic love. The way in which Dionysus enslaves the individual to the passions casts aspersions on the idea that he may be a liberator of men's hearts.

The resonances between Dionysus and Solomon give some insight to Pater's quite singular sympathy in these narratives. Pater's Dionysus is the fallible, half-mortal god who 'has suffered after a manner of which we must suppose pagan gods incapable'; 'a beautiful soft creature' who is simply unable to control his wild desires or the effect he has on others (IP 49; D 42). This 'tortured, persecuted, slain god – the suffering Dionysus' (IP 46) is Pater's innovation on the old myths, evoking Dionysus as a terribly vulnerable figure. At the end of 'A Study of Dionysus' Pater alludes to the Orphic poem in which Dionysus is violently slain by the Titans, torn limb from limb by those who once followed him in the violent frenzy of the moment he himself has unleashed in them: 'The fragments of the body [. . .] boiled in a great cauldron, and made an impious banquet' (D 47). Like the diaphanous man in 'Diaphaneitè', Dionysus is an aesthetic genius of sorts in a world which 'has no sense fine enough for [his] evanescent shades' (D 154). His is, perhaps, the ultimate fate of the diaphanous man: to be destroyed by those who neither know nor understand him. Billie Andrew Inman suggests that this image of the torn and broken Dionysus symbolises the personal crises caused by Pater's intimate relationship with undergraduate William Hardinge (1991: 20). The Hardinge episode, together with the fierce criticism of Pater's *Renaissance* and his crises of faith, indicate a man figuratively pulled apart by the forces of society, the University, and his own desires. But perhaps we should nuance Inman's suggestion. The terrible sight of Dionysus torn apart is not an image of what Pater was; it is what he might have become. Pater was not *Dionysus Zagreus* and neither was he Solomon because his sense of self-preservation was too strong – he was either too discreet or too restrained to allow himself to be destroyed. As Henry James wrote to Gosse in December 1894, 'he has had – will have had – the most exquisite literary fortune: i.e. to have taken it all out, wholly, exclusively, with the pen (style, the genius,) and absolutely not at all with the person' (293). The image of Dionysus destroyed is a nightmare vision of another possible world where Pater could be destroyed by the forces that assailed him, had he not put up barriers between himself, sensation and 'the world'. It is a possible world in which Pater would have *taken it all out* with the person and not exclusively with the pen.

Even so, the shadow of Dionysus continues to loom over Pater in works such as *Gaston de Latour* (1888) and 'Apollo in Picardy' (1893). *Gaston* in particular recalls the language of his essays on Dionysus, as it describes 'a confusion of spirit', 'physical madness', 'the strange devils' gaiety [. . .] all in gaudy evidence', '[d]elirium [. . .] in the air' (60; 60; 62; 64). Pater sums up the effects of this revelry when he explains that 'this singularly self-possessed person had to confess that [. . .] he had lost for a while the exacter view of certain outlines, certain real differences and oppositions of things in that hotly coloured world of Paris' (180). In *Gaston*, Pater is unable to bring order to the 'madness' of sadistic violence and homoeroticism in which the initially strong narrative thread loses itself. As if the violence of Paris has infiltrated Pater's literary art, the manuscripts of *Gaston* reveal how his ideas become fragmented, unfinished, sometimes hurried and often elliptical, eventually ending *in medias res*. Just as Pater withdrew *Dionysus and Other Studies*, he similarly pulled his unfinished novel from serial publication in *Macmillan's Magazine* in mid-run.

Pater understands that sensation has an ambivalent power. In the essays on Dionysus he shows at every turn that Kantian and Humean accounts of sensual experience are inadequate to grasp the conflicts which sensuality catalyses within one's self. As such they cannot understand the self they purport to reveal. Dionysian sensation also complicates Linda Dowling's view that intense sensual experience in Pater's writings may affirm the subject's autonomy (1996: 82). The conception of sensation that emerges through Dionysus effectively illustrates the limitations of this argument. Certainly sensation in Pater's writings has a transformative role which may confirm one's autonomy as Dowling has identified; but it may also seduce the individual, enslaving him to its madness. It implies the self-destruction of those who 'hardly have time to make theories' about the things they see and touch (R 152). With these visions of sensation, Pater looks anxiously back to his Conclusion to *The Renaissance* to subvert his own finest moment.

Imaginative Sensation

It is literary art that becomes for Pater a means to tame sensation. As in the letter to William Sharp, Pater aspires to 'magnificently controlled imagination' (L 85–6). His early biographer Thomas Wright identifies that his motto was 'Discipline rather than Pleasure [. . .] The beauty of Discipline is henceforward his constant theme, and one word was continually slipping from his mouth or his pen – the word *ascêsis*' (II, 65).[10] The importance of self-discipline to Pater's conception of sensuality is something missed in more recent accounts of Paterian sensation, perhaps because reserve or self-restraint are quite alien notions in our post-1968 consumerist society. Even so, art offers both Pater the man and Pater the writer a refuge from the dark possibilities of sensual pleasure because it promotes ascêsis or, what he calls, 'reserve' (Pater 1875: 202). The notion of an ascetic aesthetic sounds paradoxical, but for Pater the beauty of art is that it fuses Dionysian passion with Apollonian order or reserve: impressing restraint upon the potentially self-annihilating sensual desires which lie deep within. The creation of art is – or should be – a triumph over unruly emotions, desires and sensations that threaten to engulf the individual. It assumes a moral role, bringing reason to check the passions and sensual desires that might otherwise swirl out of control.

The Renaissance blithely disregards Immanuel Kant's conceptual distinction between the sensations created by art and those created by other sensual stimuli (Kant 1987: §§44–6, 172–4). Its Preface refers to how 'the picture, the landscape, the engaging personality in life or in a book, produces this special impression of beauty or pleasure' and 'any stirring of the senses, strange dyes, strange colours, and curious odours, or the work of the artist's hands, of the face of one's friend' (R xxx), whilst the Conclusion shifts seamlessly from 'any exquisite passion' to 'any stirring of the senses': effectively equating the physical feeling of sensation with emotional passion that it may excite (R 152). Despite his view here that sensations felt in the world and sensations evoked through art are qualitatively analogous, from the outset there is evidence to the contrary. In 'Winckelmann' Pater concedes that 'the spectacle of supreme works of art takes from the life of the senses something of its turbid fever' (R 142), and in the following years some form of distinction between aesthetic sensations and other sensations is reinstated in Pater's thinking and writing.

The unfulfilled desire for sensation satisfies Pater's respect for Matthew Arnold's Hebraic principles of 'conduct and obedience' (1869: 91). Pater may talk sometimes like a Hellenist but he cannot vanquish the Hebraic tendency that bids restraint. Thus, it is 'conduct and obedience' he feels is wanting in John Addington Symonds. In his 1875 review of Symonds' *Renaissance in Italy: The Age of the Despots* Pater deems 'reserve' essential to art and this forms the basis of the distinction between aesthetic and other sensations. It is a generally positive review, which ends on this odd note:

> Not withstanding Mr. Symonds's many good gifts, there is one quality which I think in this book is singularly absent, the quality of reserve, a quality by no means merely negative, and so indispensable to the full effect of all artistic means . . . (201)

Symonds' book, the ostensible subject of discussion, fades from view for a moment as Pater's narrative turns to 'Mr. Symonds'. It is highly likely that Pater knew of Symonds' disgraced departure from Balliol in 1863 following an affair with another man, and that he had read Symonds' unabashed affirmation of male-male desire in his poetry.[11] Reserve is indeed one quality that Symonds had not. Pater's allusion to him, like the allusion to Solomon which appeared in the following year, gestures toward the excesses of deviant sexuality. It opens a meditation in print between Pater and his reader regarding the proper mode of behaviour for a man who pursues deviant erotic sensual experiences.

Art emerges as a means to quell any such passions. George Moore recalls a lost letter written to him by Pater in 1887, in which:

> he made me understand very well that descriptions of violent incidents and abnormal states of mind do not serve the purpose of art [. . .] He made me understand that the object of art is to help us forget the crude and the violent, to lead us towards certain normal aspects of nature . . . (qtd L 74)

The final sentence is striking in its assertion of art as a normalising force against the 'crude and violent' aspects of life. In Pater's earlier writings – such as in his evocation of Giorgione's *Fête Champêtre* in *The Renaissance* – aesthetic experience may be a space in which the individual is liberated from the strictures of civil society. Nonetheless, in his letter to Moore, art is charged with a moral duty to lead the deviant individual back to the paths of what is considered to be 'normal'. Art has become not a space in which the individual may be liberated from the strictures of society, but an undefined force operating through escapism to normalise the individual. It is all terribly conventional. Here a schism emerges between the sensations of life and the meta-sensations evoked by art, in which the latter promote ascêsis from the excesses that characterise Dionysian sensuality. In making this move, Pater returns to Plato.

Pater came but gradually to admire how Plato fuses the sensual and spiritual realms in his philosophy. For Plato the fusion of spirit and senses was to take place in the realm of ideas: as in Socrates'-Diotima's conception of love in the *Symposium* (1999: 734ff): it is an imaginative idea of sensation. Of course, Pater's *Renaissance* essays also sought the fusion of sensual and spiritual experiences, but with a fundamental difference. In *The Renaissance* Pater criticises art that acts as 'only the symbol or type of a really inexpressible world' (131), asserting instead that spirit should be immanent in the sensual experience of art as in *Venus de Melos* (132). The sensual, corporeal world is granted primacy over the unseen one: it is the assertion of embodied sensuality. By 1894, though, in *Plato and Platonism* Pater inverts his early insistence on embodied sensuality, which he now surrenders for a Platonic imaginative idea of sensation:

> The lover, who has become a lover of the invisible, but still a lover, and therefore, literally, a seer of it carrying an elaborate cultivation of the bodily senses, of eye and ear, their natural force and acquired fineness [. . .] into the world of intellectual abstractions; seeing and hearing there too, associating for ever all the imagery of things seen with the conditions of what primarily exists only for the mind . . . (PP 96)

The 'lover of the invisible' privileges the imagination over the senses. 'Sensation' as Pater presents it here is the triumph of an imaginative idea of sensation which may evoke a benign illusion of sight and sound in place of embodied sensation. We are far from Venus, let alone Dionysus or Denys. For, here, Pater subverts his earlier view that imaginative ideas of sensation are like a 'somnambulistic [. . .] beautiful disease or disorder of the senses; and a religion which is a disorder of the senses must always be subject to illusions' (WM 302). This 'passion of which the outlets are sealed'; this 'wild, convulsed sensuousness' in 'Poems by William Morris' was the life-negating counterpoint to the sensuality heralded by Venus in *The Renaissance* (WM 303). Now, in *Plato and Platonism*, it is the imaginative idea of sense that liberates the individual from 'the tyranny of the senses' – the tyranny, that is, of embodied sensation. In consequence, the concept of 'imaginative reason' ascribed to Plato in *Plato and Platonism* has significantly different implications from 'the "imaginative reason"' in 'The School of Giorgione' (PP 84; R 88). Once again Pater is 'a constantly revising author', reworking his own concepts as his ideas shift across the years (Small 1991a: 36). Perhaps this is also how, over time, he came to terms with life: free in his heart to love whom he loved, desire whoever he desired – but bound by society never to let this become manifest in flesh.

Pater's own prose style is premised on an imaginative idea of sense.

His words, 'busy with themselves, but not otherwise with the world' (Donoghue 297), create a meta-sensuality to quell the ferocity of embodied sensation. With this in mind, F. R. Leavis' judgement on Paterian sensation should be recast:

> Pater may talk of burning always with a hard gem-like flame, but there is nothing answering in his prose; it notably lacks all sensuous vitality. Indeed, to point to Pater's prose – cloistral, mannered, urbane, consciously subtle and sophisticated, and actually monotonous and irresponsive in tone, sentiment and movement (the eyelids always a little weary) – is a way of giving force to the judgement that for the Victorian aesthete art is something that gets between him and life. (241)

Leavis' suggestion of a schism between Pater's affirmation of embodied sensuality and the form of this affirmation is, of course, quite right. There is an obvious irony about a book which professes to advocate the reawakening of our physical being – our body and our senses – yet immerses us entirely into the imaginative world of its prose, distancing us from embodied sensation; and the irony is heightened by the way that *The Renaissance* calls for 'the perfect identification between matter and form' (40). But what Leavis does not understand is that this irony is the point. Pater's gem-like flame must never be allowed to burn out of control. His muted prose is an endeavour to contain the flame of sensation, to tame it and contain it within the world of words he has created. His characteristic parataxis makes his sentences 'busy with themselves', to the extent that in the act of reading we too can be drawn out of our physical life and into the dense world of his prose. In *The Renaissance*, sensation is distanced by a factor of three: we are reading Pater, who is interpreting a work of fine art, which depicts a sensual being or experience.

In effect Pater chooses art for art's sake over sensation for sensation's sake. Despite his heady earlier declaration that art and sensation are analogous, he retreats to art as the fusion of sensation with reason. Although Pater sees abstract reason as a life-negating force, he recognises the need for a principle of discipline to regulate the passions. Just as he admits spirit into his conception of the world when it is implicit in matter, so he allows 'reason' when it is saturated in art. Moreover, the 'tyranny' of sensuality begs us to reconsider the relationship between the individual and world in Walter Pater's writings. The interface between the individual and the world is significantly problematised by Pater's conception of sensation and, in consequence, the clear vision of his diaphanous man becomes cloudy. After all, the quality of diaphaneitè rests on the disinterested experience of sensations, as Pater writes, 'without any struggle at all' (D 155), but it is no longer possible for the individual's relationship with the world to remain transparent once we have admitted desire and passion into the picture. Sensation offers pleasure and freedom, but it also threatens to overwhelm the individual, subverting him into an animal whose only motivation is pleasure. Art may offer an illusion of security but the individual is defined by *struggle*: whether this be a struggle for more sensations, or a struggle to assert one's right to erotic sensations, or a struggle to attain mastery over one's desire for sensation. Thus sensual experience becomes a site of tension at which one's individuality may be undermined by the forces within one's self.

With his departure from Hume, Epicurus and Kant, Pater implicitly asserts that sensation has not been adequately treated by these canonical philosophical discourses. The inherently rational discourse of philosophy could not ever hope to fully grasp the complexities of subjective, personal, passionate response to sensation and in this way 'analysis leaves off' (R 152). However, the endeavour to think the unthinkable never leaves off. It begs for new modes of 'analysis' capable of expressing the vivid, irrational relationship between the individual, sensuality and passion; new modes of discourse, flexible enough to gesture beyond the utterable. In the meandering and suggestive forms of the essay and imaginary portrait, incorporating myths and figurative language, Pater ventures to transport the reader into the intangible but pervasive realm of the sensual desire.

At the same time Pater resists the transgressive possibilities this realm offers. His literary art fuses passion with Puritanism in a vain attempt to spiritualise desire into imagination. Yet however hard he tries, the reign of aesthetic 'reserve' is never absolute. It is difficult to keep Dionysian passions under control in a world when Apollonian reason is so fragile. The violent passion of *Gaston de Latour* indicates that even one who wished to forget 'the crude and violent' through art is as vulnerable to the excesses of imaginative sensation. Removing *Gaston* from the pages of *Macmillan's Magazine* resolved an immediate practical problem in 1888, just as aborting *Dionysus and Other Studies* had in 1878, but their shadow remains. This shadow lowers over Pater's literary aesthetic as he attempts to overcome the tyrannies of sensation.

Notes

1. The most famous and expansive expression of this is Gautier's 1835 Preface to *Mademoiselle de Maupin* (3–37).
2. Following Judith Ryan, Matthew Beaumont has argued that Mansel is Pater's most significant empirical influence after Hume (Ryan 27;

Beaumont 5). I cannot see any evidence for this apart from a confluence of interests in the relationship between self and world, and Pater's admiration of Mansel's style in his essay 'Style' (1888, 1889). Curiously, there is no evidence for this assertion in Ryan's book, *The Vanishing Subject: Early Psychology and Literary Modernism* (1991), which does not otherwise focus on Pater. Mansel was not a straightforward empiricist, anyway. He was also interested in Idealism and his metaphysics were influenced particularly by Kant (Brown 1997: 27)

3. In this chapter only I am including references to both Pater's original essay and the Conclusion to *The Renaissance*, which Pater edited from the final pages of the earlier essay.

4. Chapter 6 discusses erotic touch in Pater's work at greater length.

5. For an alternative perspective, see Matthew Potolsky's 'Literary Communism: Pater and the Politics of Community', the basis of which is that 'Pater is a fundamentally political writer' (2010: 185). Having reflected deeply on this contention but searched in vain for any serious support for it in Pater's work or life, I fear this is another instance of the same sort of Whig interpretation of intellectual history which portrays him as a proto-gay activist. Such readings have more to do with the concerns of our own age, than with Pater's own actual views. I discuss Pater and society at greater length in Chapter 9.

6. This essay was republished in *The Renaissance* as, simply, 'Sandro Botticelli'.

7. 'A Study of Dionysus' and 'The Bacchanals of Euripides' were published as articles in 1876 and 1889 respectively. They were first collected after Pater's death by Charles Shadwell in *Greek Studies* (1895).

8. 'The Myth of Dionysus' was published as 'A Study of Dionysus' in the *Fortnightly Review* (December 1876); 'The Myth of Demeter and Persephone' was given at first as two lectures at the Birmingham and Midland Institute (1875) and published in the *Fortnightly Review* (January and February 1876). Charles Shadwell believes that 'The Bacchanals of Euripides' was written at about the same time, though it was not published till May 1889 in *Macmillan's Magazine* (iv). Of the less inflammatory essays, 'The School of Giorgione' was included, of course, in the second edition of *The Renaissance*. Several other essays had been published previously in the *Fortnightly Review* and appeared later in *Appreciations*. *Greek Studies*, which included these essays and others written in the late 1880s and early 1890s, was published in 1895 under the guidance of Charles Shadwell.

9. For further speculation on Pater's reasons for withdrawing *Dionysus and Other Studies* see Thomas Wright's *The Life of Walter Pater* (II, 10–18) and Edmund Gosse's 'Walter Pater: A Portrait' (257–8). Vernon Lee wrote on meeting Pater: 'What strikes me is how wholly unlike Pater is to the Mr Rose of Mallock' (1980: 294).

10. Wright glosses this as 'an ecclesiastical term meaning "restraint" – the restraint imposed upon himself by a monk' (II, 65).

11. The poems were published in 1878 in *Tales of Ancient Greece, No 1, Eudiades and a Cretan Idyll*, but they had been written c. 1868 and were known in select Oxford circles years in the interim years.

Chapter 6

Pater's Copernican Revolution: The Desiring, Dying Body

On a spring day in 1874 Walter Pater had a 'dreadful interview' with Benjamin Jowett at which he was confronted with evidence of his romantic attachment to a student called William Hardinge (Inman 1991: 1). Following this meeting Jowett permanently withdrew Pater's nomination for a University Proctorship. In the months during which they had become close friends, Hardinge had sent intimate poems to Pater, and Pater had returned with letters signed 'yours lovingly'. Details of the affair were subject to gossip and suppression but the letters alone were evidence enough for Jowett's intervention.

Although this episode was soon hushed in Oxford it was a crescendo in Pater's life and values, bringing to its height the conflict between his homoerotic ideal of sensuality and the Victorian strictures against homosexuality. Since Billie Andrew Inman brought together evidence of the romance in 1991 it has been well documented and Pater has become a familiar figure in discussions of Victorian homoerotic desire. But if Pater's flirtation with Hardinge shows his interest in desire between men, it is also necessary to understand that it illustrated to him the dangerous space between what he calls 'being' and 'doing'. It is in his essay on 'Wordsworth' (first published that same spring, 1874) that Pater reflects that 'the end of life is not action but contemplation – *being* as distinct from *doing*' (A 62). The distinction became blurred with Hardinge. However, in Pater's writings, homoerotic desire is conceived with a vivid awareness of the boundaries between 'being' in an idealised state of desirous contemplation of the male body and 'doing' or engaging in homosexual acts. After the episode with Hardinge there is no evidence that he conflated the two ever again. Yet much recent criticism on Pater has been based on the tacit assumption by some writers that he did so.

'Queer' criticism has lingered on the peripheries of the Paterian body because it mistakenly elides *being* with *doing*. To put the case more specifically, critics writing of Pater's interest in desire between men have consistently assumed that *being* interested in desire between men implies *doing* or a wish to act on such desires with the body. I have in mind, for example, Richard Dellamora's highly influential belief that Pater's writings amount to a campaign for 'a freely expressed eros' between bodies, within 'a cultural ideal expressive of desire between men' (Dellamora 1990: 110), as well as the subsequent work of Linda Dowling and Thaïs Morgan which has argued that Pater's aesthetic discourse functions as a 'homosexual code' or 'aesthetic minoritizing discourse' to covertly advocate masturbation and sodomy to his receptive readers' (Dowling 1994: 135; Morgan 1996: 142).[1] Stefano Evangelista's 2009 study, *British Aestheticism and Ancient Greece: Hellenism, Reception, Gods in Exile*, is more nuanced but it too asserts that Pater presents 'one of the earliest attempts to define a modern gay sensibility' which is integral to his 'progressive discourse of emancipation' (34). To be sure, it is true that '[i]t is no longer necessary to argue that same-sex desire is a relevant or worthwhile topic in Pater studies' and rightly so (Love 2007: 25). Now though with the battle won to integrate queer readings into Pater studies, it is high time to subject the nature of the body and same-sex desire in Pater's works to greater critical scrutiny. On balance, Paterian desire may not be conceived as an analogue to mid-twentieth-century campaigns for 'freely expressed' homoerotic desire, nor as a straightforward reprisal of Ancient Greek pederasty. Pater is a man of the mid-nineteenth century, infused with the 'reserve' he prizes (Pater 1875: 202) and which is analogous to the 'emotional reserve' or 'stoic self-control' that defines Victorian 'gentlemanliness' (Mitchell 1996: 271). Such 'reserve' has, strangely, figured very little in accounts of Paterian sexuality.[2] It is, however, most apparent when we focus on Pater's evocations of the male body, which suggests that his ideal of homoerotic desire is a state of being and not a power of doing.

To understand Paterian desire, it is necessary to begin by investigating the male body in Pater's works. Such a critical re-embodiment may both initiate a more sophisticated conception of 'desire' and its relation to the individual, and broaden the critical focus to consider the Paterian body not only as a desiring body but, also, as a fallible and dying body. Focusing on the objects of Pater's desiring narrative, we find male bodies that are not living and responsive flesh but cold, distant sculptures and mythical figures. This already weighs against any idea of Pater's male bodies as mere ciphers in a campaign for 'freely expressed' homosexuality. The remote, idealised nature of Pater's sculptural and mythical bodies is integral to his conception of what homoerotic desire can be. The desire which broils beneath the surface of Pater's aesthetic discourse may not be equated to the 'desire without limit' which Wilde speaks of (and regrets) in *De Profundis* (1986: 147). It is a mode of desire in which the unobtainable nature of the beloved – and the untouchable flesh of the beloved – are essential. Paterian 'being' is, furthermore, a state in which the desiring subject is central. Not gifted like the sculpted or mythical body with immortal beauty, this desiring subject is also increasingly conscious of the mortality of his physical existence.

The Desired Body

Pater's description of Myron's *Discobulus* (c. 460–440 BC) is emblematic of the significance of the male body in his aesthetic. In this statue the discus whirls round and around into an orbit that places the body of the individual at the centre of the universe:

> the vigorous head also, with the face, smooth enough, but spare, and tightly drawn over muscle and bone, is sympathetic with, yields itself to, the concentration, in the most literal sense, of all beside; – is itself, in very truth, the steady centre of the discus, which begins to spin; as the source of will, the source of the motion with which the discus is already on the wing, – that, and the entire form. (GS 304–5)

In this passage from 'The Age of Athletic Prizemen', published months before Pater's death in 1894, the flesh of the individual becomes the sun around which the universe and the Paterian aesthetic revolve. Re-embodying – quite literally – the Copernican Revolution by which Immanuel Kant had refigured Western philosophy around the *mind* of the individual (Kant 1929: 22; 26), Pater daringly places the body at the centre of being. In this position, the sensual body strikes a complex and ambivalent pose through which its latent eroticism must be understood.

Pater's attention to the sensuality of the body is indebted to the centrality of sensual experience in the works of Gautier, Rossetti and Swinburne. Set against the pale and languid bodies of these predecessors, though, Pater's *Discobulus* is more suggestive of his affinity to the bronzed athletes of Kingsley's 'muscular Christianity' (Adams 1995: 149). The primacy of the athletic body, 'spare and tightly drawn', is the will made flesh. Illustrated also by Pater's interest in the *Apollo Belvedere* (c. 320 BC) that had inflamed Winckelmann's imagination and Michelangelo's stocky male nudes (R 139; 147), not to mention Marius in Pater's eponymous novel (M I, 41), the athletic body exudes a power, self-control and infallibility that is the very image of self-overcoming through the discipline of physical sport. Pater certainly had inspiration for such ideas as a tutor at Brasenose College, renowned for sporting rather than academic prowess. Humphry Ward was merely articulat-ing a commonplace when he said that 'the Brasenose undergraduates [. . .] toiled at games and played at books' (qtd Higgins 1991: 80). One imagines the bookish voyeur Mr Pater sat in his favourite position – the window seat of his college sitting-room – gazing over a volume of Lucretius at the rowing eight as they straggle across Radcliffe Square after training; contemplating their youth and sculpted beauty, too soon to pass. The sublime athleticism of the male body is integral to its erotic allure. Moreover, the strength of the statue has an allure of its own, presenting its spectator with a visual symbol of self-mastery.

Utterly unlike Kingsley, Pater presents this self-mastery in radical terms which place the sensual individual, and not God, at the centre of the universe. As *Discobulus* suggests, the form of the statue visually symbolises individualism. After all, statues 'ha[ve] no background, no sky or atmosphere' (R 136): they distinguish and exult the individual above the mere mass of humanity. In Pater's oeuvre we see this individu-alism accompanied by a strong awareness of the marble or stone statue as a symbol of a pantheistic relationship between the individual and the earth. Writing of Michelangelo's *David* (1501–4) he notes, for example: 'there still remains a morsel of uncut stone, as if by one touch to main-tain its connexion with the place from which it was hewn' (R 49). In this way, then, Pater's bodies are linked to the earth – not to God – both by a golden pantheistic thread and by the grave reality that we will each return, earth to earth, ashes to ashes, dust to dust.

Pater's debt to Winckelmann's eroticism is often remarked. But he owes a debt too to 'the complex intermingling of erotically charged beauty and sublime power and elevation,' (Potts 2000: 118), which develops from the pantheistic intimations of *David*. Indeed the fusion of spirit and flesh is most clearly evident in the 'sweetness and strength' of Michelangelo's muscular figures; as Pater notes, 'Michelangelo is always pressing forward from the outward beauty . . . to apprehend the unseen beauty' (R 47; 56). The relationship between 'the unseen beauty' and hewn form is analogous to that between form and matter in Pater's discussion of art: 'form . . . should penetrate every part of the matter' (R 86). For Pater's ontology is always two-fold, with the tangible flesh inseparable from the Romantic, intangible spirit for which his favourite adjective is 'strange' (R 80). This reminds the critic to be careful not to take the radical materialism in the closing pages of *The Renaissance* too literally. Flesh is never purely flesh, for Pater: there is something of the strange and inexpressible implicit within it.

The spiritual, pantheistic and individualistic character of the Paterian body urges a cautious approach to his brief but vivid fetishisations of the male body. The desired body emerges as a complex organism, which cannot be reduced to an object of transgressive desire alone. The distance Pater creates between the desired body and its spectator begs us to reconsider the nature of transgressive desire in his narratives. Pater is at pains to stress the difference between real, flesh and blood young men and the statues on which his aesthetic discourse focuses:

> at first sight sculpture, with its solidity of form, seems a thing more real and full than the faint, abstract world of poetry or painting. Still the fact is the reverse. Discourse and action show man as he is, more directly than the play of the muscles and the moulding of the flesh; and over these poetry has command. (R 136)

Dowling and Morgan conceive the statue form as incidental to Pater's motives, suggesting that it functions merely to offer him an aesthetic cover for his expression of homoerotic desires. In effect they prioritise the discourse of desire at the expense of marginalising the materiality of the body. This is misguided. The cold, inanimate nature of Pater's bodies is not lightly attached to the desire expressed for these bodies within his narrative. The feverish desire that might be excited by Pater's evocations of the body is implicitly muted by the idealised quality of these bodies. Think, for example, of how he asserts that sculpture eradicates personal characteristics – the physical signs of personality – to create an ideal of the individual: sculpture 'unveils man in the repose of his unchanging characteristics [. . .] reveals not only what is accidental in man but the tranquil godship in him as opposed to the restless accidents of life' (R 136–7). Pater's suggestion that essential, perhaps even metaphysical, characteristics or Forms are captured in sculpture is emphasised as he continues:

> Sculpture finds the secret of its power in presenting these types, in their broad, central, incisive lines. This it effects not only by accumulation of detail, but by abstracting from it. All that is accidental, all that distracts the simple effect upon us of the supreme types of humanity, all traces in them of the commonness of the world, it gradually purges away. (R 138–9)

In this passage Pater insists on the gap between real earthly bodies and the idealised bodies of classical art, and thus in effect brings his reader back from the brink of fetishism. For desire takes its fire from that which *is* 'accidental', unique and personal to the beloved. Desire does not crave the ideal but rather the personal characteristics that individuate the lover. Therefore by stressing the difference between the real and the ideal and re-establishing the abstract unindividuated nature of the bodies on which his narrative has lingered, Pater retroactively adjusts the reader's perspective on these bodies. He seems to catch his reader in the erotic revelry stimulated by his evocations of the male body, only to recast these bodies as Platonic Forms. It is an ideal of beauty that Pater shows to us, but not of erotic beauty.

Pater thus places his readers into a complex relationship with these statuesque bodies; one defined by creativity, desire, denial and aspiration. Sculpture crucially fulfils Pater's desire to grant greater subjectivity and creativity to the spectator, who may move around to view the sculpture from different perspectives. As Lene Østermark-Johansen has suggested, this may help to explain why Pater grants such a central position to sculpture in his aesthetic, going against the grain of Swinburne's *Notes on Poems and Reviews* (1866), which had declared the death of this form in modernity (Østermark-Johansen 2011: 118).[3] Pater wants to take this subjectivity even further. His evocations of the sculptural body aspire to the same quality that he saw in Michelangelo's sculptures: 'an incompleteness, which is surely undesigned, and which, as I think, no one regrets, and trusts to the spectator to complete the half-emergent form' (R 49). Such intentional 'incompleteness' makes the Paterian body a figure of the reader's imagination as much as Pater's and that of the sculptor. The figures in Pater's prose are evoked rather than described, and the image is completed by the imagination of the reader.

Thus in 'Winckelmann', after glancing touches on Apollo, the 'distinguished beauty' of Philip of Croton and Demetrius Phalereus for his 'beautiful eyebrows' (R 133), Pater's narrative eye moves on to leave a 'half-emergent form' for the imagination of the reader to complete. So too with his abstract evocation of an unidentified statue: Pater's narrative eye lingers on the contours of this athletic male statue, locating itself in very close proximity to its object, examining, dismembering and fetishising its discrete elements: 'no member of the human form is more significant than the rest; the eye is wide and without pupil; the lips and brow are hardly of less significance than hands and breasts and feet' (R 136). Here the description ends. Its brevity permits us freedom to become imaginative creators of the form, mirroring the erotic-imaginative recreation of an absent lover. The absence of the beloved and the role of the imagination intensify and idealise the love-object. Certainly the body is objectified as a figure of sensual desire through this process, but the intentionality of the subject may not be taken for granted. So perhaps the fact that little is written about Pater's bodies is due to the simple truth that these bodies hardly exist in his writings. Rather, as with the portrait of Dorian Gray, the reader conceives a vivid visual image only to discover on returning to the text that this was but an evocation, which gained its vividness more from the imagination than from any ostensible description in words.

All in all, far from goading the reader on to desire even covertly, Pater places us at a triple remove from real flesh: in the act of reading one imagines a body out of Pater's description, itself re-imagined from the representation in fine art of a real body. At each stage the body is infused with the ideals of its interpreter so that it comes to exist in a realm far removed from touchable, living, dying reality. Rendered in Pater's prose, then, the strength and beauty of *Discobulus* is eternal, whilst the desire expressed by the narrative is as ethereal as its object is unobtainable. The gaze of Pater's narrative points to the statue expressly as an object of desire that will never be held and to the eternal beauty, youth and freedom that the mortal individual will never possess.

The Erotic Touch

One of Pater's comments on Michelangelo particularly resonates with the current critical consensus on his own homoeroticism: 'He who spoke so decisively of the supremacy in the imaginative world of the unveiled human form had not always been, we may think, a mere Platonic lover' (R 52). It is a sense that Pater too could not have been 'a mere Platonic lover', or at least not a willing one, that has governed queer readings of his writings on desire for the male marble statues evokes in his essays. To some extent this assessment is understandable, given the Hardinge episode. However, there was more of the Platonist in Pater than such critics might care to admit. A close reading of his actual writings leaves no doubt that for him erotic desire is implicitly inconsumable. As I have suggested, his narrative gaze rests not on the warm living flesh but on the body captured and idealised in marble, which, as Kenneth Clark noted over fifty years ago, 'takes the most sensual and immediately interesting object, the human body, and puts it out of reach of time and desire' (Clark 1956: 22). The 'out of reach' quality of the statue is essential to Pater's version of desire. At the centre of his narratives the body rendered in marble stands as an ambivalent idealised object: at once promising and denying love.

By directing his gaze not toward the living subject but toward the idealised body, 'out of reach of time and desire', Pater emphasises the futility of desire for both an untouchable lover and an unattainable eternity. Thus does the desiring gaze contain the knowledge of its own impossibility. The appearance of the statue tantalises the imagination with the possibility of mutual desire, only to deny its consummation. For this reason desire directed to the sculptural body is itself transformed into an ideal state of '*being*' and not a catalyst to physical love. In this context Richard Dellamora's belief that 'Pater [. . .] bases the aesthetic in bodily response' (111) is a little puzzling. As Lene Østermark-Johansen has illustrated, when it comes to sculpture 'Pater locates the sensuous element in the sculptor rather than the spectator' (2010: 87). In evoking how Winckelmann 'fingers those pagan marbles with unsinged hands' (R 143) certainly Pater privileges the unashamed tactility that he identifies with paganism. Yet at the same time, Pater was a reserved Victorian, by no means willing to adopt the unadulterated sensuality of Winckelmann in his own writings or life.

It is one of the poignant ironies of Pater's aesthetic that the pleasure of erotic touch – a reciprocal experience that requires both the frisson of bodies touching and being touched – is both desired and denied in his writing. To be precise, the objects of Pater's desiring gaze deny the pleasures of touch: these sculpted bodies stand aloof from their mortal spectator; cold and hard to the touch, impervious to their admirer. Whilst one may gaze on them in desire, their eyes, Pater notes, 'wide and directionless, not fixing anything in their gaze' (R 140), return a blank stare to the would-be lover. So the idealised male body tantalises the imagination with the possibility of touch, the most personal and intimate of sensual experiences, only to deny the reality of warm responsive flesh and reciprocal desire. Desire for the statuesque body ironically epitomises Pater's definition of love in the medieval cloister: 'a love defined by the absence of the beloved, choosing to be without hope, protesting against all lower uses of love, barren, extravagant, antinomian' (WM 302). In theory, certainly, it is true that 'Pater refuses to disengage the pleasures of the body from the pleasures of the mind' (Higgins 1993: 53). The reunification of the opposites of body and mind is his moment of Hegelian synthesis and it mirrors 'the perfect identification of matter and form' in *The Renaissance* (90). In practice though Pater knew well that the disengagement of imaginative pleasures from physical pleasures was absolutely necessary in the nineteenth century. This 'reserve' was a philosophical as well as a practical position. After all, 'the end of life is not action but contemplation – *being* as distinct from *doing*' (A 62). Homoerotic desire is for him a beautiful disposition rather than a power of action, with the emotions involved in eros unexpressed, quickening the beauty and poignancy of existence.

In addition to the romantic idea of having erotic desire rest forever in the air of eternity, Pater is dedicated to 'reserve' in the erotic experience of touch. In criticising John Addington Symonds' lack of 'reserve' in *The Renaissance in Italy: The Age of the Despots* (1875: 201), he suggests his own personal criticism of Symonds' open homoerotic relationships, as discussed in Chapter 5. This comment places Pater in opposition to

Symonds as one emphatically not calling for 'a freely expressed eros' (110), but for tact and restraint in erotic relationships. It is notable too that 'reserve' is a much admired quality in the celibate priests of his imaginary portraits, such as Prior Saint Jean in 'Apollo in Picardy' and Marius in his eponymous novel. When Henry James suggested that Pater had 'taken it out, wholly, exclusively, with the pen (the style, the genius,) and absolutely not at all with the person', he was quite right (James 293). James, who identified more with Pater than he could ever admit, probably even to himself, realised that Pater's passion and sensuality are channelled through the inconsumable homoeroticism of his ekphrasis, and thereby kept under control.

Dellamora would have us believe that 'Winckelmann's career showed Pater how a freely expressed eros could become part of a cultural ideal' (110). However, there is nothing 'freely expressed' about Pater's homoerotic desire. In his review of Symonds' *The Renaissance in Italy* Pater suggests his distaste for desire that is too freely expressed. This is where the influential recent discussions of Pater's sexuality have gone awry. While it is true that 'Pater's Winckelmann is the prototype for the persona of the homosexual aesthete that would become widespread in the *fin de siècle*, be crystallised by Wilde's effeminate style, and eventually provide one of the dominant models of twentieth-century gay identity' (Evangelista 2009: 35–6), it is a significant misstep to read Pater's Winckelmann – or any of his allusions to homoerotic desire – as analogues to late-twentieth-century conceptions of desire.

Not for Pater the defiant, flamboyant cavorting of Symonds or Wilde: his expression of homoerotic desire is muted. Moreover, this muted expression is not a 'homosexual code' or 'aesthetic minoritizing' discourse' in the senses that Linda Dowling and Thaïs Morgan, respectively, define it (Dowling 1994: 135; Morgan 1996: 142): it is not a discourse meant to covertly evoke homoerotic desires that might be expressed freely. Rather, the muted desire in Pater's *Renaissance* is a symptom of the fact that restraint is implicit in erotic desire as he conceives it. In other words, it is not that homoerotic desire is expressed through 'aesthetic minoritizing' discourse simply to avoid the detection of unsympathetic eyes but, rather, that restrained expression is *essential* to Paterian desire. While it is in *Marius the Epicurean* (1885) that Pater most explicitly embodies 'familiar norms of Victorian masculinity' (Adams 1995: 150), the implicit endorsement of the Victorian values associated with masculinity, in particular 'restraint', is a constant in his works. The physical restraint necessitated by the marble object of desire emblematises the self-restraint necessitated by the law and by decorum, but also by a belief that the frisson of unrequited desire is better than the reality of its expression. The unobtainable nature of Pater's male bodies exalts love and desire to the realm of the ideal. Without possibility of reciprocity, desire is now and forever an imaginative love: unconstrained, unsoiled and unthwarted by the real.

Pater's idealised desire recalls Plato's vision of eros and that of his other intellectual idol, Michelangelo, whose love poetry to Tommaso dei Cavalieri was significantly influenced by Neo-Platonic ideas of love.[4] For Plato's Socrates in the *Symposium*, desire is the first stage in an ascent to the Good in which it is refined into a love of the Good exalted above physical desire to the ethereal realm of the Forms (1999: 734ff). For Pater too, erotic love is a transformative mode of 'being' but instead of leading to the Good it leads to an enhanced aesthetic awareness. So, if the connection between homoerotic desire and aesthetic appreciation underlines the tensions between Pater's aesthetic and Kant's arguably naïve separation of the aesthetic from self-interest, it also suggests that desire is ultimately superseded by the aesthetic realm.

The Timeless Body

If Pater's marble bodies represent his ideal of the erotic male body, these bodies equally suggest the ideal of an infallible, eternally youthful body to their mortal spectator. The previous section of this chapter opened with Kenneth Clark's statement that: 'the nude ... takes the most sensual and immediately interesting object, the human body, and puts it out of reach of time and desire' (22). Certainly Pater's nude statues are 'out of reach' of time as well as desire. In marked contrast with Baudelaire or Swinburne, for whom sculpture was a passé form with its most famous pieces fatally marked by their antiquity, Pater suggests that sculpture transfers the body into a privileged realm that is not governed by the laws of entropy. In other words, it presents a glimpse of eternal youth to the fragile, mortal spectator – the spectator made of what Pater calls 'the perishing human clay' (A 49–50) – by presenting human bodies that are 'out of reach of time'.

Pater's sculptured bodies defy time and fragility. They capture the individual at the eternal, infallible moment of youth. Jacques Kalip has gone a little way towards grasping this when he argues that Pater only appreciates a body when it has become 'a non-sentient, [. . .] working stiff' (2002: 249). Kalip is right to pick up on the inanimate nature of Pater's bodies, yet his metaphor of the 'working stiff' misses the main point. The subjective body of the spectator and the sculpted, objective body of the statue are not distinguished by life and death in Pater's writings. The Greek sculptures on which Pater's gaze rests are emphatically not 'working stiffs' because these bodies were never alive and cannot die. They are immortal and this immortality is a significant part of their ideality. As Pater describes in 'Winckelmann':

> Greek sculpture deals almost exclusively with youth, where the mouldering of the bodily organs is still as if suspended between growth and completion, indicated but not emphasised; where transition from curve to curve is so delicate and elusive, that Winckelmann compares it to a quiet sea, which, although we understand it to be in motion, we nevertheless regard it as an image of repose. (R 140)

The 'suspended' quality of sculpture is essential to Pater's interest in the form. He evokes the statue outside of the time continuum, exempt from the natural laws of entropy that condemn the mere mortal to death. The fresh, athletic, idealistic youth captured in Pater's *Apollo Belvedere* for example is paused eternally on the brink of the future, never declining and therefore perfect. To enhance such splendour, the statue is also untarnished by the world of paid work, which defined heterosexual masculinity and male perceptions of time alike in nineteenth-century Britain.

The strong work ethic of the athlete is essential: the athletic body is created out of hard graft for its own sake. This graft of athletic exertion is fundamental and it distinguishes the athlete from wild Dionysian exertions. Graft is etched on the athlete's sculpted, economic body: 'the vigorous head also, with the face, smooth enough, but spare, and tightly drawn over muscle and bone' (GS 304). There is no excess and no extravagance; the athletic body is the determined will made flesh and in this way it is decidedly distinct from the gratuitous pleasure of Dionysian dancing that threatened to overwhelm the individual in *Dionysus and Other Studies*.[5] The 'habitual and measured discipline' of the Greek athlete (GS 293) is characteristic of Pater's endeavour to bring control to extreme emotions. The athlete brings reasonable order to the 'Asiatic, or archaic' tendencies of the individual: it is the triumph of the centripetal over the centrifugal; of Apollo over Dionysus; and, therefore, of measured, rule-governed, disciplined athletics over the 'wild dancing' of Dionysian fever. The artists of Ægina capture this in their images of ancient Greek warriors:

> not in the equipments they would really have worn, but naked, – flesh fairer than that golden armour, though more subdued and tranquil in effect on the spectator, the undraped form of man coming like an embodiment of Hellenic spirit, and as an element of *temperance*, into the somewhat gaudy spectacle of Asiatic, or archaic art. (GS 276; Pater's italics)

The naked body here symbolises Hellenic reason and pride in the secular human form. More importantly in this passage, Pater draws attention to the toned, naked flesh of the Greek warrior as evidence of temperance brought to the 'gaudy', 'Asiatic' spectacle of the spirit that is riddled with desire.

In sharp contrast to the loss of personal identity that occurs in Dionysian frenzy, athletic cultivation is a constant reaffirmation of the individual's identity and autonomy:

> Variety and novelty of experience, further quickened by a consciousness trained to an equally nimble power of movement, individualism, the capacities, the claim, of the individual, forced into their utmost play by a ready sense and dexterous appliance of opportunity . . . (PP 56)

Pater makes movement emblematic of individualism, suggesting that the power of movement is the exercise of individualism itself. Autonomy, which in 'Poems by William Morris' was affirmed by touching, is gained here by the entirely self-sufficient and fiercely disciplined exercise of one's own power. This self-cultivation is stressed by language suggesting abundance and limitless energy, giving the illusion of control over the body. Thus does the athlete evoked by Pater participate, briefly at least, in a fantasy of eternal youth and self-control that Pater will soon smash.

This self-control is strongly linked to the idealised relationship between spirit and the flesh epitomised in the athletic body. In contrast to the dominance of mind over body in later Western thought, 'Greek thought finds its happy limit,' Pater writes; 'it has not yet become too inward; the mind has not yet learned to boast its independence of the flesh' (R 132). In athletic cultivation, the individual has a heightened consciousness of the pantheistic identification of spirit and matter. The immanence of spirit in flesh is exemplified by making one's body the objectification of the will. There is 'blending and interpenetration of intellectual, spiritual, and physical elements, still folded together, pregnant with the possibilities of a whole world closed within it' (R 140). Pater's subjective individual aspires to a symbiotic relationship between spirit and body that is attained through physical cultivation. Pater suggests this when he characterises Greek gymnastics as 'one half music, [. . .], a matter, partly, of character and of the soul, of the fair proportion between soul and body, of the soul with itself' (GS 296). He terms this balanced unity of soul and body in athletic sport 'bodily soul' (GS 302). This is a feature of athletic exertion which also characterises Winckelmann, who is described by Pater as 'The quick, susceptible enthusiast, betraying his temperament even in appearance, by his olive complexion, his deep-seated piercing eyes, his rapid movements'

(R 124). The vivid appearance of the spirit manifested in the body is reminiscent of the transparent quality of the diaphanous man. Whilst the spirit affects the body, Winckelmann illustrates that the body also affects the spirit: '[his] enthusiasm, dependent as it is to a great degree on bodily temperament, has a power of reinforcing the purer emotions of the intellect with an almost physical excitement' (R 122). The effects of physical cultivation on the spirit are rendered more explicit in *Marius*. For example, when Marius walks to Rome, he experiences:

> The formative and literary stimulus, so to call it, of peaceful exercise which he had always observed in himself, doing its utmost now, the form and the matter of thought alike detached themselves clearly and with readiness from the healthfully excited brain. – 'It is wonderful,' says Pliny, 'how the mind is stirred to activity by brisk bodily exercise.' (M I, 164)

The athlete assuages the struggle, 'a *Streben*, as the Germans say, between the palpable and limited human form, and the floating essence it is to contain' (GS 28). He aspires to overcome the tension between spirit and body, and to create a symbiotic relationship between them. For in athletic cultivation there is a 'blending and interpenetration of intellectual, spiritual, and physical elements, still folded together, pregnant with the possibilities of a whole world closed within it' (R 140). Winckelmann and Marius embody this unity of soul and body – or 'bodily soul' (GS 302) – in which the spirit is vividly manifested in the body and physical health quickens the spirit. The effect is analogous to the 'perfect identification of matter and form' that describes ideal art (R 90). It makes the spirit immanent in empirical reality. The prominence of the athletic body in art illustrates the artist's 'full and free realisation' of the material world, and the athletic body demands that the artist render him 'within the limits of the visible, the empirical world' (GS 297). This assertion of the material world recalls the contrast which Pater makes between Angelico's frescos, which are 'only the symbol or type of a really inexpressible world' (R 131), and Greek art, which 'begins and ends with the finite image, yet loses no part of the spiritual motive' (R 132). It rests not on a rejection of spirit, but rather on an assertion that the spirit is immanent in the material realm; and that art must render the material realm, first and foremost, finding the spirit within it. The athlete is 'as [he] moves or rests just there for a moment, between the animal and spiritual worlds' (GS 304). The feeling is finite but within its moment the individual may feel invincible.

'The Perishing Human Clay'

Located in the tranquil realm of the ideal, the athlete and timeless statue enrapture their spectator in a moment of wish-fulfilment in which the ephemerality and fragility of the mortal body are forgotten in aesthetic contemplation. Perhaps Robert Keefe has come closest to capturing this relationship between the idealised, desired body and the mortal, 'perishing clay' (A 50) in Pater's writings. In 'Walter Pater's Two Apollo's' he suggests that, for Pater, 'The human face, the human body, the human mind have imprinted themselves, their own beauty, covering the moral void of a threatening universe, overcoming the sense of helplessness' (1987: 164). In truth the extent to which the Paterian body can really assuage the metaphysical crises facing the mortal individual is more uncertain than Keefe suggests. In Pater's ideal, human beauty offers the individual a new order of values to cover the void left by God the Father. Few knew better than he how the body had given Swinburne 'a way out of Christian discourse' in his 1866 collection *Poems and Ballads* (Armstrong 1993: 393). Yet as Pater glances at the fragile human frame he remains ever balancing on a wire above the precipice of 'the moral void of a threatening universe'. This dizzies him as it had never dizzied Swinburne because Pater lacks the poet's defiance; and it dizzies him as it never dizzied the 'muscular Christians' because Pater lacks their faith. His 'moral void' is a void of death, helplessness and erotic deviance, and it will not be stilled. Much as Pater would like to paper over the cracks of religious metaphysics and ethics with secular, embodied beauty, the body beautiful ultimately lets him down. If the body as an object of desire temporarily covers the 'void', this can only be for a moment. Ultimately the mortal spectator must return to the reality of his own often imperfect and failing, and ultimately dying, body.

Hence despite Pater's gaze on the young athletic male body, it is not this that forms the metaphorical centre of Pater's Copernican Revolution. Rather, the centre is the body as experienced by the individual who gazes on the body beautiful, the dreamer who is made of 'the perishing human clay'. These human bodies are constructed on a tension between the finite flesh and the spirit that longs for eternity. They are constantly at odds with themselves: striving for health and fitness, yet slowly dying, cell by cell. As objects of desire Pater's bodies may be magnificent in their eternal beauty, but experienced subjectively by the spectator and creator, the body is so terribly fallible. Pater was acutely aware of bodily pain and mortality. He grappled with mortality on a personal as well as a philosophical level, suffering the early deaths of his father, mother, and brother. He was also frequently in ill health. He suffered illness from an early age and after a severe beating at The King's School, he lay ill for six months, 'he never, it has been assumed, really recovered, and peculiarity of his gait which marked him all the rest of his life is attributable to it' (Wright I, 110). His health thereafter was always fragile. He knew all the symptoms of a body unwilling to cooperate with the intellectual effort necessary to write *Marius the Epicurean*, suffering from 'the intolerable languor and fatigue, the fevers and the cold fits, the grey hours of lassitude and insomnia' (Gosse 262). In his later years he was afflicted with gout: 'I am confined to my room with gout, but have been consoling myself with "The Happy Prince,"' he wrote to Wilde in 1888 (L 85).

Pater's acute consciousness of how passing time affects the fragile human body is most famously expressed in the Conclusion to *The Renaissance*, where he writes that

> Our physical life is a perpetual motion of them – the passage of the blood, the waste and repairing of the lenses of the eye, the modification of the tissues of the brain under every ray of light and sound – processes which science reduces to simpler and more elemental forces [. . .] This at least of flame-like our life has, that it is but the concurrence, renewed from moment to moment, of forces parting sooner or later on their ways. (R 150)

Time etches itself on the sinews of the body till they turn to dust because the flesh betrays us all, eventually, to death. Even the fittest and most beautiful are condemned by time as with each passing year the once-firm muscles grow weaker and the smooth skin wrinkles and sags. Throughout *The Renaissance* the young athletic bodies created in art are juxtaposed with the ageing figures of the artists on whom Pater's essays focus. For example, in 'The Poetry of Michelangelo', the 'energy', 'strength', and youth of Michelangelo's statues and paintings is contrasted with the 'frail and yielding flesh' of their creator, whose long life leads Pater to evoke him in extreme old age as 'a *revenant*, as the French say, a ghost out of another age' (R 48ff; 57–8). *Marius the Epicurean* (1885) also illustrates Pater's morbid fixation with the human body – striving for health and fitness, yet slowly dying, cell by cell – as Marius' first 'vivid sense of the value of mental and bodily health' coincides with the death of his mother: 'He came home brown with health to find that the health of his mother was failing' (M I, 41).

Though this juxtaposition between the healthy body and the dis-eased, dying body features throughout Pater's oeuvre, its balance is altered from the late 1880s. In the twenty-one years that separated *The Renaissance* (1873) from 'The Age of Athletic Prizemen' (1894, 1895), Pater's presentation of the athletic body has fundamentally altered. In the latter essay, 'emphatic historical framing distances Pater from the achievement [of athleticism] he celebrates' (Adams 1995: 181). With this, Pater renounces the possibility of recovering the Hellenic ideal he had invited his readers to share in his Conclusion to *The Renaissance*. His increasingly vivid awareness of the frailty of his own physical health may have contributed to making the attainment of the athletic ideal remote. By the age of fifty he was in 'feeble health' (Wright II, 134).[6] His appearance in the 1894 portrait by William Rothenstein suggests as much: his thick hair had receded to leave him almost bald, his slender face had become almost stout, and his grey eyes had lost the quiet intent of their youth to become quite wistful and somehow melancholy.

The remoteness of the idealised athletic body in Pater's later works may have also been influenced by the emergence of the decadent movement. Although the languor and sensual excess of decadence was arguably implicit in Paterian aestheticism from the outset, for Pater self-indulgent pleasures existed, as discussed above, only in the realm of fantasy. With the line between 'being' and 'doing' irrevocably broken down by decadent aestheticism in the early 1890s, it was no longer possible for Pater to write in the same way about the male body. Wilde's *The Picture of Dorian Gray* (1891) and the publication of Arthur Symons' 'The Decadent Movement in Literature', in November 1893 in *Harper's Magazine*, redefined the nature of the body away from that found in the early works of Pater, who was both these writers' mentor. Pater's bodies may be fated to decay and death but they are never reconciled to this fate, and aspire to beautiful athleticism. By contrast, Symons' definition of the 'new and beautiful and interesting disease' of British decadence (859) luxuriates in the inevitable decay of the flesh:

> ... the *maladie fin de siècle*. For its very disease of form, this literature is certainly typical of a civilisation grown over-luxurious, over-enquiring, too languid for the relief of action, too uncertain for any emphasis in opinion or in conduct. (859; Symons' italics)

If Pater is the father of British decadence, it is an errant child. Its conception of the individual takes Paterianism to its logical conclusion, yet it is far from clear that Pater wished to see this result. The ravaged, diseased body of the hedonist celebrated by Symons would have been mortifying to Pater who prized the unsullied athletic body over all else. What decadence does is to show that Pater's hedonism and his athletic ideal are incompatible. Coming at a time when Pater was increasingly aware of his own physical frailty, the emergence of British decadence further distanced his male ideal from reality.

The physical 'waste' of the ephemeral human life first suggested in the

Conclusion is most vividly captured in Pater's final essay, 'Pascal', which he was editing on the day he died, 30 July 1894. The spectre of sickness and decay looms large in this essay. Pater describes the 'physical malady' that blighted the final years of Pascal's life as he wrote *Pensées*, with 'long-continued physical sufferings', 'insupportable languor, alternating with supportable pain, as he died little by little through eight years of their composition' (MS 62). The idea that Pascal's writing is defined by his physical pain is important to Pater:

> Pascal's 'Thoughts,' then, we shall not rightly measure but as the outcome, the utterance, of a soul diseased, a soul permanently ill at ease. We find in their constant tension something of insomnia, of that sleeplessness which can never be a quite healthful condition of mind in a human body. Sometimes they are cries, cries of obscure pain rather than thoughts – those great fine sayings which seem to betray by their depth of sound the vast unseen hollow places of nature, of humanity, just beneath one's feet or at one's side. (MS 66)

This passage reaffirms the integral relationship between spirit and flesh that defined the human body in *The Renaissance* and *Marius the Epicurean*. Here, however, this relationship is fraught. The way in which Pater transfers Pascal's physical illness into an extended metaphor for the state of his thoughts suggests the reciprocal relationship between them. In the first part of the passage the 'soul' or 'mind' appears to be trapped within the physical body and ultimately defined by its condition. Not only is disease a metaphor for the mind, but the diseased state of the body obliterates thought with the feeling of pain. Yet in the final part of the passage, the relationship between mind and body opens an alternative mode of imaginative or intellectual achievement in which the ailing flesh enables Pascal's exploration of those 'vast unseen hollow places of nature, of humanity'. Although *Pensées* may be the product of Pascal's illness, it also defies it. Pater suggests that in the wake of Pascal's death it is as a creator and a thinker in this work that he experiences aspects of being inaccessible to those not facing death.

The way in which Pascal's masterwork is written against impending death suggests that the integral relationship between mind, or soul, and body is necessary to imagination. The ailing flesh is a terrible catalyst to the spirit so that it might see into the 'void' and even create beauty to spite it. This is clearer when Pater writes of Shakespeare's Claudio in his essay on '"Measure For Measure"' (1874, 1889):

> . . . he gives utterance to some sense of the central truths of human feeling, the sincere, concentrated expression of recoiling flesh. Thoughts as profound and poetical as Hamlet's arise in him; and but for the accidental arrest of sentence he would descend into the dust, a mere gilded, idle flower of youth indeed,

but with what are perhaps the most eloquent of all Shakespeare's words upon his lips. (A 181)

The beauty and truth of Claudio's words are quickened by his sense of the ephemerality of his physical life.

Not for too long can Pater's prose linger on decaying human flesh. Humankind, Pater knew as well as T. S. Eliot, cannot bear very much reality. Untimely death releases the individual from 'the mouldering of bones and flesh' and confirms Pater's assertion that '[s]ome of those whom the gods love die young' (R 150; R 57).[7] Untimely death captures the individual forever at the moment of his perfection, 'as if suspended between growth and completion' with the 'sweet aroma of early manhood' intact (R 140; D 158). So it is that his essays and imaginary portraits are populated by young men whose lives have been abbreviated before they could descend into the fearful ugliness of physical decay: Duke Carl of Rosenmold, Sebastian van Storck, Emerald Uthwart, Antony Watteau, Marius are amongst them. Still, physical decay haunts almost everything Pater writes. The cultivation of the body is an attempt to exalt oneself above the chaos and void of mortality at the heart of being. By his strength and beauty, the individual seems himself to fill the void as Robert Keefe suggests. However, the inevitable decay of the body means that ultimately each one is betrayed to death.

The Scope of the Paterian Body

Both as voyeur of the body beautiful and as ambivalent subject of one's own flesh, the Paterian individual is conceived on Robert Keefe's precipice with chaos just a step away, always. In the case of the objective body, chaos is defined as transgression in the real world, when desire is acted on. In the case of the subjective body, chaos emerges as something inherent in bodily degeneration. And so, the chaos that is at the heart of the body, like the chaos of Dionysus or the centrifugal forces more generally, is really the constant threat of disintegration: the disintegration of reserve, beauty and the unity of spirit and flesh. If the body offers liberation to the individual, it also sentences the individual to death. Therefore the Paterian body cannot be reduced to a mere object of desire. Focusing on the body challenges how we conceive desire in Pater's works. Understanding Pater's bodies as sentient, aesthetic objects distanced from their spectators to exist in the realm of the ideal, it becomes clear that desire in his writings is a state of 'being' and not a power of 'doing'. The significance of a rather Victorian 'reserve' in Pater's writings and life has been marginalised by an anachronistic recent critical discourse which focuses on the unembodied idea of desire and seeks and to cast Pater as a prototype for late twentieth-century homosexual identity. In truth Pater's homoeroticism bears a more complex relation to modern homosexuality, with 'freely expressed desire' significantly qualified by 'reserve' and aesthetic idealisation.

With his conception of the body, Pater positions himself somewhere on the spectrum between his mentor Benjamin Jowett and his disciple Oscar Wilde. Certainly, 'At the heart of Pater's enterprise is that which Jowett finds unspeakable: the body' (Higgins 1993: 53). However, he reclaims it not for unbridled hedonism but for the self-disciplined embodiment of one's individuality; for 'being' rather than for 'doing'. Having begun with the body, Pater ends where he always does: in the realm of imagination. Pater's homoeroticism takes place most vividly in the theatre of the imagination where it is idealised for him and for his readers. Imaginative experience was after all always more satisfying than reality for Pater.

Pater's Female Bodies

In all of this, Pater's female bodies risk being forgotten. Perhaps Pater's closest long-term relationships were with women: he lived with his sisters, Clara and Hester, for most of his working life. Whilst Hester looked after their house, Clara 'was known in the seventies as one of the best female conversationalists in Oxford and was a woman of considerable intellectual powers' (qtd Monsman 1977: 40). Yet it is unclear whether women are included in her brother's vision of the late-Romantic individual. The female body for the most part in Pater's writings barely makes ripples on the calm waters of his refined prose, after all, 'the supreme beauty is male rather than female' (R 123), whilst the idea of a female intellect is entirely absent.

Jacques Kalip suggests that 'Pater's real misogyny' is tacitly understood amongst scholars of his work (247) and it is true that Pater passes lightly over many a female body. Dante's Beatrice (D 154), Charlotte Corday (D 158), Simonetta (R 39), Judith (R 39) and Leonardo's *Medusa* (c. 1600) are but noted, functioning as barely embodied symbols of an idea or mood in Pater's writings. About the Madonnas he has more to say: those of Michelangelo, da Vinci and Botticelli, whose earthiness and energy humanise them in contrast to the sickly, ethereal Madonnas of the middle ages. Or again, in Pater's evocations of Venus and the *Mona Lisa* (c. 1503–6) the female body becomes the site where the material and spiritual spheres meet; where materiality is spiritualised and spirit becomes flesh. Yet these images function very differently from the male athlete in relation to the spirit and flesh. Whereas the male athlete reconciles spirit and flesh through athletic endeavour, the female body gestures beyond the limitations of empirical reality to the intangible.

With this in mind, Robert Keefe's comment that in Pater's writings 'The human face, the human body, the human mind have imprinted themselves, their own beauty, covering the moral void of a threatening universe, overcoming the sense of helplessness' (1987: 164) might be expanded. Female figures, including the Madonna, Mona Lisa, Venus, Charlotte Corday, Medusa, Demeter and Persephone, enter Pater's narratives as ciphers: barely embodied, symbolic spirits, whose bodies gesture from the finite to the infinite and inconceivable. Pater's evocation of women is exemplified in his comments on Angelico:

> For him, all that is outward or sensible in his work [. . .] is only the symbol or type of a really inexpressible world, to which he wishes to direct the thoughts; he would have shrunk from the notion that what the eye apprehended was all. (R 132)

The figure of woman signifies the mysterious, unknowable, divine, and her body is cloaked or distanced. In this way the absent presence of the female body is a counterpoint to the male body, transvaluing the seen world for the unseen. The image of Botticelli's Venus rising from the sea is a good example. Pater's ekphrastic description first evokes her body through 'the faultless nude studies of Ingres' (R 38). Her figure is immediately made hazy by the distancing of myth in painting evoked in words by allusion to other paintings. The image of Botticelli's Venus in truth hardly resembles Ingres' nude studies. Its typical Renaissance matte, realistic texture would later inspire Ingres' handling of the brush, but the composition and figure are wholly different. Botticelli's Venus is lithe and ethereal, in contrast to Ingres' voluptuous, often guarded and earthy women. These images are at odds, inserting a tension that undermines the reader's ability to visualise Venus. Between the mental images evoked by Botticelli and Ingres her body is lost. She becomes an unembodied style and type but not a woman; not a body, but a mythical, mysterious temptation. Elsewhere, skirting over the face and hands of Mona Lisa ('we all know the face and hands of the figure' (R79)), Pater enters into a meditation on the mystical body of Mona Lisa. He rests on her 'unfathomable smile, always with a touch of something sinister in it' in its 'subdued and graceful mystery' (R79). Her beauty points beyond itself to the unknowable.

Such passages again suggest Pater's inability to really give up metaphysics, as well as his lack of interest in the materiality of the female body. It is a moot point whether the nature of the late-Romantic individual as Pater defines it is necessarily restricted to men, and this is not a topic that we can or need to pursue for present purposes. Regardless, the Paterian individual is at the centre of the immutable conflict between a spirit that longs for immortality and a body that will inevitably die. At its youthful, beautiful zenith the body is an object to be worshipped, but it also betrays the spectator to decay and death. Previous chapters have seen a pattern emerging in which, for Pater, creativity assuages various threats to the autonomy of the individual. Yet this is not the end of the matter when we look to the body; for in the end the body is matter, and as such returns its subject always to the ultimate realities of the material world. Even creativity is turned ashes to ashes, dust to dust, and the irony is that whilst this condemns us, without it creativity would not be possible. For Pater, it is the flesh's very mortality and evanescence that make creativity possible and necessary.

Notes

1. A word on the difference between these conceptions of the relationship between discourse and desire in Pater's works: Linda Dowling's 'homosexual code' conceives this underlying discourse of male-male desire as a stable network of signifiers (1994: 135), whereas Thaïs Morgan seeks greater nuance by contending that 'homosexual code' is plural and unstable, with different writers constructing their own idiosyncratic versions. Morgan reterms 'homosexual code' as 'aesthetic minoritizing discourse' (1996: 142).
2. The most notable exception is James Eli Adams' discussion of Pater's work in *Dandies and Desert Saints: Styles of Victorian Masculinity* (1995: 183ff), discussed below.
3. Lene Østermark-Johansen gives a compelling account of how Pater's ideas on sculpture interact with those of Swinburne and Baudelaire in *Walter Pater and the Language of Sculpture* (113ff.)
4. Pater alludes to these sonnets (R 52–3). In the third edition of *The Renaissance* in 1888 he added an allusion to John Addington Symonds' 1878 translation, *The Sonnets of Michael Angelo Buonarotti and Tommaso Campanella*.
5. See discussion in Chapter 5.
6. He came down with bronchitis in 1893 (L 146), before his protracted final illness in the summer of 1894.
7. Pater does not attribute the Classical source, perhaps because the phrase had long since passed into common parlance. Attributed to Herodotus and Menander, it was rendered by Plautus: 'quem di diligunt, adolescens moritur'. Among several subsequent versions, the best known may be that of Byron in *Don Juan*: '"Whom the gods love, die young" was said of yore, / And many deaths do they escape by this' (IV, 12; 192).

Chapter 7

Evolution and the 'Species': The Individual in Deep Time

But felt through all this fleshly dress
Bright shoots of everlastingness.
O how I long to travel back
And tread again that ancient track!
> Henry Vaughan's poem 'The Retreat' (1961: 407, lines 19–22)[1]

At Oxford Pater was steeped in the continuities of tradition. Not that change was entirely absent from Oxford life in the late nineteenth century. After decades of resistance, certain key figures in government and at Oxford – Pater's friends Benjamin Jowett and Mark Pattison amongst them – accepted the need for the university to broaden its curriculum and its outlook to better serve the needs of the nation.[2] Yet despite broad alterations, as noted in an earlier chapter, 'the spirit of the place remained the same' (V. H. H. Green 152). His position as a Fellow at Brasenose allowed Pater to maintain a pace of life determined more by his body's rhythms than by external time, according to which he often stayed in bed till midday (Wright I, 89). Otherwise he organised his days according to the very principle of habit he had purported to reject in his early work when he wrote:

> In a sense it might even be said that our failure is to form habits: for, after all, habit is relative to a stereotyped world, and meantime it is only the roughness of the eye that makes any two persons, things, situations, seem alike. (R 152)

It is said that once, when asked what he had been doing one morning, Pater replied, 'Adding a comma'; when asked what he had done during the afternoon, he replied, 'taking it out.' This perhaps fanciful story captures the fact that Pater was a careful, ever-revising composer of prose: a trait which has been extensively discussed by critics.[3] At least as interesting, though, is the way that indicates the luxury of time that Pater enjoyed, and which was essential to his individualism.

Yet whilst Pater was largely able to control how he spent his own time, external pressures encroached on his conception of himself in relation to time passing. Given the leisure he seemed to have in his own day-to-day life, it might be surprising that in his writings the problem of time haunts Pater's every moment. It is truly his 'most hauntingly pervasive principle' (Leighton 2007: 38). The problem of time – for a problem it certainly was for him – he experienced most immediately through the periodical press, with which his career was inextricably bound up and which as has been well said 'operated like multiple chronometers, all marking different times' (Mussell 94). Pater did not respond well to life ruled by clockwork. He usually initiated his own publishing commitments and therefore had more flexibility, but when he sought to publish *Gaston de Latour* in instalments in *Macmillan's Magazine*, he was obliged to keep to deadlines and this may have contributed to his abandonment of the project (Monsman 1995: xvii).

Whilst the technological advances of mechanised clocks promised – or threatened – to annihilate space and time as they had hitherto been experienced (Kern 2003: 10–36), growing awareness of the vast scope of evolutionary history and the myriad species within it annihilated the individual's pretensions to grandeur. In the vast scope of deep time, human history was shrunken down and the individual almost lost, a mere speck in time. Stephen Jay Gould conceives the impact of this on the late Victorians' consciousness of their place in the universe thus: 'Consider the earth's history as the old measure of the English yard, the distance from the King's nose to the tip of his outstretched hand. One stroke of a nail file on his middle finger erases human history' (3). It is in part the realisation of humanity's insignificance in evolutionary history that Pater is coming to terms with when he writes about the individual. He is preoccupied by the contrast between the individual as Lord of All, and as now conceived by natural science and technology: as merely one of a 'species', itself subject to 'descent' and eventual extinction – and on a day-to-day basis hemmed in on every side by the iron cage of deadlines and publication schedules.

To reiterate a point made earlier: unlike today, in late Victorian times before C. P. Snow's 'two cultures' had fully and fatefully bifurcated, even a man of letters like Pater was well aware of broad trends in science and their implications. Pater conceives himself at the fulcrum of evolutionary science, looking back to the Romantic moment of Wordsworth and Goethe and forward to the Eternal Recurrence of Friedrich Nietzsche. Though his thoughts are shaped by Heraclitus, Hegel and Wordsworth's 'spots of time', he is acutely aware that the problems of time encountered in modernity are fundamentally different from those faced by such predecessors. Pater re-patterns these writers, taking inspiration from their ideas but doing so in a way that charts the immense distance between himself and them; a distance created by evolutionary science. For whilst Pater's strongest influences and inspirations tend to come from the history of philosophical thought, contemporary philosophy in his day had yet to catch up with the question of how we are to under-stand ourselves in *time* in the light of evolutionary theory.[4] Pater read Darwin's *On the Origin of Species* (1859) as an undergraduate, and his friend Matthew Moorehouse suggests that it was a significant influ-ence on his early religious scepticism (Wright I, 203). In Pater's mature writings Darwin's influence remained pervasive: it inspired his ideas and fears, and his vision of the moment evolved in dialogue with the Darwinian conception of the individual as part of a species. This is not to say that the details of evolutionary science were always important; for him, Darwin, Darwinism and evolutionary science blur into each other, along with aspects of Herbert Spencer's 'Social Organism' (1860). The vision – or spectre – of evolution poses an essential question to Pater: how might the individual reinstate his 'indefinite reprieve' from death (R 153) with meaning when he knows that he exists as a single speck in evolutionary, 'deep' time as merely one of a species.

A number of critics have speculated on Darwin's influence on Pater. Carolyn Williams gives a compelling account of how the theory of evo-lution influenced his conception of time (1989: 143ff). More recently, in his illuminating comparison between Pater and Karl Pearson, 'Two Ways Not to Be a Solipsist: Art and Science, Pater and Pearson', George Levine has suggested that Pater's allusions to Darwin show that he both accepted Darwinian evolution and, further,

> Where Arnold had tried to separate Darwin's language and ideas from the language of value, Pater absorbs it into that language, self-consciously trans-lating quantity into quality. He leans on the sciences of observation for the ideas that shape his views of art. (21)

Implicitly accepting Levine's reading of Pater on value, Angela Leighton suggests that Darwin's prevalent term 'form' is absorbed into Pater's conception of aesthetic form (2007: 81–7). Meanwhile Gowan Dawson, who like Leighton conceives Pater as a materialist, sees an allusion to Darwin's *Origin of Species* in *Marius the Epicurean* (1885) as Marius decides to consider all the 'various and competing hypotheses, which, in that open field for hypothesis – one's own actual ignorance of the origin and tendency of our being – present themselves so importunately, some of them with so emphatic a reiteration . . .' (M II, 64–5). Dawson compares this to Darwin's conclusion that 'In the future I see open fields for far more important researches . . . Much light will be thrown on the origin of man and his history' (Darwin 1899: 402; Dawson 2005: 45). Yet Pater's relationship with Darwin and the concept of evolution is not defined by the uncritical engagement and straightforwardly materialistic standpoint that these critics might suggest (Leighton 2007: 80; Dawson 2005: 50–1). Pater's interaction with Darwin and Darwinism, especially when writing of the individual, is one of resistance and reinterpretation as well as acquiescence. The latter, such as it is, is idiosyncratic: for he sees in evolution a sublime, decadent beauty. Pater's resistance to Darwinian science and evolutionary theory is subtle but ultimately damning, for whilst he mainly accepts its veracity, it does not – to adapt George Fox's phrase, from a quite different context – ever really speak to his condition. The problem of how to conceive the modern individual in deep time, which is the problem posed for Pater by Darwin, must be solved: yet not through Darwinian science, but rather by recourse to art.

Evolutionary and Dialectical History

Pater's aesthetic philosophy is founded on the assertion in his first published essay, 'Coleridge' (1866, 1889), that 'Modern thought is distinguished from ancient by its cultivation of the "relative" spirit in place of the "absolute"' (A 66). This vision of modern thought as 'relative' commits Pater to an experience of modernity defined by change and indeterminacy. It will define not only the style of his prose, 'the very fluidity' of which in 'its wandering openness to suggestion and affect, its provisional extendedness, ensure that ideas and concepts rarely harden against the flow' (Leighton 2007: 78), but also his conception of personal identity and his epistemology. Like so much of Pater's thought, his conception of history as flux emerges as a fusion of influences. He merges Heraclitean flux with Darwinism, quickened by what he calls 'the burden of Hegel' (PP 10): the knowledge that one cannot ignore the movement of history and that this would define modern philosophy.

Evolutionary flux or 'development' satisfies Pater's admiration for *reasonable* or reserved behaviour, and is accordingly characterised in 'Coleridge' as an organic materialistic flux:

> Nature, which by one law of development evolves ideas, hypotheses, modes of inward life, and represses them in turn, has in this way provided that earlier growth should propel its fibres into the later, and so transmit the whole of its forces in an unbroken continuity of life. Then comes the spectacle of the reserve of the elder generation exquisitely refined by the antagonism of the new. (A 65)

Unlike the scientific language in the Conclusion to *The Renaissance*, this passage is no mere 'tendency of modern thought' from which Pater distances himself (R 150): the scientific language here and the ideas it represents are fully assimilated into the narrative, seeming to subject all aspects of development to material forces. Pater's idea of evolution develops surprisingly in the final sentence of the passage above, though. His suggestion of history proceeding by antagonisms echoes Hegel's definition of dialectical history, in his *Lectures on the Philosophy of History (Vorlesungen über die Philosophie der Geschichte;* 1837), rather than postulating development as being smoothly evolutionary.

Hegel's idea of dialectical history was compelling to him and, as noted in Chapter 5, he adapted it to conceive history as a series of antagonisms between sensuality and spirituality. This reading of history as dialectic does not however make Pater a Hegelian, given three significant refusals. He rejects Hegel's systematising, his metaphysics, and the idea that thesis and antithesis resolve into synthesis. Defining Hegel as the philosopher who 'brings to its highest level of completeness the metaphysical reconstruction of all experience' (HP 6), Pater expands his critique of systematised philosophy, with a particular focus on Hegel's conception of history:

> the impression [Hegel] leaves . . . of a very imperfect reciprocity between the exacting reasonableness of the ideal he supposes, and the confused, imperfect, haphazard character of man's actual experience in nature and history – a radical dualism in his system, as to the extent of which he was perhaps not always quite candid, even with himself. (HP 6)

Pater's refusal of Hegel's systematisation of history is implicit in his dismissal of the idea that history could be driven by metaphysical principles. Clearly influenced by evolutionary science, Pater suggests an organic vision of temporal continuity in which history is defined not by teleology, or Victorian Progress of any other kind, but by a directionless modification of its present conditions. Moreover, his assertion, above, that temporal continuity is preserved in material fibres – which 'transmit the whole of its forces in an unbroken continuity of life' – implicitly rejects dualistic concepts of spirit and matter, and with it the basis of Hegelian metaphysics.

Pater's second refusal of Hegel in the passage above is his denial that thesis and antithesis are followed and transcended by synthesis. Recalling Heraclitus' conception of opposites, Pater in the passage above sees evolution as defined by 'unbroken' antagonisms. Whilst Heraclitus' doctrine of opposites 'contains the germ of Hegel's philosophy' (Russell 2005: 51), the two hold significantly different views on the relationship of opposites. The former proceeds as an eternal thesis-antithesis-thesis-antithesis, without *synthesis*. Each object is simultaneously its own contrary, not leading to further progressive change but integrally unstable. Thus, 'good and ill are one'; 'the way up and the way down is one and the same'; 'God is day and night, winter and summer, war and peace, surfeit and hunger . . .' (qtd Russell 2005: 51). Pater points toward this view of opposites when he comments of man, 'It seems as if the most opposite statements about him are true' (A 67). It is this same conception of history as thesis-antithesis-thesis-antithesis which characterises Paterian temporality as an 'unbroken continuity' of development and repression (A 65). We first see this eternal repeated cycle of development and repression in 'Poems by William Morris', where cultural history is figured as 'revolt' after 'revolt' (305): an epoch of spirituality is superseded by an epoch of sensuality which is in turn superseded by another epoch of spirituality, and so on for ever with no synthesis or resolution.

Returning to this vision of history in 'The Aesthetic Life' (c. 1893), Pater surveys the position of the individual, 'who might seem, at least, amid the ruins of so much abstract and artificial theory, to have completed the circle, to stand again, again, in some respects, a little child, at the point at which he set out' (AL 7). Repetition, which presented itself as an opportunity when the young Pater advocated cultural renewal through sensuality in 'Poems by William Morris', has grown more ambivalent here. The repetition of 'again, again' echoes through hollow time with a sense of futility. The knowledge that history shapes itself in ceaseless cycles asks us to revaluate our expectations and accept that historical progress and development are but a myth. There is no strong evidence that Pater came to terms with how this view might be reconciled with evolution. Yet evolution is always present in his works, if only on the margins or hanging in the air where it is crucial in defining the spirit of the Paterian individual. It is not really until the final work published in his lifetime, *Plato and Platonism*[5] (1893), that Pater offers an extensive account of how he sees the '"relative" spirit' as it is manifested in the theory of evolution, and particularly in Darwinism. Digressing from his discussion of Heraclitus's influence on Plato, Pater suggests that Darwin offers a 'cautiously reasoned' expression of Heraclitus' idea of flux (PP 11): 'The entire theory of "development," in all its various phases, proved or unprovable, – what is it but old Heracliteanism awake once more in a new world, and grown to full proportions?' (PP 10).

The Spectacle of Evolution and Entropy

In *Plato and Platonism* Pater cautiously affirms evolutionary history as a spectacle of terrible beauty: a confirmation of Herclitean philosophy, whose abstract 'development' is a thing of beautiful organicism, a ceaseless cycle 'nowhither' and slowly degenerating (PP 11). In evoking the deep time of evolutionary history Pater's metaphors and imagery not only create a vivid sense of its sublime beauty and decadence, but by capturing evolution in the imagination they attempt to aestheticise it and thus quell its devastating consequences for the Romantic individual.

Pater evokes evolution as an aesthetic spectacle, infused with Kantian sublimity, primarily to dissipate its threatening immediacy. This is evident in his aestheticised evocation of Herbert Spencer's *First Principles of a New System of Philosophy* (1862), a work which extended Darwin's theory of evolution to society. As Spencer wrote:

> . . . this law of organic evolution is the law of all evolution. Whether it be in the development of the Earth, in the development of Society, of Government, of Manufacturers, of Commerce, of Language, Literature, Science, Art, this same advance from the simple to the complex, through successive differentiation, holds uniformly. (148)

Accepting Spencer's expansion of evolutionary theory to society, Pater comments:

> Political constitutions, again, as we now see so clearly, are "not made," cannot be made, but "grow." Races, laws, arts, have their origins and end, are themselves ripples only on the great river of organic life; and language is changing on our very lips. (PP 11)

Pater's metaphor of the river transforms this multifarious, ceaseless change into an aesthetic experience, not to be feared but rather to gaze on as an autonomous spectator. The metaphor of the river has several aspects. It is, of course, an allusion to Heraclitus' river: 'The river where you set your foot just now is gone – those waters giving way to this, now this' (2003: 27); so making a link between ancient and modern thought. At the same time, as this image effectively evokes the grandeur of evolution and the relative insignificance of the individual, it distances implications of this reality for the individual's sense of self-identity. So although in evolutionary history the individual becomes an inconsequential speck of dust, 'just one of the possible outcomes' of selection and development (R 150), Pater asks us to think of this only as an aesthetic spectacle. Such an aestheticising tendency is evident elsewhere, as Pater transforms the concept of evolution into a theatrical performance, speaking of the 'great dramatic evolution' (AL 22). With this, Pater deftly takes the individual out of vast history to reposition him as its spectator.

The entropic echo of evolution's organic movement 'nowhither' comes to the fore in *Plato and Platonism*. The 'physical enquirer of to-day', Pater writes, realises that the world is

> as Heraclitus had declared (scarcely serious, he seemed to those around him) as literally in constant extinction and renewal; the sun only going out more gradually than the human eye; the system meanwhile, of which it is the centre, in ceaseless movement nowhither. Out terrestrial planet is in constant increase by meteoric dust, moving to it through endless time out of infinite space. The Alps drift down the rivers into the plains, as still loftier mountains found their level there ages ago. The granite kernel of the earth, it is said, is ever changing in its very substance, its molecular constitution, by the passage through it of electric currents. (PP 11)

This passage is among the most poetic in Pater's oeuvre. It poignantly reevokes the first part of the Conclusion to *The Renaissance*, expanding the transience, renewal and material decline that had there marked the individual's passage through life (R 150–1) in order to now define the fate of the universe, no less. The circularity of history ('in constant extinction and renewal'), familiar from 'Poems by William Morris', is revised mid-sentence by the allusion to the Second Law of Thermodynamics, formulated by William Thomson in 1852. Thomson argued that the sum of useful energy throughout the universe would be constantly reduced by the diffusion of heat until all had reached a state of entropy. Therefore Pater's characterisation of 'the sun only going out more gradually than the human eye' and the system 'in ceaseless movement nowhither' asks the reader to become a spectator of our own entropy. As in *art pour l'art*, Pater takes pleasure in historical change and entropy for their own sake. Already in *The Renaissance* Pater speaks of 'the grandeur of nothingness' (R 111), echoing Darwin's view that 'There is grandeur in the view of life' presented by evolutionary science (1899: 403). As the spectator of his own fate within evolutionary history, Pater's reader is thus invited to envisage evolution with the perverse pleasure of a decadent.

Pater's evocation of evolution in *Plato and Platonism* is at odds with the tenor of his age, according to which 'the sublime's presence was diminishing' (Colley 2010: 175).[6] Pater suggests, to the contrary, that the sublime is not past but is integral to modernity. Here the decadent grandeur of evolution and entropy has strikingly similar characteristics to the Kantian sublime. In the *Critique of Judgement*, Kant defined the sublime as a feeling aroused by the magnitude and might of a crude natural phenomenon with no determinate purpose (1987: §§25–6,

103–23). As noted above, the purposelessness, which Kant considers essential to a judgement of the sublime (§25, 109), is prominent in Pater's presentation of evolution. Using such words as 'ceaseless', 'endless', 'infinite', 'ever changing', as the passage unfolds, Pater again follows Kant's definition of the sublime as unchartable, creating a vivid sense of this quality. In mentioning the Alps, Pater – for a moment only – evokes the sublime as it was presented in English Romanticism. However, their sublimity is now undermined as the Alps too become subject to entropy in the passage from *Plato and Platonism*, the last vestiges of a now irretrievable aesthetic past. The Kantian sublime as it was taken up by Coleridge and the Romantics is rendered powerless by Pater, even quaint, against this new instance of the sublime: evolution and entropy. Only these phenomena now are truly incredible and *eternal;* all else, the Alps included, melts into air.

For Pater, whose understanding of Kant had been developing over three decades by the time he wrote *Plato and Platonism*, the allusion to the *Critique of Judgement* is likely to be calculated. Kant's third *Critique* not only identifies the characteristics of the sublime; it outlines the relation between the sublime and the imagination:

> Yet the sight of [sublime phenomena] becomes all the more attractive the more fearful it is, provided we are in a safe place. And we like to call these objects sublime because they raise the soul's fortitude above its usual middle range and allow us to discover in ourselves an ability to resist which is of a quite different kind, and which gives us the courage [to believe] that we could be a match for nature's seeming omnipotence. (Kant 1987: §28, 120)

Pater's conception of evolution as a sublime spectacle allows him to come to terms with the magnitude of its implications. He takes refuge from the assaults of scientific truth, which might provoke terror, by subjecting it to the imagination. Pater's words transform evolution into an aesthetic spectacle, and in becoming its spectators we momentarily believe that we might 'be a match for nature's seeming omnipotence'.

The 'species'

When Pater turns to consider the position of the individual within evolutionary history, it becomes more difficult for him to conceive of this as an aesthetic spectacle. After all, evolutionary science comes to challenge the very individualism on which his aesthetic is founded. Kant's 'Copernican Revolution', which positioned the individual at the centre of the world, and which underpins not only Paterian aestheticism but aestheticism more broadly, is rent asunder by evolutionary theory. The individual is shrunken down to a microscopic particle, understood not as a Romantic spirit but as just a tiny part of an evolving species in 'endless history' (PP 11). Pater cannot reject Darwin and Darwinism, nor would he want to, but when it comes to the individual he cannot come to terms with it either. Distancing himself from the conception of the individual presented by evolutionary science, ultimately he reasserts the schism between ancient and modern thought that seemed to have been vanquished by his melding of Darwin and Heraclitus. Far from disappearing as 'irrelevant' (Williams 1989: 17), the Paterian individual gains a new significance under these conditions. The individual becomes defined as the central site of resistance to the threat that evolution may crush its freedom and importance.

Pater is acutely aware of the way in which evolution's 'infinite stages of descent' (GS 27) reduce the individual to a mere instance of the species. Continuous time runs through the species, dissipating stable identity. As Pater notes, 'Darwin and Darwinism proposes a theory in which '"type" itself properly is not but is only always becoming' (PP 10). In the 'infinite stages of descent' the individual is reduced to an instance of the species, no longer ordained by God but descended, evolved, through history, his significance diminished to a speck in history's vast scope. In his essay on 'Coleridge' Pater uses metaphor, as he does in his contemplation of the shape of history, to aestheticise this terrifying phenomenon:

> Man's physical organism is *played upon* not only by the physical conditions about it, but by remote laws of inheritance, *the vibration of long-past acts* in the midst of the new order of things in which he lives. When we have estimated these conditions he is not yet simple and isolated; for the mind of the race, the character of age *sway him this way or that* through the medium of language and current ideas [. . .] he is so receptive, all the influences of nature and society *ceaselessly playing upon him*, so that every hour in his life is unique, changed altogether by a stray word, or glance, or touch. (A 67; my italics)

Pater's characterisation takes its inspiration from the Darwinian view that the individual is 'not a new and complete act of creation, but only an occasional scene, taken almost at hazard, in an ever slowly changing drama' (1899: 274). The infinite, interrelated forces of evolution are Romanticised and rendered beautiful by Pater's musical metaphors. Even so, the overall effect is ambivalent. The identity of the individual is utterly dissolved by the music of time. He becomes an instrument animated by this music as, in Pater's vision of it, its pace quickens from Darwin's 'slowly changing drama' to something more like Ravel's frenetic *La Valse*. The music of 'long-past acts' and the ever-changing present oppress the individual. These elements are insistent, as Pater's metaphors suggest by stressing the physical vulnerability of the individual to this image. No longer balanced by the 'capacities merely passive or receptive' and 'initiatory powers' of the transcendental self (GL 74), he is 'so receptive' that his identity is altered by each thing he comes into contact with. As in the nightmarish scenario of the Conclusion to *The Renaissance*, it seems for a moment that Angela Leighton is right: 'the difference between self and not self is lost' (2002: 18).

Ultimately Pater is troubled by the integral relationship between personal identity and evolutionary history, aware that this relationship cannot be aestheticised and so contained within his extended metaphor of music. When he returns to consider personal identity and evolution twenty-seven years after the publication of 'Coleridge', in *Plato and Platonism*, his figurative language suggests a darker side to our evolutionary inheritance:

> For in truth we come into the world, each one of us, "not in nakedness," but by the natural course of the organic development clothed far more completely than even Pythagoras supposed in a vesture of the past, nay, fatally, shrouded, it might seem, in those laws or tricks of heredity which we mistake for our own volitions. (PP 48)

In a striking image, Pater here conceives of evolutionary history as a weighty garment to dog one's steps through time. The outline of the individual is barely discernable beneath the garments of inheritance, 'fatally shrouded' by a history that condemns the idea of the individual as an autonomous, God-ordained being. Oscar Wilde writes, distilling Pater as often he does, 'Heredity [. . .] has hemmed us round with the nets of the hunter, and written upon the wall the prophecy of our doom' (2001: 254). Wilde's analogy between heredity and a loss of freedom is a perceptive summation of Pater's later vision of evolution. Yet despite the similarity of Wilde's assertion, the difference in tone could not be more marked: Wilde's almost flippant acceptance of the fact of heredity highlights the hesitating character of Pater's passage. Pater's all-important commas break the flow of this single sentence into a stuttering, uncertain acceptance, whilst multiple qualifications – 'each one of us', 'nay, fatally, shrouded, it might seem' – suggest a desire to distance himself from the very view he is voicing, with conviction but evident unease.

The phrase 'laws or tricks of heredity' (PP 48) is telling. Pater cannot help a note of scepticism as, mid-sentence, he revises the suggestion of veracity given by 'laws' with the possibility that these might be mere 'tricks'. As he continues, the note of dissent comes again:

in the language which is more than one half of our thoughts; in the moral and mental habit, the customs, the literature, the very houses which we did not make for ourselves; in the vesture of a past, which is (so science would assure us) not ours, but of the race, the species. (PP 48)

The parentheses are halting, undermining the rhetorical power of a list that with each stroke further cuts the individual down to size, reducing him to merely one of a species. The parenthetical qualification both distances Pater from its charge and interjects a note of scepticism and irony. If the individual becomes insignificant because in this scheme of things his heritage is ignoble and God at best a precarious notion, this is not Pater's doing but at the hands of 'science'. This distancing becomes characteristic of Pater's narrative as he portrays the individual under the conditions of evolution. Elsewhere, he entertains the idea that the individual can resist evolution with words, with the teasing parenthesis that it is '(perhaps after all only in fancy)' (PP 22). He is at least half serious. Other distancing strategies are in play when Pater addresses the contrast between ancient and modern conceptions of creation:

the Darwinian theory – that 'species,' the identifying forms of animal and vegetable life, immutable though they seem now, as of old in the Garden of Eden, are fashioned by slow development, while perhaps millions of years go by: well! every month is adding to its evidence. (PP 11)

Despite the tapestry of influences in Pater's works, he so seldom encloses borrowed words and phrases in quotation marks that his care to do so here seems to indicate some uneasiness with the language of evolutionary science. That such unease was wholly absent from his conception of abstract organic development, in the much earlier essay 'Coleridge', suggests that it is the move from evolution as a spectacle of beauty to its implications for the individual which is difficult for him to countenance, as well it might be. In this light even his view that 'well! every month is adding to its evidence' appears to come with a sigh, registering a distance between personal belief and that which is provable with 'evidence'. After all, belief has two senses: a recognition that something is factually true, but also an identification of one's self with that truth so that it saturates one's view of being. Belief in the latter sense – one is tempted to say faith – is what is missing from Pater's presentation of the individual in evolution in the passage above. His parentheses and speech marks create a duality within the narrative, in which his assertion of evolutionary theory is undercut by doubt, incredulity and even the hope that it is not so.

The suggestion that Pater might feel disaffected with evolution is supported by his dichotomy between the 'species' as conceived by 'the

Darwinian theory' and the God-ordained individuals of the Garden of Eden. With this distinction Pater reopens the gap between ancient and modern thought that he had seemed at pains to close in his identification between Heraclitus and Darwin. He develops this schism as he contrasts natural selection with Ancient Greek conceptions of the individual:

> It is humanity itself now – abstract humanity – that figures as the transmigrating soul, accumulating into its "colossal manhood" that experience of ages; making use of, and casting aside in its march, the souls of countless individuals, as Pythagoras supposed the individual soul to cast aside again and again its outworn body. (PP 49)

The formal similarity between the theories of Pythagoras and modern science marks the revolution from Pythagoras' idea of an eternal soul to the de-individuated 'species' of Darwin, as the essence of selfhood is transferred from an immutable soul to a body that will die. The repetition of 'again and again' signals a cycle, once more, but this time the individual is at its centre; not watching the spectacle from a safe distance but defined completely by it. Similarly, the individual in the first part of the Conclusion to *The Renaissance* is defined by 'birth and gesture and death' (R 150); a degenerate cycle that is internalised to become 'the whirlpool [. . .] still more rapid, the flame more eager and devouring' (R 151). Now, Pater expands this degenerative cycle to the scale of the whole species. The individual is powerless against this unceasing, unsentimental march, and one may hear echoes of Tennyson's tortured evocation of cruel Nature: 'So careful of the type she seems, / So careless of the single life' (231, lines 1047–8). In this regard too, perhaps we could think again about the significance of Pater's young ill-fated protagonists. In the context of the ailing body, the untimely deaths of Florian, Marius, Sebastian, Watteau, Duke Carl, Emerald Uthwart – and there are others – seemed to release the individual from the ravages of old age, so that they might remain forever at the zenith of their beauty and promise. When considered in terms of evolution, 'making use of and casting aside in its march, the souls of countless individuals', their deaths take on a further, broader significance: as illustrations of the cruelty and carelessness of nature.

'A Study of Dionysus' (1876) provides an earlier indication of Pater's regret about the modern Darwinian individual:

> The body of man, indeed, was for the Greeks, still the genuine work of Prometheus; the connection with earth and air asserted in many a legend, not shaded down, as with us, through innumerable stages of descent, but direct and immediate; in precise contrast to our physical theory, which never seems to fade, dream over it as we will, out in the light of common day. (GS 27)

Pater envisages the modern individual as a beleaguered shadow of the Promethean Man, and the narrative shift from impersonal third person to inclusive first person in this passage gives immediacy to the implications of this for the reader, who is subject to those 'innumerable stages of descent'. The allusion to Darwin's *Descent of Man* (1871) foregrounds the sharp contrasts between the divine man of the Greeks and Darwinian man: evolved, descended down from apes, still bearing the traces of his ignoble ancestry. In contrast, the allusion to Prometheus suggests how the individual might be extricated from history and enno-bled. In classical mythology Prometheus created Man when, in defiance of Jupiter, he modelled Man out of clay, then stole fire and took it to earth to give artistic creativity to him. Pater here seems to offer this creation myth as an alternative conception of the individual: one that cannot replace vivid reality, but might at least offer momentary relief from insistent evolution.

Or again, in his manuscript 'Aesthetic Life' (c. 1893) Pater returns to the relationship between the individual and time as it is conceived in modernity:

> Space and time, ~~though~~ if infinite, are still drearily mechanical space and time, with their hard successing of phenomena, and leave the ~~pe~~ conscious individual, the personal organism, a somewhat hopeless being, calling on upon Heaven no longer, only bracing himself to face with what stoicism he may the actual circumstances of his condition. (3)

It is the dullness, the disillusionment of spirituality, and pointlessness of the modern 'condition' that oppresses the Paterian individual. On many fronts, Pater was indeed often resistant to reform and modernity (Gosse 258), and this passage recalls his charge that empirical philosophy has 'narrowed the spiritual, the imaginative horizon' (AL 2) and the way he looks back to the 'older and more spiritual philosophy' of pantheism (GS 95). In his frustration Pater pictures the organic individual as a victim of the expansion of knowledge, oppressed by a mechanised, modern world with which he cannot identify. Still, if Pater presents a regretful image of this stoic yet 'hopeless being', at the same time he opens the possibility that the individual might again take possession of space and time from the oppressive mechanisms that define them, and thus be empowered. He reassures himself with the repetition of 'the conscious individual, the personal organism': seeming to confirm the entity of the individual, stood firm amidst yet separate from infinite, mechanised time and space. '[D]rearily mechanical space and time' alludes to the mechanisms of the public time of synchronised clocks (most clocks in England were stand-ardised to GMT from 1855) that would become increasingly at odds with the personal experience of time in early modernist works. It may also reflect the machine-like processes of periodical publishing that Pater found it so difficult to keep up with. The failure of *Gaston de Latour* was still relatively fresh in his mind.

Although he gestures to 'drearily mechanical *space* and time', here-after physical space is notable in his writings only by its absence. In his own life Pater walled out public space, preferring intimate personal and institutionalised spaces: '[his] real home was in his rooms at Brasenose, where he passed a quiet, cloistered, and laborious existence, divided between his college duties and his books' (Gosse 259). In his narratives, space is dissolved into a shapeless, imaginative realm. It is our sense of time that he perceives to be threatened. In sum, Pater's growing disillu-sionment and scepticism with evolutionary time has two main grounds. First, it takes away one's freedom by positing the self as determined by heredity and external conditions. Second, it threatens the imagination with its suggestion that science can explicate all that had once been mys-terious; all areas in which the imagination once had free rein. On both counts the individual is marginalised. The question left by this scene is how exactly Pater might deliver the 'somewhat hopeless being' from evolutionary and mechanised time to regain a sense of his individuality.

Overall, Pater's conception of evolutionary time is defined by engage-ment, resistance and reinterpretation. Evolution is not a sudden terror for him, because he can see its precedents in Heraclitus. It is felt, rather, as a dull reality nagging at the inward-facing individual and taunting him with the unthinkable truth that he is just one of a species, made insignificant by those 'innumerable stages of descent'. Pater does not reject the veracity of evolutionary theory but it does not speak to his condition; he clearly accepts its terms, but it is never properly con-fronted in his prose on its own objective, material terms. Rather it is aestheticised, where – as a 'relic' and as the aesthetic moment – it places the individual at the centre of the universe once more. Though subject to external forces and threatened by evolutionary history, the individual confirms his own significance because he can reconceive time passing and find within it eternity.

The subjective, time-ridden body that emerges here is far from the objective, ideal body discussed in Chapter 6. The contrast serves to emphasise our own position as individuals: ephemeral, imperfect beings set against these eternal Forms. Yet this is made bearable because beauty endows life with its own justification, 'simply for those moments' sake' (R 153). In aesthetic contemplation, the aesthetic imagination gives a sense of intervention in, or liberation from, continuous time. The feeling of eternity hungered after by metaphysics is ours in this moment, except that it is no longer a futile yearning for the unknowable or impossible. As aesthetic time expands, the imagination, set free, flits between the units of time; our experience of each moment is enhanced and intensified. Eternity is in each moment if only we can perceive it. The dimension of subjective time-consciousness evoked by art exalts and exults in the imagination, positioning it forever at the centre of time. Thus does art save the individual from the apparent meaninglessness of a single life under the conditions of modernity. For even if all is nothing in the end, it is at least made meaningful by the beauty of its passing. Proust – who read and admired Pater[7] – exquisitely captures this as he describes the experience of hearing Vinteul's sonata: 'We shall perish, but we shall have as hostages these divine captives (the musical notes) who will share our fate. And death in their company is somehow less bitter, less inglorious, perhaps even less probable' (I, 422).

Notes

1. This passage is quoted by Pater in *Plato and Platonism* (49–50). Pater surreptitiously introduced an exclamation in this quotation after the 'O'.
2. Such changes included, for example, the Oxford and Cambridge Extension movement, which took off from the late 1860s, the abolition of religious tests for undergraduates in 1871, and the development of new curricula in natural sciences, history and law. For a comprehensive discussion of these reforms see J. P. C. Roach's 'Victorian Universities and the National Intelligentsia'.
3. See particularly William Shuter's 'Pater's Reshuffled Text' (1989) and *Rereading Walter Pater* (1997); and Gerald Monsman's 'Editing Pater's *Gaston de Latour*: The Unfinished Work as "A Fragment of Perfect Expression"' (1991).
4. The philosophy of time consciousness does not really begin, of course, until Henri Bergson's *Creative Evolution* and *Time and Free Will*, both published in 1910.
5. There were also posthumous collections: *Greek Studies* (1895), *Miscellaneous Studies* (1895), and *Essays from the Guardian* (1895).
6. Ann C. Colley's study, *Victorians in the Mountains: Sinking the Sublime* (2010), does much to disprove this commonplace. However, the instances of sublimity that she locates in the latter nineteenth century largely reprise the Romantic sublime, looking to mountains and other such natural phenomena.
7. Proust read *The Renaissance* and possibly other works in his formative years (Painter 257; 275). Although on the subject of time he had a more rigorous interlocutor close at hand in the form of his cousin by marriage, the philosopher Henri Bergson, Proust's aesthetic moment is the greatest illustration of and literary homage to Pater's aesthetic moment.

Chapter 8

The Moment and the Aesthetic Imagination

> At the still point of the turning world. Neither flesh nor fleshless;
> Neither from nor towards; at the still point, there the dance is,
> But neither arrest nor movement. And I do not call it fixity,
> Where past and present are gathered . . .
>
> T. S. Eliot. 'Burnt Norton', *Four Quartets*, 9

Pater's preoccupation with the intensely felt *moment* of sensual or aesthetic experience goes back to the 1850s and persists throughout his career. In a poem written in the summer of 1858, just before he matriculated at Oxford, he asks with fearful innocence, 'Where are the dead?' (qtd Wright I, 136).[1] In his mature works his inability to answer this question leads him to consider how it is possible to live under the sentence of death-eternal, when the ephemeral individual life is lost in evolutionary history. The intensely felt moment is his answer.

The expanse of evolutionary history and the precious ephemerality of a single moment within it define Pater's appropriation of 'art for art's sake': 'For art comes to you proposing frankly to give nothing but the highest quality to your moments as they pass, and simply for those moments' sake' (R 153). As this celebrated declaration from the Conclusion to *Studies in the History of the Renaissance* (1868, 1873) testifies, it is time and, more specifically, the moment that distinguishes Pater's aestheticism from Gautier's conception of *art pour l'art* (1835) or Swinburne's appropriation of that term in *William Blake* (1868) (101). Pater uses time in order to open out the central tautology of 'art for art's sake': art, in other words, is not *for its own sake* exactly but for the sake of dignifying those ephemeral moments, which would otherwise be but flecks in deep time. Putting the emphasis on 'moments as they pass' Pater consciously refocuses from the impersonal spectacle of evolutionary history to the subjective experience of time as it passes moment by moment in the life of the individual.

The intensely felt sensual or aesthetic moment, held in the subjective mind against deep time, shapes Pater's essays and stories up to and including his last essay on Pascal (1894). Pascal was an apt subject for Pater's final essay. After all, it was 'Pascal's provocation' in *Pensées* (1670) that catalysed a qualitatively new and more intense speculation on the significance of the aleatory and epiphanic moment in the late eighteenth and nineteenth centuries (Rennie 2005: 10–16): the idea that faith requires one gamble with a moment. Pater's moment should be understood as the closing chapter in the epoch of the Pascalian moment, but also as the opening of a new chapter that would stretch into modernist conceptions of time. The Paterian moment bears the traces of Pascal's aleatory moment, fused with allusions to Wordsworth's 'spots of time' (429: XII, line 209)[2] and Goethe's *Augenblick*.[3] Yet Pater is primarily concerned not with time as others understood it but rather with the individual's distinct experience of time in the late Victorian period; an experience being reshaped variously by religious doubt, evolutionary theory, the regimentation of standard time, and – at least for Pater – the pressures of periodical publication.

Through the idea of the distinctly felt sensual or aesthetic moment Pater looks to prioritise the individual's subjective experience of time over the deep time of evolutionary theory. His writings take time out of the domain of objectivity and grant it back to the subjective imagination of the individual. Even so the Paterian moment has not hitherto been understood in dialogue with his reading of history. History and the moment have separately received dense critical attention. Thus Peter Allan Dale's *The Victorian Critic and the Idea of History* (1977), Carolyn Williams' *Transfigured World: Walter Pater's Aesthetic Historicism* (1989), and J. B. Bullen's essay 'The Historiography of *Studies in the History of the Renaissance*' (1991) make significant contributions to understanding Pater's historiography, while mainly eschewing the significance of sensual and aesthetic moments in his work. Meanwhile, Lee McKay Johnson's *The Metaphor of Painting: Essays on Baudelaire, Ruskin, Proust, and Pater* (1980) and Leon Chai's *Aestheticism: The Religion of Art in Post-Romantic Literature* (1990) concentrate on the aesthetic moment, but hardly speak of history. Peter Allan Dale even sets Paterian history and the Paterian moment against each other as he argues for the greater importance of the former:

> [That Pater] both as a critic and as an imaginative writer is, in the end, a good deal more concerned with tracing the historical development of speculative culture than he is with burning with a hard gemlike flame is a point that needs more recognition than it has generally received from modern writers. (188)

What does or does not interest Pater more is not something I intend to speculate on, for this is a false dichotomy. The main problem with Dale's view is its assumption that Pater's idea of history may be spoken of apart from the moment of intense sensual and aesthetic experience. In truth, Pater's sublime vision of deep time, in which the individual is reduced to an instance of the species, is integral to the significance of the Paterian moment.

Pater suggests that aesthetic contemplation can liberate the individual from the relentless ticking of the clock. Pater does not deny continuous time, the rapid pace of modernity, or the finitude of the individual life in a Godless world. But he does affirm the power of the undimmed imagination to atomise continuous, deep time into intense, subjective sensual moments, and thus retrieve these from the wastes of evolutionary history. In his writings deep time and the moment quicken and rewrite each other, urgently asserting that the individual is both subject to time's arrow and the all-powerful creator of the distinctly felt moment in time. Since the individual's brief life is merely an 'indefinite reprieve' from an eternity of non-being after death, only aesthetic and sensual experiences offer consolation by intensifying and expanding this 'interval' (R 153). Therefore, whilst Peter Allan Dale argues that 'what interested [Pater] in particular was the expression of the historical mind in art' (189), it is more useful to turn this statement inside out: to suggest that Pater is particularly interested in how the artistic or imaginative mind can reconceive time in the wake of Darwin's theory of evolution, and the multifarious technological advances of his day that threatened the individual's significance in time.

Pater's entire oeuvre is underpinned by his attempts to reimagine the shape of time. There is not one form of Paterian 'moment' but at least two: the distinct moment experienced as an isolated experience of intense, unreflective sensation, and the moment of aesthetic contemplation in which time is experienced as a fusion of past, present, and future moments, all inherent in the *now*. So whilst the individual is subject to passing time, he has the creative power to redefine time and to triumph over the diachronic movement of history that betrays the individual to death. In the rapture of aesthetic experience Pater's individual is, as T. S. Eliot would later put it, 'At the still point of the turning world': not halting time as it passes, but liberated at least from the material shackles of its conditions in order to experience it in an alternative state of consciousness where past, present and future inhere in each other, if only for a moment.

The Sensual Moment

Pater's conception of the sensual moment is his partial answer to the reduction of the individual to a mere speck in 'endless history' (PP 11). The intensely felt sensual moment prioritises one's internal, subjective sense of time over the external, objective conception of evolutionary history. Thus the Paterian moment understands that 'subjective time-consciousness defies analysis *or* measurement; contracting and expanding at will, mingling before and after without ordered sequence' (Hamilton Buckley 8). This vision of the sensual moment appears most poignantly in *The Renaissance*, which describes a number of such moments through ekphrasis and imaginative portraiture. In these works Pater effectively foregrounds the smallest unit of time and the subjective experience of it; not to invalidate the grand scale and objectivity of natural science but to recover within it the significance of concrete, sensual moments of personal experience.

Whilst continuous time defines the physical world and flows through the individual with fleeting impressions, subjective perception atomises this into distinct sensual moments. Meditating on the implications of this for the relationship between self and time in The Conclusion to *The Renaissance*, Pater writes:

> Each of [the impressions of the individual mind] is limited by time, and . . .
> **as** time is infinitely divisible, each of them is divisible also; all that is actual
> in it being a single moment, gone while we try to apprehend it, of which it
> may ever be more truly said that it has ceased to be than that it is. To such a
> tremulous wisp constantly re-forming itself on the stream, to a single sharp
> impression, with a sense in it, a relic more or less fleeting, of such moments
> gone by, what is real in our life fines itself down. (R 151)

There is a sense in which this atomism of time 'scatters the core self in pieces' (Leighton 2007: 91), especially amidst the bewildering flow of impressions and theories that come to assail Pater and the reader in this first part of the Conclusion to *The Renaissance*. However, one must always bear in mind that Pater's Conclusion is, as its opening sentence avers, concerned with the 'tendency of modern thought' (R 150). Misconstruing the dissolution of coherent personal identity here as Pater's own abiding view of the relationship between time and the individual has become the most common error in studies of Pater (Williams 1989: 27). So Leighton's assessment cannot stand as the final word on Pater's presentation of the individual. It is the 'single moment' or 'single sharp impression' to which Pater keeps returning, conceiving it as the distillation of 'what is real in our life'; a life which never reaches a state of *being* but is always *becoming*. Pater reconceives individualism around the intense experience of the single moment: in his writings the most important power that individuals have is the ability to divide experience into subjective units of significance, held in the memory against the flood of impressions in continuous time.

In the passage quoted above it would be easy to pass over the description of the sensual moment as 'a relic' – 'a relic more or less fleeting, of such moments gone by' – yet this is essential to Pater's conceptualisation. Angela Leighton has argued that amidst the constant flow of time Pater salvages 'relics' of the past, which become *memento mori*, reminding us that the decayed body will become a relic of that which was our life when our time has run its course (2007: 93ff). She takes as examples figures from the past who reappear anachronistically in Pater's stories, such as the title characters of 'Duke Carl of Rosenmold' and 'Denys L'Auxerrois' (2007: 94–6). Just so, Pater himself wants to believe that 'One day, perhaps, we may come to forget the distant horizon [of eternity], with full knowledge of the situation, to be content with '"what is here and now"' (A 104). Still he cannot realise this himself. His moments are necessarily experienced as relics in the memory, with nostalgic longing for them integral to their being, because of each moment 'it may ever be more truly said that it has ceased to be than that it is' (R 151). By definition the moment is ephemeral and it occurs at the interface between now and the future. It is ever poised on the cusp of a dialectical move from what is, to what is not. Hence it is only possible to recognise and express the experience in retrospect, because it is a state of pure receptivity which leaves no space within it for reflection. Understandably, given the intellectual history of the moment as a concept, Carolyn Williams refers to Pater's moments as 'epiphanic moments' (2010: 139; 148). But if these moments are epiphanic it is in a very different sense from the moment as conceived by Wordsworth or Woolf. The immediate experience of Pater's moments is emphatically not a moment of epiphany because their ephemeral nature makes intellectual reflection impossible. Pater's evocations suggest that the moment is part of his unrealised (and perhaps unrealisable) desire to for pure, intense sensation. The epiphany is therefore sensual rather than intellectual, and as such it suggests that there are qualitatively distinct modes of knowledge which inhere in sensuality.

In this regard Pater's moments present an analogy with the 'Sensational Mania' (Wise 1866: 266) that was unfolding in the periodical press in the 1860s and 1870s. The intense, unreflective sensations that Pater evokes, between which the individual moves 'most swiftly from point to point' (R 152), recall the structure of periodical publication: 'Sensational

Mania' was, after all, closely linked to the growth of the periodical press in which sensation fiction was serialised for a reader moving 'from point to point' or from issue to issue across weeks and months of anticipation followed by the rapt pleasures of the next instalment. In an unsigned review entitled 'Sensation Fiction', Margaret Oliphant, whose moralising critique of Paterian individualism I noted in Chapter 1, identified the effect of sensation in the periodical press with characteristic scorn:

> The violent stimulation of serial publication – of *weekly* publication, with its necessity for frequent and rapid recurrence of piquant situation and startling incident – is the thing of all others most likely to develop the germ, and bring it to fuller and darker bearing. (1862: 568)

As Oliphant suggests, the periodical reader was engaged in a culture of sensual indulgence and suspense, waiting for each new number to appear and, when it did, experiencing the intense vicarious sensation of reading its plot revelations. The 'frequent and rapid recurrence of piquant situation and startling incident' that she identifies as characteristic of serial publication is very similar to what Pater incites; but his evaluation of it is profoundly at odds with hers. Pater subverts Oliphant's condemnation of 'violent stimulation' with his argument that life lived 'under sentence of death' must be made meaningful by such intense sensual experiences. According to his reformulation of continuous time, the sensual experiences – rather than, say, clock time or routines – define the individual life.

The Conclusion to *The Renaissance* meditates on the absence of reflection implicit in the sensual moment:

> With this sense of the splendour of our experience and of its awful brevity, gathering all we are into one desperate effort to see and touch, we shall hardly have time to make theories about the things we see and touch. (R 152)

Though Pater's Conclusion itself embodies the spirit of the moment, seeming to expire too soon and at the height of its intensity, Pater returns again and again to wonder about the nature of the distinctly felt moment. His essay on 'Joachim du Bellay' (1872, 1873) ends like this:

> A sudden light transfigures some trivial thing, a weather-vane, a windmill, a winnowing-fan, the dust in the barn door. A moment – and the thing has vanished, because it was pure effect; but it leaves a relish behind it, a longing that the accident may happen again. (R 113)

The sensual moment itself occurs, here, within the space denoted by the dash: 'A moment – and the thing has vanished'. It is inexpressible in the present tense. Pater instead captures in words the 'relic' of this moment with its implicit longing, perhaps not unlike the longing for the next instalment of a periodical issue. Preserved in memory and set against an ever-changing present, the relics of such moments are subsumed into a continuous time symbolised by the weather-vane, windmill and winnowing-fan. The transfiguration of this temporal mobility into 'a moment' is not, therefore, the halting of time. Its 'effect' takes place very much within continuous time, which moves on so that 'it may ever be more truly said that it has ceased to be than that it is' (R 151).

This spirit of transience is also expressed in Pater's epigraph for the Conclusion of *The Renaissance*, from Epicurus: Λέγει που Ἡράκλειτος ὅτι πάντα χωρεῖ καὶ οὐδὲνμένει (R 150). Pater's former tutor Benjamin Jowett translates this as 'All things are in motion and nothing at rest', which in the context of the Conclusion reiterates the now familiar analogy between movement and the passing of time. In *Plato and Platonism* (1893) Pater renders this phrase as 'All things give way: nothing remaineth' (PP 6). In the space between Jowett's interpretation and that of Pater motion becomes entropic, with the relentless linear movement of time realising in the end that dust and ashes are all there is. When the subject is positioned at the centre of moving time, the excitement that defined transition is tempered by a sense of loss. Pater's 'nothing remaineth' resonates in the final words of the Conclusion: 'For art comes to you proposing frankly to give nothing but the highest quality to your moments as they pass, and simply for those moments' sake' (R 153). Like the nothingness left by Epicurean flux and history's 'ceaseless movement nowhither' (PP 11), art for art's sake celebrates the fact that art exists for nothing but itself: 'That "nothing" is both signifi-cant, and significant of nothing . . . Signifying nothing, like significant form, keeps signification in view while also emptying it of matter, and of mattering too much' (Leighton 2007: 20). The nothingness left by passing time and the nothingness of art frame the Conclusion, and the void they celebrate is crystallised by Pater's comment on 'the grandeur of "nothingness"' (R 111). This grandeur resides in the understanding that if, at the end, the reader is left with no moral truths, no definitive 'Renaissance', no God, no stability, still one is not left with a *sense* of nothingness. The sensual moment is transient but it also exists in time as longing, anticipation and memory. It is a moot point as to whether the sensual moment itself or the longing for and anticipation of this moment is the more dominant sensation: the imaginative sensation of anticipat-ing or reflecting on the moment is compelling and strongly related to imaginative desire and sensuality.

Pater's presentation of Giorgione's *Fête Champêtre* (c. 1508)[4] vividly evokes the transgressive potentiality of these sensual moments. This painting, which Pater would probably have seen on one of his visits to the Louvre, is a tableau of two men rapt in 'the musical intervals of our existence' (R 96).[5] It is in this state of heightened aesthetic awareness that the figures in the painting sit 'with intent faces [. . .] to detect the smallest sound, the smallest undulation in the air' (R 96). These young men are rapt in music and gazing with slight embarrassment and a hint of blush into each other's eyes as they sit amidst park scenery with bodies turned towards each other. Here they make a separate space, intimately their own and spatial disjunction comes to stand for the sense of a temporal pause. Pater draws on classical Arcadian ideals with images of 'rustic buildings, the choice grass, the grouped trees, the undulations deftly economised for graceful effect' and 'blent with the music of the pipes' (R 97). The traditional pipe music of Arcadia is the catalyst of this harmonious scene, and the allusion to Arcadia evokes its central and eternally seductive characteristic: sexual freedom. Autonomy from moral strictures against male-male desire is granted by location and the alternative mode of consciousness created by the music.[6] The two men are apparently oblivious of the two naked women who flank them, but the nudity of the latter offers the possibility of sexual freedom to the clothed men. In all this, the figures of the men are seized in a moment of rapt indeterminacy: no transgression has yet taken place but the air of the place is electrified by their mutual attraction, forever captured at the interval where action is undetermined. This is the sensual moment. It brims with possibilities, perhaps unrealisable, but which in the brief interval of undetermined action are at least imaginable. As with the narrative desire for those idealised Greek statues, here sexual desire is paused into an eternal moment of indeterminacy, liberating the men from the reality principle which begs desires to be acted out and bodies to be touched. The picture promises that in Eliot's words, 'There will be time to murder and create' before breaking its promise in the next moment. After all Arcadia is ephemeral. The town rising up in the background of Giorgione's painting warns that these moments of freedom must give way to the insistent realities of society. For that matter, the epigraph to 'Winckelmann' in the following essay in the *Renaissance* retroactively heightens this sense of brevity: 'Et ego in Arcadia fui.'[7] Brevity is essential to the moment, and in this moment, captured by Giorgione in paint and by Pater in ekphrasis, one sees most clearly the links the ephemeral sensual moment has with death and love. Or again, in 'The Child in the House' (1878) Flavian realises that 'the desire of physical beauty mingleth itself early [with] the fear of death – the fear of death intensified by the desire for beauty' (IP 13). This sensibility defines the sensual moment, which is conceived in anticipation of its immediate dissolution. If the rapture of this moment knows nothing else, it knows at least its own finitude.

Eros becomes identified with the sensual moment. Eros exists for Pater as a revelry in the still space between now and the future: 'Such loves were too fragile and adventurous to last more than for a moment' (WM 302). It is not love itself that is fragile; it is the moment and, as it breaks to bring forth the next moment and the next, so it breaks the rapture of love that is preserved within it. In Pater's scheme of things, and for the sake of 'reserve' of course (Pater 1875: 202), the sensual moment would have to be finite. If prolonged, this state of unreflective revelry would be tantamount to Dionysian frenzy – and that would never do. With this in mind, Andrew Eastham astutely contrasts Pater's Dionysus with Pater's Giorgione:

> while the spirit of Dionysus appears to symbolize theatricality itself, the attempt to embody this spirit transcends or ruptures the stage conditions. This is the mode of aesthetic transcendence as uncontainable sensuous spirit, a *Streben* without limits. In contrast, the Giorgionesque spirit seeks to contain theatricality ... Although in one sense Pater celebrates Titian's painting for expressing 'the feverish, tumultuously coloured world of the old citizens of Venice', it is clear that the 'admirable tact' he ascribes to Venetian painting has a more abstract function, translating the fever of Venetian lives into a ritualized civility. (Eastham 2010: 175–6)

I would add only that the Giorgionesque suggests to Pater the possibility of erotic love that recognises its own limitations. In trying to exceed these limitations, in trying to prolong intense sensation beyond the ephemeral moment of possibility, the Dionysian breaks the captivating spell of the sensual moment and releases its dangerous, anarchic potential.

The futile desire to preserve the ephemeral, sensual moment reappears in 'The History of Philosophy' (c. 1880) as Pater describes the receptive and innocent culture he imagines to have characterised Ancient Greece:

> the kind of poetry which is represented by Homer, found in that age [its] happiest opportunity in the directness of its vision, its capacity to receive as it were the photographic outline of the object before it, whether of the hero and his great action, or of the bird in the leaves of the tree. (HP 1–2)

Photography interrupts Pater's fairly familiar rumination on receptivity and sensuality in the ancient world[8] as a metaphor for the preservation of the sensual moment as a relic in continuous time. It is rather jarring to find Pater figuring literary art through photography. Quite apart from the fact that photography would come to utterly redefine the neo-

Romantic aesthetic he pursues, this is to the best of my knowledge the only reference to modern technology in Pater's oeuvre.[9] It appears like an intrusion from some other space and time, and this anachronistic appearance serves to stress how the relic of a moment is itself preserved as an anachronism in the ever-moving present. The spatial quality of 'the photographic outline' contrasts with the temporal form of Homer's poetry and the hero's action in the world. This contrast captures the immobility of the moment; recall too that 'Pater continually associates immobility with death' (Shuter 1997: 14). Further, as the passage continues, the immobility of the moment as a relic in the memory threatens the living individual:

> [Goethe] hints at the practicability of regaining just that state of unsuspecting receptivity of mind by an artificial act of reflection in which, by a sort of suicide, an all-accomplished philosophy, completing the circle, is to put one back into the state it had already superseded. (HP 2)

It is shocking, here, to see the relic of the moment come to threaten the individual with death; recourse to the past, which had been life-enhancing in 'Poems by William Morris' (1868), is now seen as life-negating. If the statement seems slightly unsure of itself – hesitating with its commas and 'sort of' – it is also uncharacteristically blunt: continuous time is the life force of the present, and to return to that which is past is to choose death. So whilst Pater recentres time around the subjective individual with his vision of the moment, set in contrast to the marginalisation of humanity in 'endless' evolutionary history, this is an ambivalent sort of empowerment. The only answer to ever-shifting modernity is to constantly create one's self anew in the stream of time passing, for the alternative is 'a sort of suicide'.

The Aesthetic Moment

Pater's conception of the aesthetic moment relates to continuous time in a qualitatively distinct way to his idea of the sensual moment. The aesthetic moment, experienced in artistic contemplation, reconciles passing time with the present so that, in effect, the individual is like Giordano Bruno: 'at every moment of infinite time, in every atom of matter, at every point of infinite space' (GL 76). Art offers to refigure the shape of time so that it is perceived not as a vast continuous flow or as a series of discrete moments but, rather, it is a reflective space created in the imagination where past, present and future inhere simultaneously in the present. This connectedness between past, present and future restores the sensual 'relic' to life, and reconciles the individual to his ephemeral life in deep time.

The aesthetic moment is a consciousness of oneself as at the centre of a long history. Time is aestheticised so that the past, present and future of 'endless history' (PP 11) exist now simultaneously in the imagination:

> [There are] profoundly significant and animated instants, a mere gesture, a look, a smile, perhaps – some brief and wholly concrete moment – into which . . . all the motives, all the interests and effects of a long history have condensed themselves, and which seem to absorb past and future in an intense consciousness of the present. (R 95)

In this passage from 'The School of Giorgione', Pater attempts to reconcile temporal movement with the 'wholly concrete moment' or 'relic'. The 'concrete moment' evolves in the second part of the sentence quoted above from a sensual moment of present, subjective sensation into a sense of oneself at the nexus of past, present and future. He reiterates this idea in his essay on 'Wordsworth' (1874, 1889): 'those strange reminiscences and forebodings, which seem to make our lives stretch before and behind us, beyond where we can see or touch anything, or trace the lines of connection' (A 54). Despite some mystical allusions, this experience is not metaphysical; it is located in the 'intense consciousness' provoked by aesthetic experience. In the particular case of which Pater is writing the imagination of the spectator is absorbed, decentring the objective critic and objective time, so that its outline is merged into a single intense and subjective impression. Whilst the individual remains subject to the ravages of time as it passes, defining and ultimately extinguishing life, Pater suggests that the individual as an imaginative subject has agency to reshape time.

As continuous time slips by, impermanent, the aesthetic moment creates a space in which time seems to be paused. Pater again uses Giorgione as a model for how aesthetic experience might capture the transient moment, as the essay continues:

> Such ideal instants the school of Giorgione selects, with its admirable tact, from that feverish, tumultuously coloured world of the old citizens of Venice – exquisite pauses in time, in which, arrested thus, we seem to be spectators of all the fulness of existence, and which are like some consummate extract or the quintessence of life. (R 95–6)

Intriguingly, this recalls the Leibnizian model of 'eternal return' as evoked by Nietzsche in *Thus Spoke Zarathustra* (*Also sprach Zarathustra*; 1883–5): 'Still! Still! Did not the world become perfect just now? Did time perhaps fly away? Did I not fall? Did I not fall – listen! – into the well of eternity' (1982: 388–9).[10] The refraction of time through the aesthetic moment is an experience catalysed by art and it occurs in the imagination of the spectator. Pater's decentring of aesthetic judgement from the objective critic to the subject is central to these passages. The paintings become absorbed into the imagination so that their outlines are merged into a single fragmented impression. Liberated from the relentless forward movement of the ticking of the clock, time seems to stop. This is the moment of aesthetic consciousness, in which objective facts, linearity and ethical values are loosened into the realms of the imagination. The power of action is arrested. Reserve, circumstance and the fragility of the acting self make action all but impossible. Still, the aesthetic moment quickens the individual's sense of himself. If the Paterian individual is held captive in time as it writes itself on the body, he is at least 'aware in that suffering body of such vivid powers of mind and sense' (M I, 219). Whilst the individual remains subject to the ravages of time as it passes, defining and ultimately extinguishing him, he nonetheless has agency to reshape time with the imagination.

Pater's belief that aesthetic experience might fuse past and future into an intense consciousness of the present is illustrated further by his ekphrasis of *La Gioconda* (*Mona Lisa*; 1503–6). The painting appears in Pater's essay on 'Leonardo da Vinci' (1869, 1873), where it is 'a specifically embodied "figure" of the trans-historical *Geist*, the over-arching unity-of-development beyond figuration, the point of view from which all specific figures are merely "phrases" in the same expression' (Williams 1989: 116). In other words, Pater's ekphrasis of *La Gioconda* reconciles deep time with a subjective impression of the present. More than this, it suggests that the individual might come to terms with deep time if it is refracted through an intense aesthetic moment of artistic contemplation. Pater's discussion of *La Gioconda* begins with standard contextual remarks on its legends, its creation, its significance in Leonardo's oeuvre and its history (R 79). Thereafter though Pater's narrative grows increasingly impressionistic. Eschewing the painting's history he presents Mona Lisa as a symbol of the aesthetic moment, who embodies the cycles of evolutionary history and biographical time in one moment of aesthetic experience. Carolyn Williams is astute in her observation that 'Nowhere is it more clear that Pater both deeply understood and deeply feared Darwin's theory than here' (1989: 122). Mona Lisa is Pater's aesthetic embodiment of the Darwinian spectre 'of a perpetual life, sweeping together ten thousand experiences' (R 80). In sharp contrast to Pater's relics she is the living embodiment of humanity's history and the spectator's organic connection with it. Her form, Pater writes, is 'wrought out from within upon the flesh, the deposit, little cell by cell of strange thoughts and fantastic reveries and exquisite passions' (R 80). The history wrought onto her body is crystallised into a moment of aesthetic consciousness that is terrifying and profoundly moving. It is distinct from the fateful pleasure of the sensual moment because pleasure is not quite the point here. This is, to reprise Williams' description, an epiphanic moment (2010: 139; 148), which contains within it a realisation and acceptance of the human condition.

Pater's vision of *La Gioconda*, while modernist in its focus on the aesthetic moment, is quintessentially Victorian in the historical scope embodied in this moment. For him aesthetic moments extend far beyond the personal realm of subjective experience and memory that was the boundary for, say, Woolf and Proust, or which defined his own idea of the sensual moment as a relic in the personal memory. Pater's 'consummate moments' of aesthetic experience span the centuries with a Victorian conceit that the individual mind could aspire to some universal understanding of experience beyond itself. This view is at odds with the solipsism Pater entertains in his 'Conclusion' and 'The History of Philosophy' but it is intimately related to his view of historical consciousness in 'The Aesthetic Life':

> precisely in the effect of time, of long centuries, since nothing seems to be without its compensation [modern man] has also the aesthetic opportunity of our generation. He has The son of the age has had the privilege of the elder brother and in becoming a scholar with and possesses the touchstones its sense of periods the authorities the critical instincts of his scholarship its sense of periods and their affinities. This faculty is has as refined itself by long usage. (AL 16)

This magisterial view of history distinguishes the nineteenth-century individual from people of the past. An analogy between this sensibility and the aesthetic moment is indicated, in that Pater calls it 'the aesthetic opportunity of our generation' because such a sensibility expands the horizon of the creative imagination. 'That historic sense' (AL 21), which Pater conceives as a distinctly modern phenomenon, illustrates the embeddedness of his aesthetic moment in history.

The well-known closing comments of *The Renaissance* gain a slightly different force in the context of a historical consciousness that:

> we are all under sentence of death but with a sort of indefinite reprieve . . . Some spend this interval in listlessness, some in high passions, the wisest, at least among 'the children of this world,' in art and song. For our one chance lies in expanding that interval, in getting as many pulsations as possible into the given time. (R 153)

The 'interval' and the 'quickened, multiplied consciousness' are the eternal moment created by art. As continuous time slips by, its brief intervals seem to be expanded because each contains within it our 'intense consciousness' of past, present and future. The aesthetic moment may be understood as a point where time expands vertically through each of the spheres of past, present and future. It is a panacea for Pater's fear that when an experience has passed it either exists only as a relic or is forever extinguished. The aesthetic moment is not extinguished with its passing. Rather, it lingers on in the imagination: resonating through the next moment and the next, enriching and expanding each with its echoes. Thus, the idea of quantitative life-eternal is replaced with a qualitative eternity not dissimilar to Nietzsche's 'eternal recurrence'. As time moves on, each moment is saturated with all that has gone before and all that might be. Time past is not past history but a constant present. In the rapture of aesthetic experience Pater's individual has not, obviously, halted the movement of time. But crucially, the individual is liberated from the material shackles of his conditions to experience time in an alternate state of consciousness where past, present and future inhere in each other, if only for a moment.

Time and History in Pater's Prose Form

George Moore suggested in 1919 that if Pater 'had lived to hear *Prélude à l'après-midi d'un faune*, he could not have done else but think that he was listening to his own prose changed into music by some sorcerei or sorcerers malign or benevolent' (195–6). The comment is perceptive, and not only because Debussy – whose work was first heard in December 1894, less than five months after Pater's death – captured the languid concupiscence of the poem by Mallarmé which inspired it. Pater's prose itself 'aspires to the condition of music' (R 86), and like Debussy's impressionistic poem for orchestra, it alters the experience of continuous time. Pater writes history like an impressionist composer, choosing notes and intervals 'according to his own peculiar sense of fact'. His pen dissolves the Renaissance into an amorphous spirit which diffuses through the centuries from twelfth-century France to eighteenth-century Germany. For Pater, 'a musical composition possesses a certain concentration of all its parts, a simple continuity' whilst, at the same time, its perfection comes from its 'unity of impression' (A 202; 203). This conception, articulated in the early 1870s, anticipates 'Impressionism' in music. It was in Pater's twilight years that Debussy's first pieces of this kind were written, with their short repeated melodies dissipating the classic symphony's structural progression into a series of impressions. Just so for Pater, as seconds, minutes and hours pass, the creative individual may unify time into an intense experience of the present: the aesthetic moment.

Like the individual, Pater's prose is bound in continuous time. The sinuous musicality of Pater's sentences instantiates the temporal consciousness characteristic of modernity, which is why he believed the essay to be the 'characteristic literary type of our time' (PP 120). Like Heraclitus' stream, Pater's prose constantly shifts in linear time, so that it seems not to have concrete presence, and ultimately leaves us without truth or facts in any straightforward sense, only with the impression of its form. At the same time his writing contains within itself echoes of the past and anticipations of the future. Such a continuous yet unified series of impressions, revisions and reiterations resembles the sonata heard by Swann in *À la recherche du temps perdu* (1913–22), as it 'opened and expanded his soul', reappearing 'to remain poised in the air, and to sport there for a moment, only, as though immobile, and shortly to expire' (Proust I, 250; 251).

According to his principle that subjective time-consciousness reshapes linear time, Pater positions the imagination at the centre of history. The suggestion of past, present and future inhering in each other is set within Pater's reconception of the relationship between art and history. History writing amongst his contemporaries, Pater complains, is 'a literary domain where the imagination may be thought to be always an intruder' (A 9). His own view is that the historian should celebrate his creative power to select and interpret facts; history should be conceived, in other words, on aesthetic criteria so that it 'comes not of the world without but of a vision within' (A 9). Pater continues by subjecting history to art:

> So Gibbon ... Livy, Tacitus, Michelet, moving full of poignant sensibility amid the records of the past, each, after his own sense, modifies – who can tell where and to what degree? – and becomes something else than a transcriber; each, as he thus modifies, passing into the domain of art proper. (A 9)

True to his own principles, Pater's pen 'modifies' or dissolves the Renaissance period into an amorphous spirit of imagination: his 'historiography ... is an integral act of self-expression', with the historical Renaissance 'intimately linked to a personal renaissance, and a process of self-discovery' (Bullen 156; 159). That is well said, for Pater's imaginative portraits of such figures as Michelangelo, da Vinci, Pico Della Mirandola or Winckelmann contain as much of him as of them.

Moreover, Pater's conception of the Renaissance period itself aspires to pass into 'the domain of art proper'. *Studies in the History of the Renaissance* is not only an audacious reconception of history writing and of aesthetic criticism, but also a radical revision of the Renaissance as a period.[11] When it was first published in 1873, it fell to his friend Mrs Mark Pattison to tell him that the title was all wrong: the book, she complained, has nothing to do with the history of the Renaissance. For the second edition Pater duly changed his title to *The Renaissance: Studies in Art and Poetry* (1877). *The Renaissance* reconceives the period as 'a many-sided but yet united movement' or zeitgeist, diffusing through Europe in the broad period between the twelfth and the mid-eighteenth centuries:

> For us the Renaissance is the name of a many-sided but yet united movement, in which the love of the things of the intellect and the imagination for their own sake, the desire for a more liberal and comely way of conceiving life, make themselves felt, urging those who experience this desire to search out first one and then another means of intellectual or imaginative enjoyment, and directing them not only to the discovery of old and forgotten sources of this enjoyment, but to the divination of fresh sources thereof – new experiences, new subjects of poetry, new forms of art. (R 1)

Time and Discrimination

Overall then, Pater engages with, resists, and reinterprets the shape of time under the conditions of modernity. Evolution is not a sudden terror for him because he can see its precedents in Heraclitus, but even if Pater accepts the veracity of evolutionary theory, sensual and aesthetic moments are his attempts to reimagine the individual at the centre of the universe, as a creative subject.

Pater argues that Coleridge's poetry suffers because 'he hungered for eternity' (A 104). Yet Pater cannot give up eternity either; he just defines it differently. Instead of thinking of eternity in terms of continuous time, as the continuation of linear time without end, he locates eternity in the perception of each ephemeral moment. Indeed, whilst Pater's prose art flows on and on, as an analogue to continuous time it creates eternal vistas within itself. The intensely personal and private moment of aesthetic contemplation yields a universal understanding as the mind traverses the centuries. In aesthetic contemplation, the imagination yields a sense of both intervention in, and liberation from, continuous time. The eternity hungered after by metaphysics may be attained by the individual in the aesthetic moment. Thus does art save the individual from the apparent meaninglessness of a single life under the conditions of modernity. For even if life leads to nothing in a metaphysical sense in the end, it is at least made meaningful by the intensity of its passing.

Pater suggests in 'Joachim du Bellay' (1873) that sensual moments are surreptitious, but the prominence he gives to the faculty of discrimination in his writings begs the questions of whether it is possible to create the circumstances in which one experiences aesthetic moments:

> Not to discriminate every moment some passionate attitude in those about us, and in the very brilliancy of their gifts some tragic dividing of the forces on their ways, is, on this short day of frost and sun, to sleep before evening. (R 152)

The ability to make informed aesthetic choices is integral to Pater's vision of what it is to be an individual. It is expounded as a principle of artistic creation in 'Style' (1888) where Pater takes inspiration from Schiller's *On the Aesthetic Education of Man* (1793; *Über die ästhetische Erziehung des Menschen*): '"The artist," says Schiller, "may be known rather by what he omits"; and in literature too, the true artist may be best recognised by his tact of omission' (A 18). Pater expands Schiller's principle to life when four years later he writes: 'one thing is plain [. . .] he will largely have to apply the faculty of selection' (AL 14). Discrimination implicitly involves the individual in value judgements and, consequently, in aesthetic discourses that Pater had sought to liberate the individual from with the primacy of touch.

In 'The Aesthetic Life' Pater writes more fully about how, in practice, discrimination shapes life in the modern world. He notes that the process of selecting necessarily involves a simultaneous process of 'ignoring or forgetting' (AL 14). This suggests that one may exert control over memories of the past; 'forgetting' like Pope's 'eternal sunshine of the spotless mind', in order to rewrite the past and countermand its ultimate mastery over the individual. Otherwise Pater's principle of 'discrimination' or 'omission' might present itself as an adaptation of Darwin's theory of natural selection, in which the memory surreptitiously selects events that most enhance its pleasure. The aestheticist reconception of natural selection wraps Darwinism into Paterianism to put selection into the service of his aesthetic.

Pater expands the idea of aesthetic discrimination to his presentation of space, where the spatial analogue of the sensual moment is the exquisitely chosen object. In contrast to the common depictions of space in late aestheticism epitomised in Aubrey Beardsley's drawings, which congeal domestic space into overblown clutter, the presence of Pater's space is defined by emptiness. Just as the moment is a sudden fracture in the banal flow of time against which it stands out, Pater's arrangement of his domestic space was empty space punctuated by certain well-chosen objects. As Mrs Humphry Ward recalled his first house in Oxford, 2 Bradmore Road, which he shared with his sisters in the 1870s:

The drawing-room which runs the whole breadth of the house from the road to the garden behind was 'Paterian' in every line and ornament. There were a Morris paper; spindle-legged tables and chairs; a sparing allowance of blue plates . . . framed embroidery of the most delicate design and colour . . . engravings, if I remember right, from Botticelli, or Luini, or Mantegna; a few mirrors, and a very few flowers, chosen and arranged with a simple yet conscious art. I see that room always with the sun in it, touching the polished surfaces of wood and brass and china, and bringing out its pure, bright colour (123)

The troubling question that one is left with, though, and the crisis point of Pater's aesthetic is where his vision of a life lived for sensual experience leaves ethics.

Notes

1. Pater burnt most of his poems in self-conscious homage to Goethe. Only this and 'Oxford Life' (mentioned in Chapter 4) exist in fragments, quoted by Wright.
2. 'There are in our existence spots of time,
   That with distinct pre-eminence retain
   A renovating virtue . . .' (429: XII, lines 209–12).
3. Meaning, literally, *in the blink of an eye.*
4. Since the twentieth century this painting has been reattributed to Titian, Giorgione's contemporary and a fellow student of Giotto, but when Pater wrote it was taken to be by Giorgione.
5. In recent studies, both Carolyn Williams and Andrew Eastham have successfully refocused criticism of 'The School of Giorgione' (1877, 1888) away from its theory of Anderstreben, to its theorisation of theatrical tableau (2010: 135ff; 2010: 173ff).
6. A real life correlate is Andre Gide's first unashamed homosexual desire for Mohammed the Algerian flautist, whose music Gide describes as so entrancing that 'you forgot the time and place and who you were' (Gide 1935: 251).
7. 'I too have been in Arcadia.'
8. Chapter 5 discussed Pater's presentation of sensuality in Ancient Greece.
9. This comment notwithstanding, it should be noted a propos Pater and technology that Carolyn Williams makes a compelling case for Pater as anticipating film with his presentation of tableaux and epiphanic moments in the context of temporal movement (2010: 135ff).
10. The interconnectedness between past, present and future is more famously discussed by Nietzsche in his early essay, 'On the Uses and Disadvantages of History for Life.' Take for example Nietzsche's comment that 'in opposition to all historical modes of regarding the past . . . the past and present are one' (1997a: 66). Patrick Bridgwater considers whether there could have been any direct influence between Nietzsche and Pater in his *Anglo-German Interactions in the Literature of the 1890s* (10–43). Most of Nietzsche's

works were not published until the 1890s and were unavailable in Britain until 1897, after Pater's death. However, 'On the Uses and Disadvantages of History for Life' was published in a German journal in 1874: a year when Pater – who knew German well – spent the summer in Germany studying in Heidelberg, and three years before he published 'The School of Giorgione' which was later included in the third edition of *The Renaissance* (1888).

11. Pater's focus on the Renaissance was itself a rebellion against the most prominent aesthetic critics of his day: rejecting both John Ruskin's moral imperatives and William Morris' medievalism.

Chapter 9

Ethics, Society and the Aesthetic Individual

The deepest problems of modern life derive from the claim of the individual to preserve the autonomy and individuality of his existence in the face of overwhelming social forces, of historical heritage, of external culture, and of the technique of life.

Georg Simmel, 'The Metropolis and Mental Life' (409)

Ce grand malheur, de ne pouvoir être seul.

Edgar Allan Poe's epigram to 'The Man of the Crowd' (101)[1]

The subject of Pater's second paper for the Old Mortality Society was Fichte's Ideal Student, and it focused on self-culture. Its effect portended the moral outrage that his *Renaissance* would ignite nine years later. Audaciously eschewing the social conscience that was a feature of the Old Mortality meetings where they addressed subjects including education for the poor, Pater's paper focused on self-culture. Pater found ideas in Fichte's work which 'seem to have become personal insights or personal ideals to Pater, or to have justified tendencies that were intrinsic to his personality' (Inman 1981a: 70). As Gerald Monsman says, 'it is evident that for Pater in 1864 the criterion of right conduct is not an external standard of morality, but the comeliness of the individual life' (1970: 371). As noted in Chapter 3 Pater's paper was, according to one of Old Mortality's more conservative members, S. R. Brooke, vociferous in advocating 'selfish principles' and he summed it up as 'one of the most infidel productions it has ever been our pain to listen to' (qtd Monsman 1970: 371). When Pater's one-time mentor William Wolf Capes weighed in to condemn the form of hedonistic individualism espoused in *The Renaissance* in his 1873 University Sermon at Oxford, the complaint against Pater was familiar: 'For such a system [Pater's philosophy of art] keeps self too steadily in view, it fosters a morbid interspection [sic], and finds quite a secondary place for the motive energies of social effort, and the self-sacrifice of loftier morality' (Inman 1981a: 328).[2] The evidence of Pater's later works suggests that these criticisms cut deep. The relationship between the individual, intense aesthetic experience, and social ethics that were a source of muted tension throughout his career became more central from the mid-1880s till the end of his life.

In the last quarter of the nineteenth century, Pater is writing at a time when normative views of ethics as a socially cohesive realm of determined value were being placed under threat (Schneewind 6). He attempts to redefine the bases of moral judgement in response to the intellectual shifts that threatened social and ethical norms. His is an attempt which interweaves constant fluctuation into its own fabric, and its success is mixed. In 1886 Pater had intended to write a trilogy, with *Marius* followed by novels dealing, he explained, 'with similar problems, under different conditions: in France at the end of the sixteenth century; and in England, at the end of the eighteenth' (L 66). By the close of 1888, *Gaston de Latour* had been discontinued in *Macmillan's Magazine*, though unfinished, and the third novel unbegun in spite of various attempts that lasted until Pater's death. There were various reasons why he could not complete the trilogy: some practical, for Pater never overcame the painfully slow process of writing that made it difficult for him to deliver instalments on time; some theoretical, for *Gaston* came to crystallise the problem of ethics in Pater's aesthetics. Having attempted to ground morality in aesthetic contemplation in *Marius the Epicurean*, the sadomasochistic violence of *Gaston*'s later fragmentary chapters – which remained unpublished in his lifetime[3] – challenged his own belief that 'descriptions of violent incidents and abnormal states of mind do not serve the purpose of art' (George Moore qtd L 74).

Pater was aware that to reconcile his vision of discriminated sensual and aesthetic moments it would be necessary to define a 'new "Ethick"' (AL 1). However, it is emblematic that this phrase, 'new "Ethick"', is a quotation from Pater's unfinished essay, 'The Aesthetic Life' (c. 1893), an essay which descends into the illegible – scribbled out sentences and paragraphs as Pater reaches a dead end with his own vision of aesthetics and morality. The centrality of the late-Romantic individual is at the crux of the 'confusion between aesthetics and ethics' that characterises Pater's writings (Tucker 108). For John Ruskin, individuals and society revolve around ethics; while for Henry Sidgwick, individuals and ethics revolve around society. For Pater, society and ethics revolve around the individual and art. He does not believe in society and he is sceptical, to say the least, about its ethical terms. Moral values can only be understood in terms of individuals and personal friendships between them.

This chapter focuses on the tense dynamics between four elements in Pater's writings: the individual, aesthetic experience, ethics and society.

It argues that Pater's 'new "Ethick"' is constructed on a nexus of unresolved issues which centre on his inability to fuse personal aesthetic experience and individualism with social ethics. In this Pater is very much a would-be Romantic visionary coming to terms with the confident high ideals of Romantic, and particularly Schillerean, aesthetics, in the shrunken scope of late-Victorian modernity. Under the strain, ultimately the scope of art becomes determined by the limitations of his individualism.

Society

When Mallock parodied Pater as Mr Rose, in 1877, he understood the centrality of individualism to Pater's aesthetics. With this in mind, he astutely captured the view of society suggested by Pater's published works: '"I," said Mr Rose, "look upon social dissolution as the true condition of the most perfect life. For the centre of life is the individual, and it is only through dissolution that the individual can emerge"' (56). The Paterian individual is premised on a strong sense of his singularity; a singularity that takes its poignancy from Pater's own position. Pater himself was ever an outsider. Perhaps this is why he and Gerard Manley Hopkins took to each other despite their theological differences: they understood one another because each knew what it means to feel alone. Pater began at Oxford on a scholarship and without the financial means of many of his contemporaries. His second-class degree suggested he was less able than others, and made it hard for him to find an academic position. The fellowship he gained at Brasenose College from 1864 placed him a world away from the opulence of Christ Church or the academic prowess of Balliol or Corpus Christi; Brasenose, 'a college for the average man' (Higgins 1991: 80), positioned him outside the intellectual circles that dominated Oxford as one who would have to make his presence felt, as he did in the Old Mortality Society. His sexuality too marked him as an outsider because at Oxford, unlike Cambridge, 'the cult of homoeroticism was not encouraged by the dons'; it was in the main, like aestheticism, an undergraduate cult (Annan 196). Furthermore, Pater was a non-clerical don who denounced Christianity at a time when, in spite of recent reforms, Churchmen still ran the university. Even in the Old Mortality Society, he was one of the only members from outside Balliol and his anti-religious views made him enemies in the group.[4] At times Pater seemed to delight in his difference: 'he had been the first man in Oxford to decorate college rooms'[5] and, in an oft-narrated episode, 'he flashed forth at the Private View of the

Royal Academy in a new top hat and a silk tie of brilliant apple-green' (Wright I, 215; Gosse 254; 253). Such audaciousness was relatively rare in a career lived quietly and studiously. The Paterian individual is an outsider to society, like Pater himself, and he was deeply troubled about exactly how to reconcile the individual with society.

To an extent Schiller offers Pater a solution. Schiller bridges the gap between art and morality left by Kant's *Critique of Judgement* by confidently making the move from self-realisation in aesthetic experience to ethical sensibility. He situates moral sensibility in the imagination, brought into being by the feelings of freedom, unity and autonomy evoked in aesthetic experience and educated by the individual's contemplation of art. Thus moral feelings are determined by passionate impulses: 'Morality [. . .] consists not in the formal obedience to moral law based on rational assent to principle, but rather in the heartfelt, unpremeditated inclination to do good' (2006: 128).[6] Here Schiller suggests that passionate feelings are autonomous of law and convention, which indeed they may transgress. He declares his faith rather in the individual, whom he places at the centre of moral judgement.

In this Pater concurs. He shares Schiller's view that personal morality emanates from 'a direct sense of personal worth' (D 157) cultivated within one's self and not determined by any abstract system:

> The theory or idea or system which requires of us the sacrifice of any part of this experience, in consideration of some interest into which we cannot enter, or some abstract morality we have not identified with ourselves, or what is only conventional has no real claim on us. (R 153)

Pater's words hark back to Ancient Greek ethics which ask 'What am I to do if I am to do well?' in contrast to modern ethics which ask 'what ought I to do if I am to do right?' (J. P. Ward 114). He empowers the individual by defining morality within one's self against 'some abstract morality'. The individual is made arbiter of *the good*, which itself is defined simply by the individual's heartfelt inclination toward it.

Pater takes up Schiller's belief that moral sense resides in the imagination with a rather nebulous assertion. As he puts it, the diaphanous character 'does not take the eye by breadth of colour; rather it is that fine edge of light, where the elements of our moral nature refine themselves to burning point' (D 154). Once again, light evokes the creative spirit and it does so here to effectively identify the imagination with the moral faculties. But just what is signified by *our moral nature* and what would it mean to refine this *to the burning point* is not quite clear. Perhaps Pater is relying on his audience – in this case the Old Mortality Society, so well he might – to identify the gestures to Schiller in this most

Schilleresque of essays. Since ethics are not his central concern here, he may feel this needs no further explanation. Even so, the grand sweeping nature of his phrase discloses the indistinctness of his notion of what this would mean in precise terms, or how it could possibly be realised in the context of his modernity. Pater defines morality as a compassionate response located in the senses, the heart and the passions, and not in the intellect. The intensity of aesthetic perception and the heightened emotions it excites teach one to notice and respond virtuously in life. Thus he praises Botticelli for his ability to create 'a sympathy for humanity in its uncertain condition'. The sympathy is created at least in part by the delicate attention of Pater's narrative as he describes Botticelli's Madonnas: 'they shrink under the pressure of the divine child, and plead unmistakable undertones for a warmer, lower humanity' (R 39). Here the beauty and scale of the painting defamiliarise the subject from the emotion to show it to us as an archetype. Art assumes the role of moral educator in a way that engages the individual to make personal judgements. For this reason the individual is made central, displacing God or any other authority from the role of determining ethical good: he is set free.

Schiller saw that the concept of a subjective judgement with claim to universality, introduced by Kant in his *Critique of Judgement*, is absolutely necessary to make the leap of faith from personal morality centred in the imagination to ethical judgement in society. A priori universality means that moral values are subject to universal agreement and may be the basis of civil society. Art evokes an ephemeral experience of intense compassion, which it expands to benefit all society because art ennobles the imagination, allowing us to transcend habitual conditions and recognise that which is universally considered to be the moral good. With art, the individual 'in his own hut [. . .] discourses silently with himself and, from the moment he steps out of it, with all the rest of his kind, [. . .] there will the tender blossom of beauty unfold' (1982: 26.2, 191). So whilst self-culture is a private endeavour – a solitary dialectic of self in dialogue with itself, mediated through art – the individual is nonetheless yoked to society, and the tender ethical sensibility cultivated in private is only fully realised in society. The last of Schiller's letters in the *Aesthetic Education* asserts that the quickened spirit and sense of freedom evoked in aesthetic experience 'recalls to us our freedom as moral agents and we return to the everyday world with a disposition ready to face the challenges and a mind emboldened to make certain moral choices' (Kooy 40). This integration of art, society and ethics was a significant element in Schiller's appeal to educated middle-class Victorians, for whom, often, 'the primary function of art was to socialise individual readers or spectators into the moral values of their culture' (Guy 314). Such an integration is foundational to John Ruskin's *The Stones of Venice* (325ff), and to Matthew Arnold's view, in *Culture and Anarchy*, that

> Perfection, as culture conceives it, is not possible while the individual remains isolated. The individual is required, under pain of being stunted and enfeebled in his own development if he disobeys, to carry others along with him in his march towards perfection, to be continually doing all he can to enlarge and increase the volume of the human stream sweeping thitherward. (9)

Expanded to the grand scale which Schiller imagines, the proliferation of aesthetic education would create the 'aesthetic State': a society in which men do good deeds out of a sense of freedom and autonomy (1982: 27.7, 213ff). The aesthetic State is contrasted with the dynamic State, where one acts out of oppression, and the ethical State in which one acts out of duty (1982: 24.1, 171). Schiller explains that in those circles where conduct is governed by beauty in the aesthetic State, none may appear to the other except as an object of free play. To bestow freedom by means of freedom is the fundamental law of the kingdom (1982: 27.9, 215). In the aesthetic State the individual is enabled to act in freedom in accord with the impulses of his heart for the good of society. These subjective impulses will necessarily cohere with the general good because of their a priori universality. Pater departs from Schiller as aesthetic contemplation opens out into an ethical sensibility realised in society. Pater accepts Schiller's view that unity and freedom create a sense of personal value which is fundamental to morality. However, he flounders at Schiller's turn from the solitude of aesthetic contemplation to society as he is unable or unwilling to reconcile the individual with any social role.

Whereas Schiller's 'aesthetic education' reaches its zenith when the aesthetic subject returns to society, Pater's ethics remain wedded to individual experience. He is unable or unwilling to follow Schiller's confident turn to society, for two main reasons. First, he was intensely aware of the relative nature of moral judgement, and secondly he did not believe in society. Writing almost a century after Schiller, amidst the debris of philosophical systems and religious faith and with an acute sense of the material world in flux, it is clear to Pater as it never was to Schiller that moral values too are subject to relativity: 'Modern thought,' as we have already noted, 'is distinguished from the ancient by its cultivation of the "relative" spirit in place of the "absolute"' (A 66). Moral sensibilities are ever shifting through time and vary between people, as he was well aware from the changed perception of male-male desire as between Ancient Greece and its condemnation in his own society. In short, he could not subscribe to Schiller's universality. Rather, he insists that relativism must be reflected in moral principles:

> The moral world is ever in contact with the physical, and the relative has invaded moral philosophy from the ground of inductive sciences. There it has started a new analysis of the relations of mind, good and evil, freedom and necessity. (A 67)

There is, perhaps, a touch of irony in his use of *invasion* here: a nod toward those who resented this, like his contemporary, F. H. Bradley, who harboured pretensions to systematise ethics in apparent defiance of the emergent spirit of relativism. For Pater, by contrast, relativism has a positive side: it reveals afresh the truth of the human condition, sets the individual free from 'facile orthodoxy' (R 152), and in the sphere of ethics grants him the authority to legislate his own values. With all moral absolutes eradicated, morality is redefined as an unending empirical investigation. Such a spirit of relativism would reach its apotheosis soon after in the figure of Friedrich Nietzsche.[7] With the distinction between good and evil in question, we are left to wonder if Pater's teleological language is but the relic of a learnt language of ethics, or whether he aspires still to this apparently impossible ideal.[8] Or is he like Nietzsche gesturing *beyond* good and evil to some other form of perfection?

   In part, Pater also finds society a difficult concept because of the emergent evolutionary view that society has 'spontaneously evolved' and its values are irredeemably relative (Spencer 1860: 92). Sounding a modern note, he faults the *Republic* as ahistorical: 'Plato is certainly less aware than those who study these matters in the "historical spirit" of the modern world that for the most part, like other more purely physical things, states "are not made, but grow"' (PP 162). But in truth Pater is inherently suspicious of any integral relationship between the individual and society on which the visions of Plato, Hobbes and Hegel are all founded: 'Plato then assumes rather than demonstrates that so facile parallel between the individual consciousness and the social aggregate' (PP 162). Indeed, Pater says precious little about society: anticipating the modernist interiority which he would influence, he mainly turns inward, away from it. This refusal rests on a further critique. Society, Pater suggests, 'reduces us to an almost colourless existence' (D 157): it stands for a norm of dull mediocrity against which the creative individual is judged, and rebels.

   Thus 'Diaphaneitè' is his swansong to society. Written right at the beginning of his career, it is the justification for his disregard of society thereafter. Billie Inman has noted that Pater appropriates and reworks

Schiller's tripartite concepts of the dynamic State, ethical State and aesthetic State into the three types of individual in 'Diaphaneitè', where they become respectively 'doctrinaires', 'the saint, the artist, even the speculative thinker' and the diaphanous man in 'Diaphaneitè' (Inman 1981a: 100; D 154). The significance of this lies in how Pater shrinks the broad social significance of Schiller's vision into an optic limited to just one: the solitary self. In 'Diaphaneitè' the individual and society become dichotomies. The diaphanous type is first defined by the way that he 'crosses rather than follows the main current of the world's life' (D 154). This singularity is confirmed as Pater evokes the threat of 'collective life' and he stresses that the diaphanous type, the self-cultured individual could never be expanded to society: 'Society could not be conformed to their image' (R 158). The principle of self-culture could never be expanded to all. For in a world that is irredeemably banal, the self-cultured individual becomes defined by this exceptionality. Far now from Schiller, here Pater agrees with Nietzsche, who writes with a certain predictability in *Thus Spoke Zarathustra*: 'A high culture is a pyramid, it can stand only on a broad base, its very first prerequisite is a strongly and soundly consolidated mediocrity' (1982: 646).

In 'The Soul of Man Under Socialism' (1891), Wilde with typical audacity reasserted a supposedly unproblematic relationship between individual and society: 'propos[ing] a welfare and industrial State as precondition of a "New Individualism" characterised not by machinery or wealth but by Christlike inwardness' (Gagnier 2000b: 325). This 'Christlike inwardness' resembles Paterian 'contemplation', but Wilde's vision inverts Pater; taking the more sociological view, dominant in Britain at the time, that individualism is predicated on appropriate political and social conditions (Lukes 41–5). Pater refused any such causality; thus failing to practise the historicism he preached when criticising Plato. It is a cruel irony that Wilde would himself become a butterfly crushed upon society's wheel.

As though Pater is himself that 'solitary prisoner [in his] own dream of a world' (R 151), his Schilleresque gestures towards humanity at large are undermined by his inability to envisage how self-culture could expand beyond the individual. Symons' conjecture that '[Pater] was quite content that his mind should keep as a solitary prisoner its own dream of the world; it was that prisoner's dream of the world that it was his whole business as a writer to remember to perpetuate', comes to mind (2003: 98). I beg to quibble on one point. Even if Pater ultimately seems like that 'solitary prisoner', he was never 'content' with this. The inclusive pronouns of Pater's essays consciously and consistently reach out to people, just as Pater himself reached out to his students as a kindly friend and teacher. It is the move from ethical feelings founded on personal friendships to an abstract conception of ethics in society that Pater finds difficult. His gesture towards this broader vision of self-culture at the end of 'Diaphaneitè' is indicative: 'A majority of [diaphanous people] would be the regeneration of the world' (D 158). This hyperbolic flourish does not make up in gusto what it lacks as a tenable idea. Its irreverent idealism belies ambivalence about society, which remains a blank somewhere in between the particularity of the individual and the ideal of the whole world. That blank is the space in which the individual is reduced to 'a dull, colourless existence', which Pater does not care to discuss. Hence he cannot envisage the social regeneration implicit in his theory. Like the end of *The Renaissance*, 'Diaphaneitè' burns itself out with this voracious flame, leaving such dull practicalities unresolved.

Pater's desire to prioritise the individual allows space for social deviance and relativity. Yet it also means that he writes against the prevailing tenor of social responsibility. His dichotomy between the individual and society not only separates him from Schiller, but puts a gulf between him and many others: both eminent contemporaries, and the earlier thinkers he elsewhere identifies with. He cannot, for example, take up Hobbes' conception of civil society or Hegel's *Sittlichkeit*. Such concepts ring hollow to Pater.

Moreover, is there a risk that this radical kind of 'Individualism [. . .] destroys the very idea of obedience and duty, thereby destroying both power and law; and what then remains but a terrifying confusion of interests, passions and diverse opinions?' (Lukes 6). Pater's defiant turn away from society risks the solipsistic, unchecked supremacy of the individual against whom there is no authority. He stresses this quality when he describes the diaphanous man as 'a revolutionist' who is 'not disquieted for the desire for change' and whom the world regards with 'indifferentism' (D 157; 155; 157). Such a vision is ultimately unrealisable, but it knows that. It is a pipe dream of Romantic individualism, curiously out of time, in an age that had long since given up such notions in favour of a different model of individualism.

Solipsism in aestheticism is a familiar story. The relationship between individual and society in the aesthetic movement lends itself to parody, and 'could all too easily be seen as a self-serving apology for an amoral, selfish, hedonism – for an attitude to life (and a lifestyle) which threatened the very basis of civil society' (Guy 318). Such sweeping generalisations are, like Mrs Oliphant's dismissal of Paterian self-culture (1873: 604ff), at fault in ignoring the cultural and intellectual nuances of aestheticism. In truth, the disjunction between the individual and society has more complex implications for ethics. Having ostracised the individual from society and relegated God – at best – to the realms of the possible, there is a need to establish an alternative basis for ethical judgement: a 'new "Ethick"'.

Ethics as Aesthetics

Katherine Bradley, one half of Michael Field, wrote of Pater in her journal on 25 August 1890: 'He has struck out the Essay on Aesthetic Poetry in *Appreciations* (for the 2nd ed.) because it gave offence to some pious person – he is getting hopelessly prudish in literature, & defers to the moral weaknesses of everybody. Deplorable!' (qtd L 113, n. 3). This is not the enduring image left to us of Pater. Neither does it exemplify the amoral individual characterised in 'Diaphaneitè'. But quite apart from the fact that Pater could never dare to be the diaphanous man he envisaged, he was always more moral than he is remembered. This section concentrates on his attempts to reconcile the individual with morality through aesthetic experience in his 'new "Ethick"'. This is defined in *Marius the Epicurean*, 'The Aesthetic Life' and ultimately challenged by *Gaston de Latour*.

The genesis of Paterian moral sympathy lies in the expansive, unified aesthetic moment discussed in earlier chapters. Chapter 4 discussed how Pater's pantheism involves the individual in a network of sympathies with other individuals, and in Chapter 8 the aesthetic moment expands the sympathies of the individual to other historical periods. In each of these visions, the individual empathises with others and realises a sense of common humanity through aesthetic experience. As Regenia Gagnier notes, 'Pater dramatically extended his meditation on the precise way the solipsistic prison of the self could be opened to the higher life in *Marius the Epicurean*' (2000b: 328). This 'higher life' is the ethical life and it is Pater's most successful development of aesthetics into ethics. In the final days of Marius' life, as he is dying, his ailing body quickens his senses and noticing the minutiae of the natural world that surrounds him his sympathy with those around him is expanded. Thus, 'the scent of the new-mown hay', 'the sunlight' and 'the sounds of the cattle' (M II, 216) open out into a broader sense of common human- ity as Pater describes: 'the faces of those people, casually visible, took a strange hold on his affections; the link of general brotherhood, the feeling of human kinship, asserting itself most strongly when it was about to be severed forever' (M II, 217). Marius' senses are heightened by their own form of 'elaborate and lifelong' aesthetic education (M II,

219), charted by the novel, and to which this is the climax just prior to his death. For a moment at least it takes us back to Schiller's aesthetic education as we see Pater make the easy link from aesthetic contemplation to kinship with those around to sympathy with humanity at large.

The neat beauty of the vision is such that one hesitates to add a note of cynicism. And yet, placed in the broader terms of Pater's writing, one might justly ask whether Marius' common sense of humanity is sustainable and whether it could ever go beyond a beautiful *sense* of common humanity to a shared experience or a power of action. Sure, 'Pater is not a philosophy professor and it would be a mistake to look to him for a rigorous moral theory to serve as the basis of a rigorous aesthetic theory' (Guyer 346–7). Even so, given the antipathy between the individual and society elsewhere, it is necessary to question whether Pater's apparent reconciliation of the individual, aesthetics and ethics is not in fact an example of that 'confusion between aesthetics and ethics' noted by Paul Tucker (108). In *Marius the Epicurean* the matter is settled by Marius' immanent death, which preserves it, like the sensual moments discussed in the previous chapter, as a moment of exquisite unsustainable beauty: 'for a moment he experienced a singular curiosity, almost an ardent desire to enter upon a future, the possibilities of which seemed so large' (M II, 221). Like the moment in evoked by Giorgione's *Fête Champêtre*, it is premised on the impossibility of expanding beyond the individual. It is poised between being and not-being, where it is vanquished by its extinction before it ever could be realised. After his insight into 'human kinship' Marius has to die. He never could cheapen this imaginative experience into an ethical life where it would be tarnished by the ugliness of the world. As in the intense climatic moment of the Conclusion to *The Renaissance* and 'Diaphaneitè' Pater ends his works before he has to address such inconveniences. *Being* is, after all, higher than *doing* (A 62) and this is the realm Pater reserves for art.

Violence

The 'reserved' quality of art, discussed primarily in Chapter 5, presents it as an apt link from the sensual self to ethics and if Pater does not fully realise this in *Marius*, this novel at leaves some possibility that it could be realised. The same could not be said of *Gaston de Latour*. Indeed, refocusing from the site of Pater's literary triumphs to his apparent failures – 'The Aesthetic Life', which he never published, 'A Study of Dionysus' and 'The Bacchanals of Euripedes', which he withdrew from publication, and *Gaston de Latour*, his abandoned novel – we see how the ethical solution of *Marius* is thwarted. Pater's loosely woven tapestry of the good, the beautiful and pleasure is most revealingly glimpsed in these pieces, written in the late 1870s and 1880s, when he attempted to theorise the ethics vaguely glimpsed in his earlier writings. Here he tussles in an attempt to reconcile ethics with aestheticism; and here he must confront the genesis of evil in sensual beauty once we abandon the measured, intellectual realm of idealist metaphysics. Just as an aesthetic *sense* of common humanity cannot be equated with the power of ethical action, neither can art be equated with the good. Whilst *Marius* illustrates the climax of ethical possibility, *Gaston* subverts its very basis, suggesting that art is not a safe haven from the 'descriptions of violent incidents and abnormal states', which Pater entreated George Moore to avoid. *Gaston de Latour* illustrates how 'flowers of evil' may bud in art by placing Gaston in Paris in 1572, on what would afterwards be called the St Bartholomew's Day massacre. In stark contrast to Pater's advice to Moore, his narrative becomes saturated in 'the horror of supernatural darkness' (GL 60). Pater sums it up when he explains that 'this singularly self-possessed person had to confess that [. . .] he had lost for a while the exacter view of certain outlines, certain real differences and oppositions of things in that hotly coloured world of Paris' (GL 64). All of which is very well if it is spiritualised into the realm of art, but art fails. It is overcome by the madness within. In art as in life 'reserve' can all too easily break down. As Gerald Monsman has explained, the standard edition of this 'unfinished romance', edited by Charles Shadwell after Pater's death, smoothes out these issues: 'for Shadwell the unfinished and unpolished must be decorously hidden away . . . [A] certain amount of his editorial energy seems to have gone into constructing the equivalent of those fig leaves which so proliferated on nineteenth-century statuary' (1991: 2). Prior to this though Pater's text becomes so steeped in the centrifugal tendency that it cannot proceed. He is unable in the end to reconcile the violence and passion of life with art. Art is therefore an unreliable moral educator. There might have been other reasons as well Pater's withdrawal of *Gaston de Latour* in 1888, but its subversion of his design to bring ethics and aesthetics together may have been decisive.

It is not without trepidation that Pater turns from art to sensual experience in the world for moral guidance. Of course, sensuality has attractions for the relativist in him: a direct link between morality and sensuality enables him to approach morality on its own ever-shifting terms. Hume has no qualms about this. In accordance with his sceptical empiricism, Hume bases moral principles entirely on sensual impressions, arguing that vice and virtue are not discoverable merely by reason, or the comparison of ideas, [so] it must be by means of some impression or sentiment they occasion, that we are able to mark the difference betwixt them [. . .] An action, or sentiment, or character, is virtuous or vicious; why? Because its view causes a pleasure or uneasiness of a particular kind. (1964: II. iii, 179)

In 'The Aesthetic Life' Pater seems to adopt Hume's straightforward view of ethical judgement in which good and evil correspond to pleasure and pain as he writes that 'The life of sensation suggests its own moral code, has its own conscience, clear and near, and with no problematic assumptions' (AL 9). The brief and uncomplicated form of this statement seems to assume the reader's assent to Humean ethics. Only, Pater must have been aware – more aware than Hume perhaps – that nothing so concrete as a 'moral code' is possible if morality is founded on sensations. The particularity, subjectivity and ever-shifting nature of sensations could afford no such thing. The sensual pleasure evoked by beauty contains its own morality not because it stimulates an a priori, universal realisation of the good, but because the good is implicit in it. The distinction is significant because it eradicates Schiller's metaphysical idea that ethical values could be a priori universals. It also decentres ethical judgement from the Church or State. Rather, as in Epicurean ethics and Hume's empirical ethics, moral judgements are implicit in sensual experience, where fluctuation and subjectivity are integral. In this way Pater's 'code' is more like a faith that aesthetic judgements correlate to just ethical judgements; a faith that no longer has the guarantee of God. This is all very well for Hume, who believes in custom as the basis for social stability and whose idea of sensation is, in comparison to Pater's, naïvely free from desire. However, Pater's rejection of Hume's constructive thesis, discussed in Chapter 2, and the dangerous desire for sensual pleasure, discussed in Chapter 5, make sensual pleasure a most unreliable moral compass. Perhaps if desire truly is kept in check by 'reserve' there might be a semblance of order but reserve only extends to the sphere of action The problem is neatly illustrated in an exchange between Pater and a student who asked, 'But Mr Pater, why should we be good?' to which he replied, 'Because it is beautiful' (qtd Conlon 453). It is an apocryphal tale but its veracity is not as important as the truth it captures: that Pater's ethics are conditional on beauty. Quite simply, the individual is to act according to his aesthetic sense of beauty and ugliness, which correlate to right and wrong. But is it possible to found ethical values on a subjective judgement of beauty? And even if it is, does he mean that we should be good because the good is always beautiful or that we should be good only when the good is beautiful?

There is evidence for both interpretations in 'The Aesthetic Life'. In the first case, it seems that we should only be good when the good is beautiful because the sensual pleasure of the individual is the highest criterion to determine action. For example, in a passage also noted in the previous chapter, Pater discusses London: 'aesthetically the least promising scene' (AL 14) and a city in which he never really felt comfortable:

> one thing is plain if he is to prosecute the life of aesthetic culture he will have to apply largely the faculty of selection. Well! does not all right conduct of artistic matters always involve selection? Does not the aim of all art lie in the establishment of an ideal depending partly on negative qualifications culture in its most general sense being largely in large measure negative or renunciant[:] a fine taste habit of ignoring or forgetting. (AL 14)

It is difficult to reconcile 'ignoring and forgetting' with ethical being; one is reminded that by contrast the literary ethics of, say, Dickens and Gaskell were premised on noticing the 'ugly' or degraded areas of society. The reality is that virtuous acts are often most needed amid the ugliness, but this is somehow at odds with Pater's aesthetic imperative. He disdains what he refers to as 'real life and its sordid aspects', or at least affects to disdain it (2003: 87). When Pater's friend, the painter Simeon Solomon, was imprisoned and financially ruined because of homosexual offences and cast into London's seedy underworld, Pater's response is contested. Laurel Brake has argued that Pater helped him financially (1994: 14) whilst Richard Dellamora claims that he turned his back on him (117). There is scant evidence either way. Of course Pater memorialised Solomon in his 'Study of Dionysus' (GS 37) but the truth and depth of his moral response actually depends on whether he really believed in 'ignoring or forgetting' that which offends the delicate eye.

The question of whether the beautiful is always good raises inherent problems in Pater's aesthetic. He suggests that beauty informs moral sensibility: '[the individual's] apprehension of moral fact will identify itself with his nature and acquired appreciation of a sensible charm in things' (AL 10). Gesturing toward a notion that individualism may be reconciled with universal values – 'moral fact' – in the subjective imagination, Pater seems unable to follow through the implications. The problem is that he locates ethical sensibility in the sensual pleasure of the beautiful. His comparison elsewhere of sensual desire to being in 'service to a band of madmen' (PP 94) overshadows his idea of morality with the possibility that sensual 'ecstasy' may become uncontrollable, obscuring all distinctions between good and evil as the individual, intoxicated by his desire for greater and greater sensations, becomes aware only of his own pleasure. The vision of uncontrollable Dionysian sensuality which emerged in Chapter 5 shows that there are 'flowers of evil' amongst beauty (GL 71). Certainly Pater realises the intrinsic capacity for 'evil' in the beautiful: Dionysian frenzy shows that desire may come between beauty and ethics, subverting both with the primal urge for ever greater sensations. The beautiful becomes ugly; the good becomes evil, and all is obscured because the individual is alone in his revelry, with only his distorted judgement for a guide.

Pater revisited the ethical dilemmas of *Gaston de Latour* when he reviewed *The Picture of Dorian Gray* in *Bookworm* three years after Gaston had ceased to be published in *Macmillan's Magazine*. The critical scorn heaped on his admirer's work could equally have been directed at him had he continued to publish his novel. But by 1891 Pater had all but given up his novelistic ambitions. Until his death he would tinker with *Gaston*, but his move back to Oxford from London in 1893 was in many ways a retreat from the ambition to fully realise his vision of literary art in his own novels; a realisation of sorts that he would not fulfil his own artistic vision. In the past he had solicited favourable reviews from his protégé Oscar Wilde but he felt unable to return the compliment by 1891. His criticisms centre on Wilde's presentation of 'a dainty Epicurean theory' (2003: 87), thus offering an insight into Pater's own conception of Epicurean morality in the latter part of his career:

> A true Epicureanism aims at a complete though harmonious development of man's entire organism. To lose the moral sense therefore, for instance, the sense of sin and righteousness, as Wilde's heroes are bent on doing so speedily [. . . is] to pass from a higher to a lower form of development. (2003: 87–8)

This may be Pater's most convincing word on ethics. In terms of his own broad vision of the individual and art, it is difficult for him to make ethics necessary in way other way than to suggest that 'moral sense' is essential to the 'harmonious development of man's entire organism'. Morality is justified because it is of value to the holistic cultivation of one's individuated self. It is difficult to accept for a moment that Pater himself pursued this self-involved, self-important way of living, but it is evidence of the intellectual difficulty of reconciling a pursuit of beauty with the supremacy of the individual and relativity. The problem defeats him because it outrages art. Pater's ultimate refuge in the individual is not a solution; it is a statement that he cannot move beyond the individual on any other basis.

While Pater the man may have 'beg[u]n as an aesthete and ended as a moralist', as his friend Vernon Lee put it (1980: 295), Pater the writer never found a way to fully reconcile his vision of the individual with ethics. Given that glaring gap, and though his position was misinterpreted by over-zealous followers who gave it a hedonistic and decadent twist, T. S. Eliot's famously snooty admonishment cannot be quite gainsaid: 'His view of art, as expressed in *The Renaissance*, impressed itself upon a number of writers in the 'nineties, and propagated some confusion between life and art which is not wholly irresponsible for some untidy lives' (1951: 441).

Pater wanted to believe that art and beauty could fulfil the spiritual needs of the individual and liberate him from the world. In this way, his turn to beauty is a self-consciously aesthetic response to modernity; it is the hope that man may embrace the liberation offered by relativity and, instead of learning the rules of society, to cultivate a personal response through art. Yet what Dowling calls 'Pater's task to complete the "aesthetic education of man" that Schiller had begun' (1996: 86) is doomed to failure.⁹ It is difficult to imagine Pater completing any metaphysical system, least of all Schiller's extensive philosophical system. His rejection of systematisation in philosophy commits him to a philosophical aesthetic which cannot be completed. By editing society out of his 'aesthetic education' Pater presents a form of self-culture that is always and forever incomplete. Without it, he finds it hard to muster the moral authority to legislate for humanity. Art, in Pater's aesthetic, may educate hearts and imaginations but, despite his declaration at the close of 'Diaphaneitè', it cannot alter the world without.

Held in abstract from society, the Paterian individual – the diaphanous, glass man – appears as a fragile form which risks breaking if put in contact with others. However, the resistance that defines the individual against and in contrast to the external forces that threaten him, is the same resistance that ultimately prevents the expansion of moral feelings to moral actions. Pater's imagination sets him against the fragmentary and oppressive nature of modernity and society, promising him the possibility of transcending all of this, but by asserting the autonomy of the individual through aesthetic experience alone, Pater has created for himself a tautology and a trap: society is not required, ethics are unleashed into the relative space of an isolated personal judgement.

For these reasons, a study of Walter Pater's ethics is a study of creative failure. His 'confusion between aesthetics and ethics' (Tucker 108) exemplifies the self-contradictory, stuttering position from which he wrote. Like Friedrich Nietzsche's *übermensch*, Pater's aesthetic subject, rapt in sensual experience, goes beyond good and evil. Beauty becomes a fickle teacher, subject to the desires of the individual. But Pater, more so than Nietzsche, is possessed by these categories still; whilst attempting to cast off the shackles of religious ethics, his own sensibility is still enmeshed in Christian values of good and evil. In consequence, his individualism is left as an exquisite disposition without the power of action, except for resistance.

Notes

1. This is quoted from *The Characters of Man* by Jean de la Bruyère. The meaning is: 'Such a great misfortune, not to be able to be alone.'
2. The University Sermon was an annual event and as such these comments were a high profile disavowal of Capes' devotee and his work.
3. Chapters 6 and 7 were edited and published by Charles Shadwell in 1896. Gerald Monsman has pieced together a further six chapters from the fragments of Pater's notes in his critical edition of the novel (Pater 1995: 84–308).
4. The notion of Old Mortality as a liberal brotherhood in which radical ideas could be voiced is sometimes overdone. As noted in Chapters 3 and 4, Samuel Brooke, a co-member in the 1860s, was vehement in speaking against Pater's conception of 'self-culture' and warned Gerard Manley Hopkins against him.
5. 'The sitting-room whose panelling, which extends from floor to ceiling, Pater coloured primrose, has two windows, and the one which projects, became, when furnished with cushioned seats, his favourite reading place' (Wright I, 215).
6. Schiller's views may have been influenced by both Catholicism and Hume's concept of 'natural virtues' (1964: I. ii, 271ff) but they are made distinct by their secular basis and the central role of aesthetics.
7. Of course, Pater was rather more reserved than Nietzsche; no doubt the lengths to which Nietzsche takes his often very Pateresque ideas would have shocked Pater beyond measure. The comparison between them has been made several times. Though I am not aware of any extensive comparison of their views on ethics, as noted above, Patrick Bridgwater touches on some of the issues involved in *Nietzsche in Anglosaxony* (1972) and *Anglo-German Interactions in the Literature of the 1890s* (1999). One can read Nietzsche's comments on ethics in *Beyond Good and Evil* and *The Genealogy of Morals*.
8. Even as he expresses this teleology, Pater criticises teleological conceptions of humankind (A 60–1). In matters of ethics he argues that teleologies neglect 'the intangible perfection of those whose ideal is rather in being than in doing' (A 61). To some extent this may be addressed through his conception of time, which attempts to reconcile synchronic with diachronic in the 'consummate moments' of aesthetic contemplation (R 88).
9. More broadly, Linda Dowling's downplaying of Schiller's significance may be questioned. The idea that his philosophy survived, as she goes on to assert, 'only [as] a ghostly idealized vestige [. . .] to puzzle readers' (87) does a great disservice to him. In fact Schiller's aesthetic philosophy exerted great influence on Coleridge and Schelling in the late eighteenth century, Nietzsche, Carlyle and Pater in the nineteenth century, and Walter Benjamin

in the twentieth century, to name but a few. In the twenty-first century so far, Germany has celebrated Schiller Year (2005) and academics such as George Steiner continue to engage with his aesthetic, declaring 'Say it Loud – It's Schiller and It's Proud'!

Chapter 10

Conclusion: 'the elusive inscrutable mistakable self'

In such of us as not merely, live, but think and feel what life is and might be, there is erected an inner drama full of conflicting emotions, long drawn out through the years, and, in many cases, never brought to a conclusion.
Vernon Lee, *Gospels of Anarchy and Other Contemporary Studies* (9)

Vernon Lee might have had Walter Pater in mind as she wrote these lines. His meandering aesthetic philosophy, itself 'never acquiescing in a facile orthodoxy' (R 152), was on no account ever brought to a conclusion. And so, to write a conclusion about Pater is already to engage in an exercise quite foreign to the man himself.

The extent to which one may make conclusions about Pater's late-Romantic individual is limited to a notional sense of an ending, never to be confused with resolution. A feather on the breath of time is Pater's ever-shifting thought. His Prufrockian 'visions and revisions' understand themselves to be – like his idea of the late-Romantic individual – subject to ever-fluctuating time, even as he strives to overcome this limitation. It is with these qualifications that Pater has emerged in this study as a Romantic 'aesthetic philosopher', who engages in the history of modern philosophy in order to explore the 'elusive inscrutable mistakable self' (HP 23).

Oppression, resistance and creativity characterise the relationship between the individual, modernity and aesthetics in Pater's writings. The late-Romantic Paterian individual is assailed on every side by the relativity, the strictures of society, deep time and the theory of evolution, inevitable physical decay and death, and even the secret passions and desires within. Stood ever on the brink of its own destruction, the Paterian individual affirms its 'uniqueness, originality, self-realization' (Lukes 17) with each subjective and creative act. Whilst all that is solid melts into air, the imagination, which can appreciate beauty and create that which is beautiful becomes the ultimate justification of being. This is exemplified by the artist's work and in subjective aesthetic experience, in Kantian 'initiatory powers' (GL 74) that make experience possible, and in the self-cultivation of physical exercise even though it is ultimately doomed to fail.

It is true that 'the importance of Pater's thought lies in its subjectivity [and the view that] we create ourselves and that we are the measure of our own value' (Pittock 15–16), but this must come with qualifications. Pater realises that autonomy is hard-won and it is always but a moment away from dissolution. Even as he positions the individual at the creative centre of the universe he points out his ephemeral nature, and as he suggests the potential of self-cultivation he vividly evokes the individual's self-destructive potential and physical frailties. So Pater believes in the individual almost in spite of himself. The 'illusive inscrutable mistakable self' is a secular faith. This is why he is at the centre of each and every one of Pater's published writings[1] as they ask again and again how 'I' am formed and what I mean when I refer to my self.

Pater's Romanticism emerges in the present study as more than an excavated 'relic', like Dionysus in Auxerre. As Chapter 8 suggested, dwelling with relics ultimately severs the very life-force of the individual. Rather, I have suggested that Pater's Romanticism is a dynamic force through which Pater comes to terms with modernity. This is what Nikolas Kompridis would define as 'philosophical romanticism' (2): Romanticism not founded on a period or a specific set of influences but as an ever-emerging philosophy based on common principles. Pater's late-Romanticism, like his aesthetic moment, spans past, present and future. It engages with thinkers of the past but its real stimulus comes from the issues of his day. The obliqueness of Pater's views on contemporary thought and literature were explained to some extent in Chapter 1 which noted that Pater did not read contemporary writers, but it would be a mistake to deduce that he did not engage with contemporary thought. Recent criticism has been deft in explaining how Pater addresses emerging contemporary concerns. In expanding on their work in the current study, it has been my aim to contend that a conception of the Paterian late-Romantic individual is absolutely crucial to understanding exactly how Pater engages with his contemporary world. I do not think that it would be an exaggeration to say that Pater's whole aesthetic is in some sense an attempt to ascertain how the individual may cease to be 'a somewhat hopeless being' in the face of modernity (AL 3). In other words, the motivating question of his aesthetic philosophy is, how might one retain a sense of one's individuated self and a sense of the mystery in the individual's experience of life in the face of modernity? Pater died as he lived, contemplating this question. Having spent June and July 1894 convalescing with rheumatic fever and pleurisy, he seemed to be recovering. He was working on his nearly complete 'Pascal' essay when, on 30 July 1894, he collapsed on the stairs of the house he shared with his sisters; 64 St Giles. He died there at the age of 54. If his burial in Holywell Cemetery, now next to the very Oxford English Faculty he had hoped would never exist, would have raised a wry smile from Pater, the plaque unveiled in his memory on the wall of the Brasenose College Chapel might, I think, have moved him. It reads: 'Philosophy being the grandest of music'.

I have suggested in this study that Pater's writings are more than even the grandest music: that his works engage vigorously and carefully with philosophical ideas and problems so that it is not possible to reduce him to a mere stylist, a musician of mellifluous words. Even so, philosophy was, to him, beautiful and sublime as all art should be. It did not offer him eternal and systematic truths but suggested insights and moods to make meaning of the secular, ephemeral life of the individual. There is no reason to think that Pater ever really believed that aesthetic experience might save the Romantic individual against the forces of modernity and modern thought that threatened to vanquish it. As he writes in 'Coleridge', 'Forms of intellectual and spiritual culture sometimes exercise their subtlest and most artful charm when life is already passing from them' (A 65). Such is his Romanticism. In *Culture and Society* Raymond Williams suggests that what we understand by Victorian sensibility had all but ceased to be by 1880. Pater's late-Romantic individual is defined across this fault line. Conceived on this transition, Pater's Romantic individualism is defined by creativity, quickened by a sense of possibility and contradictoriness. His late-Romantic individual of 'uniqueness, originality, self-realization' incorporates both elements that seem at once, Romantic, Victorian, and startlingly modern. As such it is a picture of the individual in his 'uncertain condition' (R 39), characterised by a very modern notion of flux and subjectivity. Yet quite unlike the modernist vision this spawned, Pater suggests that the individuated mind could span the centuries; he is subject to Victorian Doubt, but ultimately rooted in Protestant Christian sensibility; and his values are defined by 'strange' metaphysics. He might most usefully be conceived as neither Victorian nor modernist; but as one who writes on the cusp, capturing this moment of transition in his thoughts and echoing his own presentation of the Renaissance as a creative transition.

If ultimately Pater is unable to meet modernity on its own terms; if in the end he retreats to art to shut out reality, this does not undermine the significance of his endeavour. Like the book of self-portraiture that captivates Marius, Pater's writings on the individual are 'a creature of efforts rather than of achievements, in the matter of apprehending truth, but at least conscious of lights by the way, which he must needs record, acknowledge' (M II, 47). Part of his significance lies in his sincere attempt to conceive the inconceivable: an individual without God but with metaphysical spirit, without society but with ethical values, without historical eternity but with a sense of eternity.

In the first of his *Imaginary Portraits*, Pater writes of Antoine Watteau that 'He was always a seeker after something in the world, that is there in no satisfying measure, or not at all' (IP 43). The same may be said of Pater himself, and the way he seeks this *something* characterises his terribly unphilosophical philosophical aesthetics.

As a thinker Pater engages with the history of philosophy on his own terms. Whilst he is extremely well-read in philosophy, exhibiting an implicit understanding of the debates surrounding the issues he discusses, he is in no way entrenched in it. As he turns to Hume, to Kant, to the ancients as well as to Romantic thought, intellectual ideas indeed become 'painted ideas, painted and visible philosophy' in his prose (MS 43). Like history, philosophy is subsumed into the realm of art where reason and imagination are brought together. Moreover, ultimately, this study has argued that Pater ultimately rejects philosophy. A discourse centred in the rational mind, conventional philosophy is too narrow to address the full scope of human experience as Pater sees it. Concretely, as discussed in Chapter 5, Pater's conception of sensation bursts the boundaries of its philosophical treatment by Kant, Epicurus and Hume: sensation cannot for Pater be disinterested from the desires of the individual. The relationship between sensation and desire that he prioritises in his aesthetic quite simply makes it impossible to think of sensation philosophically. Pater also recognises that systematised philosophy does not befit the fluctuations of continuous time which, as he says, is 'a tremulous wisp constantly re-forming itself on the stream' (R 151). Pater's criticism that philosophical writings do not account for the temporal nature of being in the post-Darwinian, modern world means that he must depart from systematised forms to find a mode of writing to befit the discussion of time. Like Pater's late-Romantic individual, thought in his writings must ride the wave of ever-moving time: to concretise truth is to kill it. Finally, Pater demurs from the metaphysical conceits of idealist and Platonic philosophies. Chapters 4 and 5 suggested that he trusts the faculty of reason too little to believe its metaphysical extrapolations, leaving his view of 'spirit' in ambivalence. He shies from the 'pretensions to pass beyond the limits of individual experience' on which philosophical universalism is founded (MS 1). The radical subjectivity which he sets out in his Preface to *The Renaissance* makes each individual the measure of all things, with no claim to legislate for the experience of another. Yet this rejection of philosophical universalism is more problematic than it could have seemed at first. Surrounded by 'that thick wall of personality', the individual ends up 'imprisoned now in the narrow cell of its own subjective experience' (R 151; MS 2): not exactly freed from the world and objectivity, so much as alienated. It is then very difficult for Pater to find a way to reconcile his individualism and aesthetics with ethics and society. As suggested in Chapter 9, it is simply not possible for him to move from personal experience to a broader sympathy for the other whilst defending an aesthetic premised on 'ignoring and forgetting' all that does not please the eye (AL 14).

Having thus rejected the form of philosophical discourse as he knew it, the question to which Pater always returns is what philosophy would have to be to account for the nature of the irrational, fluctuating and mysterious modern world. He finds the answer in literary art. Time and time again, art emerges as his terribly Romantic answer to the questions of modernity. Ultimately Pater goes beyond philosophy to *art* – which always 'aspires to the condition of music' (R 66) – in order to explore the individual. It is an inverse move to that of Hegel, who believed that art and religion would be subsumed into philosophy in the realm of Absolute Spirit. Pater's fusion of art and philosophy or, more accurately, the encapsulation of philosophy in art, is founded on the intellectual assertion that imagination can reach into the corners of experience which range beyond the rational mind. Whereof he cannot speak he does not remain silent, but instead looks to the imagination to at least gesture to the inexpressible. The philosophical theories Pater read are diffused through the imagination, which vanquishes the false dichotomy between philosophy and literary art. The claim is that, properly understood, philosophy is not an abstract theory about the world, much less a systematising endeavour. Rather, it infuses how Pater thinks and is subject to the unsystematic and inconsistent mind of the individual. Given that philosophy merges into art and art is the expression of personality in Pater's works, it follows that Pater's aesthetics are an expression of his self. He engages with opposing thinkers from across the vast scope of history without commitment to any, entertaining their ideas to measure them against his own, to take from them what he wishes and to make it into an art that reflects the problems he grappled with in his own life.

The terms on which this philosophical literary art is successful are debatable. Certainly Pater personifies his declamation of 'facile orthodoxy' using his own principle of 'selection' or discrimination to work through these theories, finding in them enough 'to rouse, to startle it to a life of constant and eager observation' (R 152; AL 14; R 152; R 152).

However, as a result of vanquishing systems and absolute truths, Pater has difficulties in defining a constructive aesthetic vision. His unpublished manuscripts are his clearest attempts at this; but they peter out into pages increasing in crossings out and large blank spaces, eventually ending still in *medias res*. His failure to conclude his enquiry is inevitable failure as soon as he admits the fluctuating character of existence. The only sense of unity he perceives is in those brief moments, when all is condensed in an intense experience of the present. The suggestion that this could be reflected in prose and exemplified in his own work has no claim to rational, intellectual unity; it claims only an impression of unity.

Pater's attempts to forge new modes of thinking in the modern world are inhibited by his inability to fully vanquish metaphysics. Although he ostensibly returned to religion only at the end of his life, Chapter 4 showed that he never really went away from it. Elliptical allusions to the 'strange', a hankering after 'the other sort of knowledge' and a censorious comment that empiricism had 'narrowed the spiritual, the imaginative horizon' point to his sense that there is some inconceivable but nonetheless real thing beyond human understanding (R 69; HP 12; AL 2). It is true that he is no conventional religious believer: he mocks 'that mythical personage' (R 148) at the beginning of his career and even at the end 'he never returned to Christianity in the in the orthodox, or intellectual sense' (Mrs Humphry Ward 121). Neither are his flirtations with pantheism or Romantic gestures to some unknowable void ever fully developed in his works. Even so, that intangible *something* lurks behind them, where it becomes essential to 'the initiatory powers' (GL 74), the animating force of genius, and the threatening void invoked by the body. If Pater seems to 'privilege the concrete over the abstract' (Higgins 1991: 86) this is not to say that the material world is all there is. It is one of many ironies that whilst he declares the primacy of the seen world, he is captivated by that which cannot be understood. Much as he believes that we must live as though there is no God, the Paterian individual is defined at the interface between the seen and the unseen, the tangible body and the intangible spirit. Hence it is not so much a desire to know, as a desire to explore the parameters of our *not* knowing, which engages Pater. His legacy is not consistency, to be sure; he had far too much imagination to be consistent.

At the time of Pater's death there was a sense, summed up by Henry James, that he is 'not of the little day – but of the longer time' (1980: 293).[2] Ironically for one who embraced the ephemeral, he is indeed of 'the longer time'. For the terrible beauty of Pater's writing is that it expresses the individual in his uncertain condition on the brink of the modernist sensibility that Pater would in part define. The poignancy of his writings is that they express above all the uncertain condition of one particular individual, Walter Pater. Beneath the poses and imaginary portraiture his warm, sometimes faltering voice calls out to his readers, reassuring them that they are not alone. He is not an authority but one of them, vulnerable and unsure, as he wanders through the debris of old beliefs: a gentle spirit raging, with 'reserve', against the dying of the light.

Notes

1. This is not true of the two unpublished essays I have quoted from: 'The History of Philosophy' and 'The Aesthetic Life'. In these works Pater attempts more speculative enquiries, dealing directly with ideas rather than focusing these through individuals. One wonders whether this conceptual distinction is not part of the reason why Pater could not make these essays work and ultimately abandoned them. Pater writes best when he focuses his ideas through the stories of individuals: they concentrate and unify his ideas.
2. This is a response to Gosse's biographical article, which expresses a similar closing sentiment (271).

Bibliography

Primary Works

Alighieri, Dante (1995), *The Divine Comedy*, Allen Mandelbaum (trans.), London: Alfred F. Knopf.

Arnold, Matthew [1864] (1925), 'Pagan and Mediaeval Religious Sentiment', in Matthew Arnold (ed.), *Essays in Criticism*, London: Macmillan, pp. 187–213.

(1865), 'The Function of Criticism at the Present Time', in Matthew Arnold (ed.), *Essays in Criticism*, London: Macmillan, pp. 1–41.

—(1867a), *On the Study of Celtic Literature*, London: Smith, Elder and Co.

—(1867b), 'Dover Beach', in Matthew Arnold (ed.), *New Poems*, London: Macmillan, pp. 112–14.

—(1869), *Culture and Anarchy: An Essay in Political and Social Criticism*, London: Macmillan.

—(1882), 'Literature and Science', *The Nineteenth Century*, 12.66 (August 1882), pp. 216–30.

—(1873), *Literature and Dogma: An Essay Towards a Better Appreciation of the Bible*, London: Macmillan.

Baudelaire, Charles [1964] (2006), 'The Painter of Modern Life', in Jonathan Mayne (trans. and ed.), *The Painter of Modern Life and Other Essays*, London: Phaidon Press, pp. 1–41.

—(1983a), 'The Salon of 1846', in Eric Warner and Graham Hough (trans and eds), *Strangeness and Beauty: An Anthology of Aesthetic Criticism, 1840–1910*, Cambridge: Cambridge University Press, vol. I, pp. 173–82.

—(1983b), 'The Salon of 1859', in Eric Warner and Graham Hough, *Strangeness and Beauty: An Anthology of Aesthetic Criticism, 1840–1910*, Cambridge: Cambridge University Press, vol. I, pp. 197–205.

—[1986] (1991), *Les Fleurs du Mal*, in Francis Scarfe (trans. and ed.), *The Complete Verse*, London: Anvil Press Poetry, vol. I.

Berkeley, George [1709] (2008), *An Essay Towards a New Theory of Vision*, New York: Cosimo.

—[1710] (1999), *A Treatise Concerning the Principles of Human Knowledge*, Oregon: Oregon University Press.

—[1732] (1963), *A New Theory of Vision and Other Writings*, London: J. M. Dent & Sons.

Bosanquet, Bernard (1899), *The Philosophical Theory of the State*, London: Macmillan.

Bradley, F. R. (1876), *Ethical Studies*, London: Henry S. King & Co.

Browning, Oscar (1892), *Goethe: His Life and Writings*, London: Swan Sonnerschein & Co.

Burke, Edmund [1757] (1998), *A Philosophical Enquiry into the Origins of our Ideas of the Sublime and Beautiful*, Oxford: Oxford University Press.

Bussell, F. W. [1894] (1980), 'Sermon in Memory of Walter Pater', in R. M. Seiler (ed.), *Walter Pater: The Critical Heritage*, London: Routledge & Kegan Paul, pp. 284–8.

Byron, George [1819] (1984), *Don Juan*, T. G. Steffan, E. Steffan and W. W. Pratt (eds), London: Penguin.

Bywater, Ingram (1917), *Ingram Bywater: The Memoir of an Oxford Scholar, 1840–1914*, W. W. Jackson (ed.), Oxford: Clarendon Press.

Campbell, Lewis (ed.) (1861), *The Theaetetus of Plato*, Oxford: Oxford University Press.

Carlyle, Thomas [1825] (1992), *The Life of Friedrich Schiller*, Richmond Hill: Camden House-Firefly.

—[1836] (1929), *Sartor Resartus and On Heroes and the Heroic in History*, London: J. M. Dent & Sons Ltd.

Coleridge, S. T. (1817), *Biographia Literaria; or Biographical Sketches of my Literary Life and Opinions*, London: Best Penner.

Darwin, Charles [1859] (1899), *On the Origin of the Species*, London: John Murray.

—[1871] (2002), *The Descent of Man and Selection in Relation to Sex*, London: Gibson Square.

Debussy, Claude [1894] (2008), *Prélude à l'après-midi d'un faune*, on *Debussy, Satie and Roussel*, BBC Symphony Orchestra, David Robertson (cond.), BBC Music.

Dilke, Lady [1887] (1980), 'Unsigned Review', in R. M. Seiler (ed.), *Walter Pater: A Critical Heritage*, London: Routledge, pp. 165–7.

Eliot, T. S. [1917] (1961), 'The Love Song of J. Alfred Prufrock', in T. S. Eliot (ed.), *Selected Poems*, London: Faber and Faber, pp. 11–16.

—[1930] (1951), 'Arnold and Pater', in T. S. Eliot (ed.), *Selected Essays*, London: Faber & Faber, pp. 431–43.

—[1943] (1944), *Four Quartets*, London: Faber & Faber.

Epicurus (1994), *The Epicurus Reader: Selected Writings and Testimonials*, Brad Inwood and L. P. Gerson (eds), Ambridge: Hackett Publishing.

Euripides [1904] (2007), *The Bacchae*, Gilbert Murray (trans.), place unknown: Clarke Press.

Fichte, Johann Gottliebe [1800] (1987), *The Vocation of Man*, Peter Preuss (trans.), Indiana: Hackett.

Field, Michael [1895] (1890), 'Poetic Tribute to Walter Pater', in R. M. Seiler (ed.), *Walter Pater: The Critical Heritage*, London: Routledge, p. 280.

Fox Bourne, H. R. (1876), *The Life of John Locke*, II vols, New York: Harper and Brothers, Publishers.

Gautier, Théophile [1835] (2005), *Mademoiselle de Maupin*, Helen Constantine (trans.), London: Penguin.

Gide, André (1935), *If It Die*, Dorothy Bussy (trans.), London: Vintage.
—*Fruits of the Earth* [1935] (2002), trans. unknown, London: Vintage.
Goethe, Johann Wolfgang von (1870), *Aus meinem Leben: Dichtung und Wahrheit*, Leipzig: Reclam.
Green, T. H. (1874), 'Introduction', in David Hume, *A Treatise on Human Understanding*, David Hume, London: Longmans, Green & Co, pp. 1–305.
—(1883), *Prolegomena to Ethics*, A. C. Bradley (ed.), Oxford: Clarendon Press.
Hamilton, William (1859), *Lectures on Metaphysics and Logic*, H. L. Mansel and John Veitch (eds), IV vols, Boston: Gould and Lincoln.
Harrold, Charles Frederick (1935), 'Review', *Modern Philology*, 33 (1935), pp. 110–12.
Hegel, G. W. F. [1886] (1993), *Introductory Lectures on Aesthetics*, Bernard Bosanquet (trans.), London: Penguin.
—(1991), *Elements of the Philosophy of Right*, H. B. Nisbit (trans.), Allen Wood (ed.), Cambridge: Cambridge University Press.
—(1998), *The Hegel Reader*, Stephen Houlgate (ed.), Oxford: Blackwell.
Heraclitus (1979), *The Art and Thought of Heraclitus*, Charles H. Kahn (trans. and ed.), Cambridge: Cambridge University Press.
—(2003), *Fragments*, Brooks Haxton (trans.), James Hillman (ed.), London: Penguin.
Hopkins, Gerard Manley (1959), *The Journals and Papers of Gerard Manley Hopkins*, Humphrey House and Graham Storey (eds), London: Oxford University Press.
—(2006), *Oxford Essays and Notes*, vol. IV, *The Collected Works*, Lesley Higgins (ed.), Oxford: Oxford University Press.
Hugo, Victor (1982), *Les Misérables*, Norman Denny (trans.), London: Penguin.
Hume, David (1875), *Essays Moral, Political and Literary*, II vols, T. H. Green and T. H. Grose (eds), London: Longmans, Green, & Co.
—[1739–40] (1964), *A Treatise of Human Nature*, II vols, London: Everyman-Dent.
—[1748] (1999), *An Enquiry Concerning Human Understanding*, Oxford: Oxford University Press.
Huxley, T. H. [1886] (1894), 'Science and Morals', *Evolution and Ethics, and Other Essays*, T. H. Huxley (ed.), vol. IX, available at http://aleph0.clarku.edu/huxley, accessed 30 August 2012.
Huysmans, Joris-Karl (2003), *Against Nature*, Robert Baldick (trans.), London: Penguin.
James, Henry [1894] (1980), untitled letter to Edmund Gosse, in R. M. Seiler (ed.), *Walter Pater: The Critical Heritage*, London: Routledge, pp. 292–3.
—(1999), *Henry James: A Life in Letters*, Philip Horne (ed.), New York: Penguin.
Johnson, Lionel (1894), 'Walter Pater', *Fortnightly Review*, 56 (1894).
Kant, Immanuel (1929), *Critique of Pure Reason*, Norman Kemp Smith (trans.), Basingstoke: Palgrave.
—(1987), *Critique of Judgement*, Werner S. Pluhar (trans.), Cambridge: Hackett Publishing Group.

—(2002), *Critique of Practical Reason* Werner S. Pluhar (trans.), Cambridge: Hackett Publishing Group.

—(2004), *Prolegomena to Any Future Metaphysics* Guy Hatfield (trans.), Cambridge: Cambridge University Press.

King James Bible (1952), London: Thomas Nelson & Sons.

Lee, Vernon (1884), *Euphorion: Being Studies of the Antique and Medieval in the Renaissance*, London: T. Fisher Unwin.

—[1895] (1980), untitled extract, in R. M. Seiler (ed.), *Walter Pater: The Critical Heritage*, London: Routledge, pp. 294–7.

—[1908] (2006), *Gospels of Anarchy and Other Contemporary Studies*, place unknown: Wildeside Press.

Lewes, George Henry (1853), *The Biographical History of Philosophy*, vol. IV, London: Smith, Elder and Co.

—[1855] (1873), *The Story of Goethe's Life*, London: Smith, Elder and Co.

—[1874–9], *Problems of Life and Mind*, IV vols, Boston: James R. Osgood.

Locke, John [1690] (1997), *An Essay Concerning Human Understanding*, London: Penguin.

Mallock, W. H. [1877] (1975), *The New Republic*, Leicester: Leicester University Press.

Mansel, H. L. (1863), unsigned review of 'Sensation Novels', *The Quarterly Review*, 113.226 (April 1863), pp. 481–514.

Merz, John Theodore (1896), *A History of European Thought in the Nineteenth Century*, IV vols, Edinburgh: Blackwood.

Mill, John Stuart (1843), *A System of Logic*, II vols, London: John W. Parker.

—[1859] (1982), *On Liberty*, London: Penguin.

Moore, George (1919), *Avowals*, Internet Archive, available at http://www.archive.org, accessed 11 August 2011.

Nietzsche, Friedrich (1967), *The Birth of Tragedy*, Walter Kaufmann (trans.), New York: Vintage.

—(1982), *Thus Spoke Zarathustra*, in Walter Kaufmann (trans. and ed.), *The Portable Nietzsche*, London: Penguin, pp. 103–439.

—(1997a), 'On the Uses and Disadvantages of History for Life', in R. J. Hollingdale (trans.), Daniel Breazeale (ed.), *Untimely Meditations*, Cambridge: Cambridge University Press, pp. 57–124.

—(1997b), *Twilight of the Idols or, How to Philosophize With a Hammer*, trans. Richard Polt, Cambridge: Hackett Publishing.

Oliphant, Margaret (1862), Unsigned review of sensation fiction, *Blackwood's Magazine*, 91 (May 1862), pp. 565–74.

—(1873), Unsigned review of *The Renaissance*, *Blackwood's Magazine*, 114 (November 1873), pp. 604–9.

Pater, Walter (1868), 'Poems by William Morris', *Westminster Review*, 34.2 (October 1868), pp. 300–12.

—[1873] (1997), *Studies in the History of the Renaissance*, Oxford: Oxford University Press.

—[1875] (1980), 'Review of *The Renaissance in Italy: The Age of the Despots* by John Addington Symonds', in Donald L. Hill (ed.), *The Renaissance: Studies in Art and Poetry*, London: University of California Press, pp. 196–202.

—(c. 1880), 'The History of Philosophy', bMS. Eng 1150 (2), Houghton Library, Harvard University.

—[1885] (1985), *Marius the Epicurean*, London: The Soho Book Company.
—(c. 1886–8), 'Art and Religion', bMS Eng 1150 (11), Houghton Library, Harvard University.
—[1887] (1997), *Imaginary Portraits*, New York: Allworth Press.
—(1889), 'Aesthetic Poetry', in *Appreciations, with an Essay on Style*, London: Macmillan, pp. 213–27.
—[1889] (1987), *Appreciations, With an Essay on Style*, Evanston, IL: Northwestern University Press.
—[1888–9] (1995), *Gaston de Latour: The Revised Text*, Gerald Monsman (ed.), Greensboro, NC: ELT Press.
—[1891] (2003), 'A Novel by Mr. Oscar Wilde', in Karl E. Beckson (ed.), *Oscar Wilde: The Critical Heritage*, London: Routledge, pp. 87–9.
—(1892) 'Introduction', in Charles Lancelot Shadwell (trans.), *The Purgatory of Dante Alighieri: Purgatorio*, London: Macmillan, pp. xiii–xxviii.
—(c. 1893), 'The Aesthetic Life', bMS. Eng 1150 (7), Houghton Library, Harvard University.
—[1893] (2005), *Plato and Platonism*, New York: Barnes & Noble.
—(1895), *Greek Studies*, Charles L. Shadwell (ed.), London: Macmillan.
—[1895] (1910), *Miscellaneous Studies*, Charles L. Shadwell (ed.), London: Macmillan.
—[1895] (1918), *Essays from the Guardian*, London: Macmillan.
—[1895] (1997), 'Diaphaneitè', in Adam Philips (ed.), *Studies in the History of the Renaissance*, Oxford: Oxford University Press, pp. 154–8.
—(1970), *The Letters of Walter Pater*, Lawrence Evans (ed.), Oxford: Oxford University Press.
—(date unknown), 'Hobbes', bMS Eng 1150 (18), Houghton Library, Harvard University.
—(date unknown), 'Moral Philosophy', bMS Eng 1150 (17), Houghton Library, Harvard University.
Pattison, Mark (1876), 'Philosophy at Oxford', *Mind*, 1.1 (January 1876).
—[1885] (1969), *Memoirs*, Fontwell Press, Sussex: Centaur Press.
Plato [1871] (1999a), *Phaedrus*, in Benjamin Jowett (trans.), *The Essential Plato*, London: TSP, pp. 781–851.
—[1871] (1999b) *Symposium*, in Benjamin Jowett (trans.), *The Essential Plato*, London: TSP, pp. 679–762.
—[1871] (2004), *Republic*, Benjamin Jowett (trans.), New York: Barnes & Noble.
Poe, Edgar Allan [1840] (1912), 'The Man of the Crowd' in *Tales of Mystery and Imagination*, London: J. M. Dent & Sons, pp. 101–9.
Proust, Marcel (1996), *In Search of Lost Time*, Scott Moncrieff, Terence Kilmartin and D. J. Enright (trans), London: Vintage.
Rossetti, Dante Gabriel [1850] (1983), Untitled essay on Chiaro dell' Erma, in Eric Warner and Graham Hough (eds), *Strangeness and Beauty: An Anthology of Aesthetic Criticism, 1840–1910*, Cambridge: Cambridge University Press, vol. I, pp. 124–31.
Ruskin, John [1843–1860] (1906), *Modern Painters*, V vols, Orpington, Kent: George Allen.
—[1849] (1889), *The Seven Lamps of Architecture*, Orpington, Kent: George Allen.

—[1851–3] (1886), *The Stones of Venice*, III vols, Orpington, Kent: George Allen.

Schiller, Johann Christoph Friedrich von [1967] (1982), *On the Aesthetic Education of Man*, Elizabeth Wilkinson and L. A. Willoughby (trans and eds), Oxford: Clarendon Press.

—(2005), *On Naïve and Sentimental Poetry*, William F. Wertz, Jr (trans.), The Schiller Institute, available at http://www.schillerinstitute.org/transl/Schiller_essays/naive_sentimental-1.html, accessed 22 May 2009.

—(2006), 'On Grace and Dignity', in Tapio Riikonen and David Widger (trans and eds), *Aesthetical and Philosophical Essays*, place unknown: The Echo Library, pp. 127–51.

—'On the Use of the Chorus in Tragedy' (2007), *The Bride of Messina*, trans. unknown, Kissinger Publishing, pp. 139–46.

Schopenhauer, Arthur (1886), *The World as Will and Idea*, R. B. Haldene and J. Kemp (trans.), III vols, London: Trübner & Co.

Shadwell, Charles (1895), 'Preface', *Greek Studies: A Series of Essays*, Walter Pater, London: Macmillan, pp. v–ix.

Shelley, Percy Bysshe [1840] (1904), *A Defence of Poetry*, Indianapolis: Bobbs-Merrill.

Sidgwick, Henry (1895), 'The Philosophy of Common Sense', *Mind* 4.14 (April 1895), pp. 145–58.

Simmel, Georg (1950), 'The Metropolis and Mental Life', in Kurt Wolff (trans.), *The Sociology of George Simmel*, New York: Free Press, pp. 409–24.

Spencer, Herbert (1860), 'Art IV. – The Social Organism', *Westminster Review* XVII (January 1860), pp. 90–121.

—[1862] (1865), *First Principles of a New System of Philosophy*, New York: D. Appleton & Company.

Swinburne, Algernon Charles [1866] (1917), 'Hymn to Proserpine', *Poems and Ballads*, London: William Heinemann, pp. 67–73.

—(1866), *Notes on Poems and Reviews*, London: John Camden Hotten.

—[1868] (1925), *William Blake*, London: Heinemann.

Symonds, John Addington (1875), *The Renaissance in Italy: The Age of the Despots*, London: Smith, Elder, and Co.

—(1878), *Tales of Ancient Greece, No 1, Eudiades and a Cretan Idyll*, London: Arrowsmith.

—(trans.) (1878), *The Sonnets of Michael Angelo Buonarotti and Tommaso Campanella*, London: Smith, Elder, and Co.

Symons, Arthur [1887] (1980), 'Signed Review', in R. M. Seiler (ed.), *Walter Pater: The Critical Heritage*, London: Routledge, pp. 175–82.

(1893), 'The Decadent Movement in Literature', *Harper's New Monthly Magazine* 87.522 (November 1893), pp. 858–69.

—[1897] (1993), 'Preface: being a word on behalf of patchouli', *Silhouettes and London Nights*, Oxford: Woodstock Books, pp. xiii–xv.

—(1919), 'Introduction', *The Renaissance*, Walter Pater, New York: The Modern Library, pp. xi–xxiv.

—[1931] (2003), 'Unspiritual Adventures in Paris', in Roger Holdsworth (ed.), *Selected Writings*, Manchester: Carcanet Press, p. 98.

Tennyson, Alfred Lord [1850] (2000), *In Memoriam*, in Valentine Cunningham (ed.), *The Victorians: An Anthology of Poetry and Poetics*, Oxford: Blackwell, pp. 219–52.

Vaughan, Henry [1650] (1961), 'The Retreat', in Arthur Quiller-Couch (ed.), *The Oxford Book of English Verse, 1250–1918*, Oxford: Clarendon Press, pp. 406–7.

Wilde, Oscar [1881] (1993), 'Hélas!', in Merlin Holland (ed.), *Oscar Wilde: Plays and Poems*, London: The Folio Society, p. 449.

—[1887] (2004), 'Mr Pater's *Imaginary Portraits*', in Anya Clayworth (ed.), *Oscar Wilde's Selected Journalism*, Oxford: Oxford University Press.

—[1891] (1999), *The Picture of Dorian Gray*, Oxford: Oxford University Press.

—[1891] (2001a), 'The Critic as Artist', in Linda Dowling (ed.), *The Soul of Man Under Socialism & Selected Critical Prose*, London: Penguin, pp. 213–79.

—[1891] (2001b), 'The Soul of Man Under Socialism', Linda Dowling (ed.), *The Soul of Man Under Socialism & Selected Critical Prose*, London: Penguin, pp. 125–50.

—[1949] (1986), *De Profundis*, in Hesketh Pearson (ed.), *De Profundis and Other Writings*, London: Penguin, pp. 97–211.

Wise, J. R. (1866), Unsigned 'Belles Lettres', *Westminster Review*, 30.1 (July 1866), pp. 266–80.

Wordsworth, John [1873] (1980), Untitled letter to Walter Pater, in R. M. Seiler (ed.), *Walter Pater: The Critical Heritage*, London: Routledge, pp. 61–3.

Wordsworth, William [1850] (1979), *The Prelude: 1799, 1805, 1850*, Jonathan Wordsworth, M. H. Abrams, Stephen Gill (eds), London: Norton.

Yeats, W. B. [1935] (1955), *Autobiographies*, London: Macmillan.

Secondary Works

Aarsleff, Hans (1971), 'Locke's Reputation in Nineteenth-Century England.' *The Monist* 55.3 (July 1971), pp. 392–422.

Adams, James Eli (1992), 'Gentleman, Dandy, Priest: Manliness and Social Authority in Pater's Aestheticism', *ELH*, 59 (1992), pp. 441–6.

—(1995), *Dandies and Desert Saints: Styles of Victorian Masculinity*, Ithaca: Cornell University Press.

—(2002), 'Transparencies of Desire: An Introduction', in Laurel Brake, Lesley Higgins, Carolyn Williams (eds), *Walter Pater: Transparencies of Desire*. Greensboro, NC: ELT Press, pp. 1–11.

Andrews, Kit (2002), 'Walter Pater and Walter Benjamin: The Diaphanous Collector and the Angel of History', in Laurel Brake, Lesley Higgins, Carolyn Williams (eds), *Walter Pater: Transparencies of Desire,* Greensboro, NC: ELT Press, pp. 250–60.

—(2011a), 'Walter Pater as Oxford Hegelian: *Plato and Platonism* and T. H. Green's *Prolegomena to Ethics*', *Journal of the History of Ideas*, 72.3 (July 2011), pp. 437–9.

—(2011b), 'Pater and the British Reception of German Idealism.' *Journal of the History of Ideas*, 72.3 (July 2011), pp. 437–59.

Annan, Noel (2001), *The Dons: Mentors, Eccentrics and Geniuses*, London: Harper Collins.

Armstrong, Isobel (1993), *Victorian Poetry: Poetry, Poetics and Politics*, London: Routledge.

Ashton, Rosemary (1980), *The German Idea: Four British Writers and the Reception of German Thought, 1800–1860*, Cambridge: Cambridge University Press.

Ayer, A. J. (1980), *Hume*, Oxford: Oxford University Press.

Ball, Patricia (1967), *The Central Self*, London: Athlone Press.

Bann, Stephen (ed.) (2004), *The Reception of Walter Pater in Europe*, London: Continuum.

Barthes, Roland (2000), *Camera Lucida: Reflections on Photography*, Richard Howard (trans.), London: Vintage.

Beaumont, Matthew (2011), 'Pater as Psychagogue: Psychology, Aesthetics, Rhetoric', *19: Interdisciplinary Studies in the Long Nineteenth Century*, 12 (2011), available at http://19.bbk.ac.uk/index.php/19/issue/view/80/showToc, accessed 2 September 2012.

Becker-Leckrone, Megan (2002),'Pater's Critical Spirit', in Laurel Brake, Lesley Higgins, Carolyn Williams (eds), *Walter Pater: Transparencies of Desire*. Greensboro, NC: ELT Press, pp. 286–97.

Benson, A. C. (1906), *Walter Pater*, London: Macmillan.

Bizzotto, Eliza (2000), 'The Legend of the Returning Gods in Pater and Wilde', in Franco Marucci and Emma Sdegno (eds), *Athena's Shuttle: Myth, Religion, Ideology from Romanticism to Modernism*, Milan: Cisalpino, pp. 161–74.

Bowie, Andrew [1990] (2003), *Aesthetics and Subjectivity: From Kant to Nietzsche*, Manchester: Manchester University Press.

Brake, Laurel and Anne Humphreys (1989), 'Critical Theory and Periodical Research', *Victorian Periodicals Review*, 22.3 (1989), pp. 1–17.

Brake, Laurel and Ian Small (eds) (1991), *Pater in the 1990s*, Greensboro, NC: ELT Press.

Brake, Laurel (1991), 'The Discourses of Journalism: "Arnold and Pater" Again – And Wilde' in Laurel Brake and Ian Small (eds), *Pater in the 1990s*, Greensboro, NC: ELT, pp. 43–61.

—(1994), *Walter Pater*, Tavistock, Devon: Northcote House Publishing.

—(2001) *Print in Transition, 1850–1910: Studies in Media and Book History*, Basingstoke: Palgrave Macmillan.

—(2002), 'The Entangling Dance: Pater after *Marius*, 1885–1891', in Laurel Brake, Lesley Higgins, Carolyn Williams (eds), *Walter Pater: Transparencies of Desire*, Greensboro, NC: ELT Press, pp. 24–36.

—(2006), 'Vernon Lee and the Pater Circle', in Patricia Pulham and Catherine Maxwell (eds), *Vernon Lee: Decadence, Ethics, Aesthetics*, Basingstoke: Palgrave Macmillan, pp. 40–57.

Bridgwater, Patrick (1972), *Nietzsche in Anglosaxony: A Study of Nietzsche's Impact on English and American Literature*, Leicester: Leicester University Press.

—(1999), *Anglo-German Interactions in the Literature of the 1890s*, Oxford: Legenda.

Brown, Daniel (1997), *Hopkins' Idealism: Philosophy, Physics, Poetry*, Oxford: Oxford University Press.

Bruns, Gerald L. (1975), 'The Formal Nature of Victorian Thinking', *PMLA* 90.5 (October 1975), pp. 904–18.

Bullen, J. B. (1991), 'The Historiography of *Studies in the History of the Renaissance*', in Laurel Brake and Ian Small (eds), *Pater in the 1990s*, Greensboro, NC: ELT Press, pp. 155–67.

Cevasco, G. A (ed.) (1993), *The 1890s*, London: Garland Publishing.

Chai, Leon (1990), *Aestheticism: The Religion of Art in Post-Romantic Literature*, New York: Columbia University Press.

Clark, Kenneth (1956), *The Nude: A Study of Ideal Art*, London: Penguin.

Clements, Elicia and Lesley J. Higgins (eds) (2010), *Victorian Aesthetic Conditions: Pater Across the Arts*, Basingstoke: Palgrave Macmillan.

Cohen, Ed (1994), *Talk on the Wild Side: Towards a Genealogy of a Discourse of Male Sexualities*, London: Routledge.

Colley, Ann C. (2010), *Victorians in the Mountains: Sinking the Sublime*, Farnham, Surrey: Ashgate.

Collins, Randall (1998), *Sociology of Philosophies: A Global Theory of Intellectual Change*, London: Harvard University Press.

Conlon, John (1982), *Walter Pater and the French Tradition*, Lewisburg, PA: Bucknell University Press.

Copleston, Frederick [1966] (2011), *Utilitarianism to Early Analytic Philosophy*, vol. VIII in *A History of Philosophy*, London: Continuum.

Court, Franklin (ed.) (1980), *Pater and His Early Critics*, Victoria: University of Victoria.

Crinkley, Richmond (1970), *Walter Pater: Humanist*, Lexington: Kentucky University Press.

Crompton, Louis (2003), *Homosexuality and Civilization*, London: Belknap Press.

Cruise, Colin (2005), *Love Revealed: Simeon Solomon and the Pre-Raphaelites*, London: Merrell.

Dale, Peter Allan (1977), *The Victorian Critic and the Idea of History*, London: Harvard University Press.

Daley, Kenneth (2001), *The Rescue of Romanticism: Walter Pater and John Ruskin*, Athens: Ohio University Press.

Dames, Nicholas (2005), '"The Withering of the Individual": Psychology in the Victorian Novel', in Francis O'Gorman (ed.), *A Concise Companion to the Victorian Novel*, Oxford: Blackwell, pp. 91–113.

Daunton, Martin (ed.) (2005), *The Organisation in Knowledge in Victorian Britain*, Oxford: Oxford University Press.

Davis, Michael F. (2002), 'Walter Pater's "Latent Intelligence" and the Conception of "Queer Theory"', in Laurel Brake, Lesley Higgins, Carolyn Williams (eds), *Walter Pater: Transparencies of Desire*, Greensboro, NC: ELT Press, pp. 261–85.

Dawson, Gowan (2005), 'Walter Pater's Marius the Epicurean and the Discourse of Science in *Macmillan's Magazine*: "A Creature of the Nineteenth Century"', *English Literature in Transition, 1880–1920*, 48.1 (2005), pp. 38–54.

—(2007), *Darwin, Literature and Victorian Respectability*, Cambridge: Cambridge University Press.

De Laura, David J. [1969] (2000), *Hebrew and Hellene in Victorian England:*

Newman, Arnold and Pater, available via www.victorianweb.org/books/delaura, accessed 30 October 2012.

Dellamora, Richard (1990), *Masculine Desire: The Sexual Politics of Victorian Aestheticism*, London: North Carolina University Press.

Dixon, Thomas (2008), *The Invention of Altruism: Making Moral Meanings in Victorian Britain*, Oxford: Oxford University Press.

Docherty, Thomas (2003), 'Aesthetic Education and the Demise of Experience', in John J. Joughin and Simon Malpas (eds), *The New Aestheticism*, Manchester: Manchester University Press, pp. 23–35.

Dodd, Philip (ed.) (1981), *Walter Pater: An Imaginative Sense of Fact*, London: Frank Cass.

Donoghue, Denis (1995), *Walter Pater: Lover of Strange Souls*, New York: Alfred A. Knopf.

Dowling, Linda (1994), *Hellenism and Homosexuality in Victorian Oxford*, Ithaca: Cornell University Press.

—(1996), *The Vulgarization of Art: The Victorians and Aesthetic Democracy*, Charlottesville: Virginia University Press.

Eastham, Andrew (2010), 'Haunted Stage: Walter Pater and the "Theatrical Mode of Life"', in Elicia Clements and Lesley J. Higgins (eds), *Victorian Aesthetic Conditions: Pater Across the Arts*, Basingstoke: Palgrave Macmillan, pp. 167–81.

—(2011), *Aesthetic Afterlives: Irony, Literary Modernity and the Ends of Beauty*, London: Continuum.

Eldridge, Richard (2003), *An Introduction to the Philosophy of Art*, Cambridge: Cambridge University Press.

Evangelista, Stefano (2002), '"Outward Nature and the Moods of Men": Romantic Mythology in Pater's Essays on Dionysus and Demetre', in Laurel Brake, Lesley Higgins, Carolyn Williams (eds), *Walter Pater: Transparencies of Desire*, Greensboro, NC: ELT Press, pp. 107–18.

—(2004), 'Walter Pater Unmasked: Impressionistic Criticism and the Gender of Aesthetic Writing', *Literature Compass*, 1 (2004), pp. 1–4.

—(2006), 'Eros and the Text: The Past, Present, and Future of Pater and Gender', *The Pater Newsletter*, 51 (2006), pp. 23–4.

—(2009), *British Aestheticism and Ancient Greece: Hellenism, Reception, Gods in Exile*, Basingstoke: Palgrave Macmillan.

Evans, Lawrence (1970), 'Introduction', in Lawrence Evans, *The Letters of Walter Pater*, Oxford: Oxford University Press, pp. xv–xliv.

Foucault, Michel (1998), *History of Sexuality*, II vols, Robert Hurley (trans.), London: Penguin.

Fraser, Hilary (1986), *Beauty and Belief: Aesthetics and Religion in Victorian Literature*, Cambridge: Cambridge University Press.

Gagnier, Regenia (1991), *Subjectivities*, Oxford: Oxford University Press.

—(2000a), *The Insatiability of Human Wants: Economics and Aesthetics in Market Society*, London: Chicago University Press.

—(2000b), 'The Law of Progress and the Ironies of Individualism in the Nineteenth Century', *New Literary History*, 31.2 (2000), pp. 315–36.

—(2005), 'Cultural Philanthropy, Gypsies and Interdisciplinary Scholars: Dream of a Common Language', *19: Interdisciplinary Studies in the Long*

Nineteenth Century, 1 (2005), pp. 1–24, available via http://www.19.bbk. ac.uk/BackIssuePage.htm#Issue1, accessed 9 November 2011.

Garratt, Peter (2010), *Victorian Empiricism: Self, Knowledge, and Reality in Ruskin, Bain, Lewes, Spencer and George Eliot*, Madison, NJ: Fairleigh Dickinson University Press.

Gilmour, Robin [1993] (1996), *The Victorian Period* Harlow, Essex: Longman.

Gosse, Edmund [1894] (1913), 'Walter Pater: A Portrait', *Critical Kit-Kats*, London: William Heinemann, pp. 241–71.

Gould, Stephen Jay (1987), *Time's Arrow, Time's Cycle: Myth and Metaphor in the Discovery of Geological Time*, London: Harvard University Press.

Green, V. H. H. (1974), *A History of Oxford University*, London: B. T. Batsford Ltd.

Greenslet, Ferris [1903] (2008), *Walter Pater*, Charleston: Bibliobazaar.

Guy, Josephine M. (ed.) (1998), *The Victorian Age: An Anthology of Sources and Documents*, London: Routledge.

Guyer, Paul (2003), 'Art and Morality: Aesthetics at 1870', in Thomas Baldwin (ed.), *The Cambridge History of Philosophy 1870–1945*, Cambridge: Cambridge University Press, pp. 337–47.

Hamilton Buckley, Jerome (1966), *The Triumph of Time: A Study of the Victorian Concepts of Time, History, Progress, and Decadence*, London: Oxford University Press.

Hext, Kate (2008), 'Recent Scholarship on Walter Pater: "Antithetical Scholar of Understanding's End"', *Literature Compass*, 5 (2008), pp. 407–23.

—(2010), 'The Limitations of Schilleresque Self-Culture in Pater's Individualist Aesthetics', in Lesley Higgins and Elicia Clements (eds), *Walter Pater Across the Arts*, Basingstoke: Palgrave Macmillan, pp. 285–302.

—(2012), 'Literary Form and Philosophical Thought in Nineteenth-Century Britain', *Literature Compass*, 9.11 (November 2012), pp. 695–707.

Higgins, Lesley (1991), '"Essaying W. H. Pater Esq.": New Perspectives on the Tutor/Student Relationship Between Pater and Hopkins', in Laurel Brake and Ian Small (eds), *Pater in the 1990s*, Greensboro, NC: ELT Press, pp. 77–93.

—(1993), 'Jowett and Pater: Trafficking in Platonic Wares', *Victorian Studies* 37.1 (1993), pp. 43–72.

—(2002a), 'No Time for Pater: The Silenced Other of Masculine Modernism', in Laurel Brake, Lesley Higgins, Carolyn Williams (eds), *Walter Pater: Transparencies of Desire*, Greensboro, NC: ELT Press, pp. 37–54.

—(2002b), *The Modernist Cult of Ugliness: Aesthetic and Gender Politics*, Basingstoke: Palgrave Macmillan.

—(2006), 'Introduction', *The Collected Works of Gerard Manley Hopkins: Oxford Essays and Notes*. Vol. 4. Oxford: Oxford University Press, pp. 1–87.

—(2007), 'Walter Pater: Painting in the Nineteenth Century', *English Literature in Transition, 1880–1920*, 50.4 (2007), pp. 415–53.

Hough, Graham [1947] (1961), *The Last Romantics*, London: Methuen.

Houghton, Walter E. [1957] (1985), *The Victorian Frame of Mind, 1830–1870*, London: Yale University Press.

Inman, Billie Andrew (1981a), *Walter Pater's Reading: A Bibliography of his Library Borrowings and Literary References, 1858–1873*, New York: Garland Publishing Inc.

—(1981b), 'The Intellectual Context of Walter Pater's "Conclusion"', in Philip

Dodd (ed.), *Walter Pater: An Imaginative Sense of Fact*, London: Frank Cass, pp. 12–30.

—(1989), 'Review: *Walter Pater and the Gods of Disorder* by Robert Keefe and Janice A. Keefe', *Nineteenth-Century Literature*, 43.4 (1989), pp. 539–42.

—(1991), 'Estrangement and Connection: Walter Pater, Benjamin Jowett and William M. Hardinge', in Laurel Brake and Ian Small (eds), *Pater in the 1990s*, Greensboro, NC: ELT Press, pp. 1–20.

Iser, Wolfgang (1987), *Walter Pater: The Aesthetic Moment*, David Henry Wilson (trans.), London: Cambridge University Press.

Jay, Martin (1996), 'Modernism and the Specter of Psychologism', *Modernism/ Modernity*, 3.2 (1996), pp. 93–111.

Jessop, Ralph (1997), *Carlyle and Scottish Thought*, Basingstoke: Palgrave Macmillan.

Johnson, Lee McKay (1980), *The Metaphor of Painting: Essays on Baudelaire, Ruskin, Proust, and Pater*, Michigan: UMI Research Press.

Johnson, R. V. (1969), *Aestheticism*, London: Methuen.

Kaiser, Matthew (2002), 'Marius at Oxford: Paterian Pedagogy and the Ethics of Seduction', in Laurel Brake, Lesley Higgins, Carolyn Williams (eds), *Walter Pater: Transparencies of Desire*, Greensboro, NC: ELT Press, pp. 189–201.

Kalip, Jacques (2002), 'Pater's Body of Work', in Laurel Brake, Lesley Higgins, Carolyn Williams (eds), *Walter Pater: Transparencies of Desire*, Greensboro, NC: ELT Press, pp. 236–49.

Kaylor, Michael Matthew (2006), *Secreted Desires: The Major Uranians: Hopkins, Pater and Wilde*, Brno: Masaryk University Press.

Keefe, Robert (1987), 'Walter Pater's Two Apollos', *Nineteenth Century Literature*, 42.2 (1987), pp. 159–70.

Keefe, Robert and Janice A. Keefe (1988), *Walter Pater and the Gods of Disorder*, Athens: Ohio University Press.

Kern, Stephen [1983] (2003), *The Culture of Time and Space, 1880–1918*, London: Harvard University Press.

—(2006), 'When Did the Victorian Period End? Relativity, Sexuality, Narrative', *Journal of Victorian Culture*, 11.2 (2006), pp. 326–38.

Kerry, S. S. (1970), *Schiller's Writings on Aesthetics*, Manchester: Manchester University Press.

Knickerbocker, William S. (1925), *Creative Oxford: Its Influence in Victorian Literature*, Syracuse, NY: Syracuse University Press.

Kompridis, Nikolas (ed.) (2006a), *Philosophical Romanticism*, London: Routledge.

—(2006b), 'Re-Inheriting Romanticism', in Nikolas Kompridis (ed.), *Philosophical Romanticism*, London: Routledge, pp. 1–17.

—(2006c), 'The Idea of a New Beginning: A Romantic Source of Normativity and Freedom', in Nikolas Kompridis (ed.), *Philosophical Romanticism*, London: Routledge, pp. 32–59.

Kooy, Michael John (2002), *Coleridge, Schiller and Aesthetic Education*, Basingstoke: Palgrave.

Lackey, Michael (2006), 'Modernist Anti-Philosophicalism and Virginia Woolf's Critique of Philosophy', *Journal of Modern Literature*, 29.4 (Summer 2006), pp. 76–98.

Laity, Cassandra (2009), *H. D. and the Victorian Fin de Siècle: Gender, Modernism, Decadence*, Cambridge: Cambridge University Press.

Lane, Christopher (1994), 'The Drama of the Impostor: Dandyism and Its Double.' *Cultural Critique*, 28 (1994), pp. 29–54.

Le Gallienne, Richard [1894] (1980), 'Obituary Notice' in R. M. Seiler (ed.), *Walter Pater: The Critical Heritage*, London: Rouledge, pp. 80–4.

Leavis, F. R. [1936] (1972), *Revaluation*, London: Penguin.

Leighton, Angela (2002), 'Aesthetic Conditions: Returning to Pater', in Laurel Brake, Lesley Higgins, Carolyn Williams (eds), *Walter Pater: Transparencies of Desire*, Greensboro, NC: ELT Press, pp. 12–23.

—(2005), 'Pater's Music', *The Journal of Pre-Raphaelite Studies*, 14 (2005), pp. 67–89.

—(2007), *On Form: Poetry, Aestheticism, and the Legacy of a Word*, Oxford: Oxford University Press.

Lennox, James (2004), 'Darwinism', Stanford Encyclopedia of Philosophy, available http://plato.stanford.edu/entries/darwinism, accessed 22 May 2009.

Levey, Michael [1962] (2003), *From Giotto to Cézanne: A Concise History of Painting*, London: Thames & Hudson Ltd.

—(1978), *The Case of Walter Pater*, London: Thames & Hudson Ltd.

—(1985), 'Introduction', *Marius the Epicurean*, Harmondsworth: Penguin, pp. 7–26.

Levine, Caroline (2003), *The Serious Pleasures of Suspense: Victorian Realism and Narrative Doubt*, London: University of Virginia Press.

Levine, George (2000), 'Two Ways Not to Be a Solipsist: Art and Science, Pater and Pearson', *Victorian Studies*, 43.1 (Autumn 2000), pp. 7–41.

—(2008), *Realism, Ethics and Secularism: Essays on Victorian Literature and Science*, Cambridge: Cambridge University Press.

Loesberg, Jonathan (1991), *Aestheticism and Deconstruction: Pater, Derrida and De Man*, Princeton: Princeton University Press.

Longbaum, Robert (1970), *The Modern Spirit: Essays of the Continuity of Nineteenth and Twentieth-Century Literature*, London: Chatto & Windus.

Love, Heather (2007), 'Exemplary Ambivalence', *The Pater Newsletter*, 52 (2007), pp. 25–30.

Lukes, Steven (1973), *Individualism*, Oxford: Blackwell.

Lyons, Richard S. (1972), 'The "Complex, Many-Sided" Unity of the Renaissance', *Studies in English Literature, 1500–1900*, 12 (1972), pp. 765–81.

McGrath, F. C. (1986), *The Sensible Spirit: Walter Pater and the Modernist Paradigm*, Tampa, Florida: Florida University Press.

Maxwell, Catherine (2008), *Second Sight: The Visionary Imagination in Late Victorian Literature*, Manchester: Manchester University Press.

Meisal, Perry (1981), *The Absent Father: Virginia Woolf and Walter Pater*, New Haven: Yale University Press.

—(2001), 'Psychoanalysis and Aestheticism', *American Imago*, 58.4 (Winter 2001), pp. 749–66.

Miller, Andrew and James Eli Adams (1996), *Sexualities in Victorian Britain*, Bloomington: Indiana University Press.

Mitchell, Sally (1996), *Daily Life in Victorian England*, Westport, CT: Greenwood Press.

Moliterno, Frank (1998), *The Dialectics of Sense and Spirit in Walter Pater and James Joyce*, Greensboro, NC: ELT Press.

Monsman, Gerald (1967), *Pater's Portraits: Mythic Pattern in the Fiction of Walter Pater*, London: Johns Hopkins University Press.

—(1970), 'Old Mortality at Oxford', *Studies in Philology* 67.3 (July 1970), pp. 359–89.

—(1977), *Walter Pater*, place unknown: G. K. Hall & Co.

—(1979), 'Gaston de Latour and Pater's Art of Autobiography', *Nineteenth-Century Fiction*, 33.4 (1979), pp. 411–33.

—(1980), *Walter Pater's Art of Autobiography*, London: Yale University Press.

—[1991] (2009), 'Editing Pater's *Gaston de Latour*: The Unfinished Work as "A Fragment of Perfect Expression"', in Laurel Brake, Lesley Higgins, Carolyn Williams (eds), *Walter Pater: Transparencies of Desire*, available via http://www.eltpress.org/pater/pater_chap3.pdf, accessed 20 May 2009.

—(1995), 'Introduction', in Gerald Monsman (ed.), *Gaston De Latour: The Revised Text*, Greensboro, NC: ELT Press.

—(2002), 'The Platonic Eros of Water Pater and Oscar Wilde: "Love's Reflected Image" in the 1890s', *Literature in Transition, 1880–1920*, 45.1 (2002), pp. 26–45.

Moran, Maureen (2007), 'Walter Pater's House Beautiful and the Psychology of Self-Culture', *English Literature in Transition*, 50.3 (2007), pp. 291–312.

Morell, J. D. (1846), *An Historical and Critical View of Philosophy in the Nineteenth Century*, II vols, London: William Pickering.

Morgan, Thaïs E. (1996), 'Reimagining Masculinity in Victorian Criticism: Swinburne and Pater', in Andrew H. Miller and James Eli Adams, *Sexualities in Victorian Britain*, Indianapolis: Indianapolis University Press, pp. 140–57.

Morris, C. R. [1937] (1963), *Locke, Berkeley, Hume*, Oxford: Oxford University Press.

Morris, William Edward (2001), 'David Hume', Stanford Encyclopaedia of Philosophy, available at www.plato.stanford.edu, accessed 5 March 2009.

Muirhead, John H. [1931] (1965), *The Platonic Tradition in Anglo-Saxon Philosophy*, London: George Allen and Unwin.

Mussell, James (2007), *Science, Time and Space in the Late Nineteenth Century*, Aldershot: Ashgate.

Najarian, James (2002), *Victorian Keats: Manliness, Sexuality and Desire*, Basingstoke: Palgrave Macmillan.

Nettleship, R. L. (1906), *Thomas Hill Green: A Memoir*, London: Longmans, Green & Co.

Norton, David Fate (2001), 'Editor's Introduction', in David Fate Norton and Mary J. Norton (eds), *A Treatise of Human Nature*, David Hume, Oxford: Oxford University Press, pp. 9–106.

Nye, Mary Jo (2003), *The Cambridge History of Science: The Modern Physical and Mathematical Sciences*, vol. V, Cambridge: Cambridge University Press.

Østermark-Johansen, Lene (2011), *Walter Pater and the Language of Sculpture*, Farnham, Surrey: Ashgate.

Painter, George D. [1959] (1996), *Marcel Proust: A Biography*, London: Pimlico.

Peckhaus, Volker (1999), '19th Century Logic Between Philosophy and Mathematics', *Bulletin of Symbolic Logic* 5.4 (December 1999), pp. 433–50.

Pereboom, Derek (2006), 'Kant on Transcendental Freedom', available via http://www.uvm.edu/~phildept/pereboom, accessed 4 May 2007.

Perry, Ralph Burton (1927), *Philosophy of the Recent Past*, London: Charles Scribner's Sons.

Perry, Seamus [1998] (1999), 'Romanticism: The Brief History of a Concept', in Duncan Wu (ed.), *A Companion to Romanticism*, Oxford: Blackwell, pp. 3–11.

Peterson, Linda H. (1999), 'Sage Writing', in Herbert F. Tucker, *A Companion to the Victorian Literature and Culture*, Oxford: Blackwell, pp. 373–87.

Pfau, Thomas (2002), 'Pater', *Paris Review*, 163 (2002), pp. 248–9.

Pittock, Murray (1993), *The Spectrum of Decadence: Literature of the 1890s*, London: Routledge.

Poovey, Mary (1989), *Uneven Developments: The Ideological Work of Gender in Mid-Victorian England*, London: Virago.

Porter, Roy [2003] (2004), *Flesh in the Age of Reason*, London: Penguin.

Potolsky, Matthew (2010), 'Literary Communism: Pater and the Politics of Community', in Elicia Clements and Lesley Higgins (eds), *Walter Pater Across the Arts*, Basingstoke: Palgrave Macmillan, pp. 185–204.

Potts, Alex (2000), *Flesh and the Ideal: Winckelmann and the Origins of Art History*, London: Yale University Press.

Powys, John Cowper (1955), *Visions and Revisions: A Book of Literary Devotions*, London: MacDonald.

Prettejohn, Elizabeth (2007), *Art for Art's Sake: Aestheticism in Victorian Painting*, London: Yale University Press.

—(1999), 'Walter Pater and Aesthetic Painting', in Elizabeth Prettejohn (ed.), *After the Pre-Raphaelites: Art and Aestheticism in Victorian England*, Manchester: Manchester University Press, pp. 36–58.

Prewitt Brown, Julia (1997), *Cosmopolitan Criticism: Oscar Wilde's Philosophy of Art*, Charlottesville: Virginia University Press.

Pulham, Patricia and Catherine Maxwell (eds) (2006), *Vernon Lee: Decadence, Ethics, Aesthetics*, Basingstoke: Palgrave Macmillan.

Quinton, Anthony (1958), 'The Neglect of Victorian Philosophy', *Victorian Studies* 1.3 (March 1958), pp. 245–54.

Rennie, Nicholas (1996), 'Ut Pictura Historia: Goethe's Historical Imagination and the *Augenblick*', *Goethe Yearbook*, 8.1 (1996), pp. 120–41.

—(2000), 'Between Pascal and Mallarme: Faust's Speculative Moment', *Comparative Literature*, 52.4 (2000), pp. 269–90.

—(2005), *Speculating on the Moment: The Poetics of Time and Recurrence in Goethe, Leopardi, and Nietzsche*, Göttingen: Wallstein.

Richter, Simon (2008), 'Speculating on the Moment: the Poetics of Time and Recurrence in Goethe, Leopardi, and Nietzsche', *Goethe Yearbook*, 15.1 (2008), pp. 225–7.

Roach, J. P. C. (1959), 'Victorian Universities and the National Intelligensia', *Victorian Studies*, 3.2 (December 1959), pp. 131–50.

Robbins, Ruth (2003), *Pater to Foster, 1873–1924*, Basingstoke: Palgrave Macmillan.

Roberts, Gabriel (2008), 'Analysis leaves off': The Use and Abuse of Philosophy in Walter Pater's *Renaissance.*' *The Cambridge Quarterly* 36 (2008): 407–25.

Russell, Bertrand [1897] (1999), 'Seems Madame? Nay, it is', in Charles

R. Pigden (ed.), *Russell on Ethics: Selections from the Writings of Bertrand Russell*, London: Routledge, pp. 79–86.

—[1934] (2001), *Freedom and Organisation 1814–1914*, London: Routledge.

—[1946] (2005), *History of Western Philosophy*, London: Routledge.

Ryan, Judith (1991), *The Vanishing Subject: Early Psychology and Literary Modernism*, Chicago: University of Chicago Press.

Rylance, Rick (2000), *Victorian Psychology and British Culture 1850–1880*, Oxford: Oxford University Press.

—(2004), 'The Disturbing Anarchy of Investigation' Psychological Debate and the Victorian Periodical', in Louise Henson, Geoffrey Cantor, Gowan Dawson, Richard Noakes, Sally Shuttleworth, and Jonathan R. Topham (eds), *Culture and Science in the Nineteenth-Century Media*, Aldershot: Ashgate, pp. 239–50.

Schneewind, Jerome B. [1977] (1986), *Sidgwick's Ethics and Victorian Moral Philosophy*, Oxford: Oxford University Press.

Searle, John M. (2004), *Mind*, Oxford: Oxford University Press.

Seel, Martin (2006), 'Letting One's Self Be Determined: A Revised Concept of Self-Determination', in Nikolas Kompridis (ed.), *Philosophical Romanticism*, London: Routledge.

Seiler, R. M. (1973), 'Walter Pater Studies: 1970–1980' in David J. De Laura (ed.), *Victorian Prose: A Guide to Research*, New York: Modern Language Association of America.

—(ed.) (1980), *Walter Pater: The Critical Heritage*, London: Routledge.

—(1987), *Walter Pater: A Life Remembered*, Calgary: Calgary University Press.

—(ed.) (1999), *The Book Beautiful: Walter Pater and the House of Macmillan*, London: Athlone Press.

Shuter, William (1971), 'History as Palingenesis in Pater and Hegel', *PMLA*, 86.3 (1971), pp. 411–21.

—(1989), 'Pater's Reshuffled Text', *Nineteenth-Century Literature*, 43.4 (1989), pp. 500–25.

—(1994), 'The "Outing" of Walter Pater', *Nineteenth-Century Literature*, 48.4 (1994), pp. 480–506.

—(1997), *Rereading Walter Pater*, Cambridge: Cambridge University Press.

Sinfield, Alan (1994), *The Wilde Century: Effeminacy, Oscar Wilde and the Queer Moment*, London: Cassell.

Small, Ian (1978), 'The Vocabulary of Pater's Criticism and the Psychology of Aesthetics', *British Journal of Aesthetics*, 18.1 (1978), pp. 81–7.

—(1990), 'Intertextuality in Pater and Wilde', *Literature in Transition, 1880–1920*, Special Series 4 (1990), pp. 57–66.

—(1991a), 'Editing and Annotating Pater', in Laurel Brake and Ian Small, *Pater in the 1990s*, Greensboro, NC: ELT, pp. 33–42.

—(1991b), *Conditions for Criticism: Authority, Knowledge, and Literature in the Late Nineteenth Century*, Oxford: Clarendon Press.

Smith, Alison (1997), *The Victorian Nude: Sexuality, Morality and Art*, Manchester: Manchester University Press.

Snyder, Laura J. (2006), *Reforming Philosophy: A Victorian Debate on Science and Society*, London: University of Chicago Press.

Sontag, Susan [1977] (2002), *On Photography*, London: Penguin.

Sorrell, Martin (2005), 'The Glass Man', performed by Karl Prekopp, Saskia Reeves, BBC Radio 4.

Steiner, George (2005), 'Say it Loud – It's Schiller and It's Proud', *Sign and Sight*, available via http://www.signandsight.com/features/152, accessed 4 May 2007.

Sussman, Herbert (1995), *Victorian Masculinities: Manhood and Masculine Poetics in Early Victorian Literature And Art*, Cambridge: Cambridge University Press.

Sychrava, Julia (1989), *Schiller to Derrida: Idealism in Aesthetics*, Cambridge: Cambridge University Press.

Taylor, Benjamin (1995), *Into the Open: Reflections on Genius and Modernity*, New York: New York University Press.

Toynbee, Philip (1970), 'Rebel into Pussycat', *The Observer*, 16 August 1970, p. 21.

Treuherz, Julian [1993] (2001), *Victorian Painting*, London: Thames & Hudson Ltd.

Tucker, Paul (1991), 'Pater as "Moralist"', in Laurel Brake and Ian Small (eds), *Pater in the 1990s*, Greenboro, NC: ELT Press, pp. 107–25.

Turner, Frank M. (1981), *The Greek Heritage in Victorian Britain*, West Hanover, MA: Yale University Press.

—(1993), *Contesting Cultural Authority: Essays in Victorian Intellectual Life*, Cambridge: Cambridge University Press.

—(2005), 'Victorian Classics: Sustaining the Study of the Ancient World', in Martin Daunton (ed.), *The Organisation in Knowledge in Victorian Britain*, Oxford: Oxford University Press, pp. 159–72.

Uemura, Morito (2006), '"Diaphaneitè": Pater's Enigmatic Term', presented at Walter Pater: New Questions, Questionings, Rutgers University, USA, 28 July 2006.

Varty, Anne (1991), 'The Crystal Man: A Study of "Diaphaneitè"', in Laurel Brake and Ian Small (eds), *Pater in the 1990s*, Greensboro, NC: ELT Press, pp. 205–15.

Ward, Anthony (1966), *Walter Pater: The Idea in Nature*, London: Mac Gibbon and Kee Ltd.

Ward, J. P. (1991), 'An Anxiety of No Influence: Walter Pater on William Wordsworth', in Laurel Brake and Ian Small (eds), *Pater in the 1990s*, Greensboro, NC: ELT Press, pp. 63–75.

Ward, Mrs Humphry (1918), *A Writer's Recollections (1856–1900)*, London: W. Collins, Sons & Co.

Warner, Eric, and Graham Hough (eds) (1949), *Strangeness and Beauty: An Anthology of Aesthetic Criticism, 1840–1910*, Cambridge: Cambridge University Press, vol. I.

Watson, Nick, Stuart Weir, Stephen Friend (2005), 'The Development of Muscular Christianity in Victorian Britain and Beyond', *Journal of Religion and Society*, 7 (2005), available via http://moses.creighton.edu/JRS/2005/2005-2, accessed 14 January 2009.

Watson, William [1889] (1880), 'Signed Review', in R. M. Seiler (ed.), *Walter Pater: The Critical Heritage*, London: Routledge, pp. 205–9.

Watt, Ian (1996), *Myths of Modern Individualism: Faust, Don Quixote Don Juan, Robinson Crusoe*, Cambridge: Cambridge University Press.

Whiteley, Giles (2010), *Aestheticism and the Philosophy of Death: Walter Pater and Post-Hegelianism*, Oxford: Legenda.

Wilkinson, Elizabeth and L. A. Willoughby (1982), 'Introduction', in Elizabeth Wilkinson and L. A. Willoughby (trans and eds), *On the Aesthetic Education of Man*, Friedrich Schiller, Oxford: Clarendon Press, pp. ix–cxci.

Williams, Carolyn (1989), *Transfigured World: Walter Pater's Aesthetic Historicism*, London: Cornell University Press.

—(2010), 'Walter Pater, Film Theorist', in Elicia Clements and Lesley Higgins (eds), *Walter Pater Across the Arts*, Basingstoke: Palgrave Macmillan, pp. 135–51.

Williams, Raymond (1983), *Culture and Society: 1780–1950*, New York: Columbia University Press.

Wollheim, Richard (1995), 'Walter Pater: From Philosophy to Art', in E. S. Shaffer (ed.), *Comparative Criticism: Walter Pater and the Culture of the Fin-de-Siècle*, Cambridge: Cambridge University Press, pp. 21–40.

Wright, Thomas (1907), *The Life of Walter Pater*, II vols, London: Everett.

Zepp-LaRouche, Helga (2003), 'Poetry and Agape: Reflections on Schiller and Goethe', The Schiller Institute, available via www.schillerinstitute.org/educ/poetry_agape.html, accessed 23 May 2007.

Ziolkowski, Theodore (1969), *Dimensions of the Modern Novel*, Princeton: Princeton University Press.

Index

Adams, James Eli, 129n
Aesthetic Afterlives (Eastham), 6, 10
aesthetic education, 169, 170, 174
The Aesthetic Education of Man
    (Schiller), 43n, 95, 162, 169
aestheticism
    dying body, 124
    ethics, 173, 174–5
    evolution and the 'species', 138–9
    individualism and the 'aesthetic
        philosopher', 1, 4, 8
    sensuality, 86
*Aestheticism and the Philosophy of
    Death* (Whiteley), 10
*Aestheticism: The Religion of Art in
    Post-Romantic Literature* (Chai),
    147
aesthetic judgement, 86, 91, 157, 177
'The Aesthetic Life' (Pater)
    empiricism, 26, 33
    ethics, 21, 166, 174, 175, 177, 178
    evolution and the 'species', 135,
        143
    metaphysics, 66, 72, 83n
    the moment, 158, 162
    Pater's manuscripts, 18, 23n
    philosophy and art, 189n
    sensuality, 89
    subjectivity and imagination, 45, 46
aesthetic moment, 21, 145n, 155–9,
    160
aesthetics
    empiricism, 38
    ethics, 21, 166–7, 174–6, 180
    individualism and the 'aesthetic
        philosopher', 18
    subjectivity and imagination, 59
aesthetic spectator, 20, 59
'The Age of Athletic Prizemen' (Pater),
    111, 123

À la recherche du temps perdu (Proust),
    160
aleatory moment, 20, 147
Alighieri, Dante, 78, 81, 84n, 127
Also sprach Zarathustra (*Thus Spoke
    Zarathustra*) (Nietzsche), 71, 156,
    172
Anders-streben, 92–3, 163n
Andrews, Kit, 10
Angelico, Fra, 121, 128
Anglicanism, 65, 66
*Anglo-German Interactions in
    the Literature of the 1890s*
    (Bridgwater), 163n, 181n
Apollo, 114, 119
Apollo Belvedere, 111, 119
'Apollo in Picardy' (Pater), 20, 78,
    80–2, 84n, 102, 117
Arnold, Matthew
    conduct and obedience, 103
    Culture and Anarchy, 17, 68, 83n,
        170
    empiricism and the imperilled self,
        26
    ethics, 170
    evolution and the 'species', 132
    'The Function of Criticism at the
        Present Time', 51
    'Literature and Science', 46
    metaphysics, 67, 68, 71, 83n
    'On Translating Homer', 62n
    Pater as 'aesthetic philosopher', 9,
        13, 14–15, 17
    subjectivity and imagination, 46, 51,
        59, 62n
art
    art pour l'art, 86, 88, 137, 146
    desiring body, 112, 121
    ethics, 166, 169, 175, 176, 179, 180
    evolution and the 'species', 145

individualism and the 'aesthetic
  philosopher', 1, 5, 7, 10, 17
metaphysics, 75, 76
the moment, 146, 152, 155, 157, 160
and philosophy, 186, 187
sensuality, 86–8, 92, 103–7
subjectivity and imagination, 51,
  59–60
'Art and Religion' (Pater), 18, 23n
artistic genius, 57–8, 70
ascêsis, 103, 104
atheism, 66, 77
athletic body, 111, 119–21, 123, 124,
  128
autonomy, 4, 41, 102, 120, 180, 184

'The Bacchanals of Euripides' (Pater),
  98, 100, 108n, 175
Bacon, Francis, 24, 42n
Bain, Alexander, 28
Balliol College, Oxford, 44, 62n, 63n,
  104
Baudelaire, Charles, 48, 56, 59, 118
Beardsley, Aubrey, 66, 162
Beaumont, Matthew, 39, 107n
beauty
  the body, 112, 114, 122, 127
  ethics, 21, 177, 178, 179, 180
  evolution and the 'species', 142, 144
  Pater as 'aesthetic philosopher', 7, 14
  Pater's post-Romantic individual,
    183
Belgravia (magazine), 97
Benjamin, Walter, 182n
Bergson, Henri, 145n
Berkeley, George
  empiricism and the imperilled self,
    24–7, 32, 42n
  Johnson's riposte, 90
  subjectivity and imagination, 45, 46,
    49–54, 62n
Beyond Good and Evil (Nietzsche),
  181n
Birth of Venus (Botticelli), 93–4
Blake, William, 57
body, 109–29
  desired body, 111–15
  dying body, 122–6
  erotic touch, 115–18
  flesh, 112, 120, 124, 125, 128
  overview, 20, 109–11
  Pater's female body, 127–9
  scope of Paterian body, 126–7
  sensuality, 90, 93
  spirit and matter, 74, 75
  timeless body, 118–21
Bosanquet, Bernard, 54, 63n

Botticelli, Sandro, 92–5, 127, 128,
  169
Bradley, F. H., 11, 54, 63n, 171
Bradley, Katherine, 174
Brake, Laurel, 15, 178
Brasenose College, Oxford, 15, 45, 54,
  111–12, 130, 167, 185, 187
Bridgwater, Patrick, 22n, 163n, 181n
*British Aestheticism and Ancient
  Greece* (Evangelista), 15, 110
Brooke, S. R., 47, 62n, 82n, 165, 181n
Browne, Sir Thomas, 42n
Bruno, Giordano, 76, 155
Bruns, Gerald L., 7–8
Bullen, J. B., 147
Burke, Edmund, 69
'Burnt Norton' (Eliot), 146
Byron, George Gordon, 129n
Bywater, Ingram, 22n, 24

Campbell, Lewis, 24, 42n
Capes, William Wolfe, 23n, 24, 165
Carlyle, Thomas, 8, 44–5, 71, 182n
The Case of Walter Pater (Levey), 82n
causality, 30
Cavalieri, Tommaso dei, 118
Chai, Leon, 147
chaos, 126
The Characters of Man (la Bruyère),
  181n
childhood, 36, 90
'The Child in the House' (Pater), 19,
  34–7, 40, 153
Christianity
  'Art and Religion', 18
  ethics, 167, 181
  metaphysics, 64, 65, 67, 72–4, 76,
    77–80
  philosophy and art, 188
Clark, Kenneth, 115, 118
Clements, Elicia, 15
Clifford, William Kingdon, 28
'Coleridge' (Pater), 8, 27, 38, 40, 48,
  133, 139, 141, 185
Coleridge, Samuel Taylor, 138, 161,
  182n
Colley, Ann C., 145n
Comte, Auguste, 40, 43n
consciousness, 26, 29, 35, 37–41, 46,
  50, 53
continuous consciousness, 35, 37–41,
  60
Copernicus, 56
Copleston, Frederick, 62n
cosmos, 21
Creation of Man (Michelangelo), 90
Creative Evolution (Bergson), 145n

creativity
  artistic genius, 57–8, 70
  empiricism and the imperilled self,
    30, 42
  metaphysics, 66, 69, 70, 72–7, 81
  subjectivity and imagination, 19,
    54–8, 60, 61
Crinkley, Richmond, 18
'The Critic as Artist' (Wilde), 62–3n
criticism, 59, 62–3n, 68, 83n
Critique of Judgement (Kant), 46, 55,
    86, 137, 138, 168, 169
Critique of Practical Reason (Kant), 46
Critique of Pure Reason (Kant), 46,
    55–6
Culture and Anarchy (Arnold), 17, 68,
    83n, 170
Culture and Society (Williams), 185

Dale, Peter Allan, 147, 148
Daley, Kenneth, 22n
Dandies and Desert Saints (Adams),
    129n
Dante Alighieri, 78, 81, 84n, 127
Darwin, Charles
  evolution and the 'species', 132–3,
    136–7, 139, 142–3
  the moment, 148, 157, 162
Darwinism
  empiricism, 28
  evolution and the 'species', 20,
    132–3, 135–7, 139, 141–3
  individualism and the 'aesthetic
    philosopher', 5, 16, 17
  the moment, 148, 157, 162
  see also evolution
*Darwin, Literature and Victorian
    Respectability* (Dawson), 15
David (Michelangelo), 112
Dawson, Gowan, 15, 28, 43n, 132–3
death
  the body, 123, 126, 129
  evolution and the 'species', 132, 142
  the moment, 146, 153, 155
Debussy, Claude, 159
decadent movement, 124
'The Decadent Movement in Literature'
    (Symons), 124
deep time, 136, 146, 147, 148, 156,
    157
The Defence of Guinevere (Morris),
    88
Dellamora, Richard, 68, 83n, 110, 116,
    117, 178
Demetrius Phalereus, 114
'Denys L'Auxerrois' (Pater), 84n,
    99–100, 150

De Profundis (Wilde), 111
Descartes, Rene, 26, 32, 60, 62n
Descent of Man (Darwin), 143
desire
  body, 109–29: desired body, 111–15;
    dying body, 122–6; erotic touch,
    115–18; overview, 20, 109–11;
    Pater's female bodies, 127–9; scope
    of Paterian body, 126–7; timeless
    body, 118–21
  ethics and violence, 177, 178, 179
  Hellenism, 69
  Pater as 'aesthetic philosopher', 6
  sensation, 186
dialectical history, 134
'Diaphaneitè' (Pater)
  ethics, 171, 172–3, 180
  metaphysics, 19, 67, 69, 72, 80, 81,
    84n
  sensuality, 101
  subjectivity and imagination, 44, 45,
    47–9, 62n
diaphanous man, 46, 68, 69, 101, 106,
    121, 171, 173–4
Dickens, Charles, 178
Dionysus, 97–102, 119, 126, 154, 176,
    179
Dionysus and Other Studies (Pater), 96,
    97, 102, 107, 108n, 119
discipline, 103, 106
Discobulus (Myron), 111, 112, 115
discrimination, 161–3, 178, 187
Don Juan (Byron), 129n
Donoghue, Denis, 6, 16, 83n
Dowling, Linda, 91, 99, 102, 110, 113,
    117, 129n, 180, 181n
'Duke Carl of Rosenmold' (Pater), 150

The Earthly Paradise (Morris), 92
Eastham, Andrew, 6, 10, 154, 163n
'Editing Pater's *Gaston de Latour*'
    (Monsman), 145n
ego, 2, 67, 72, 79
ekphrasis, 117, 128, 149, 153, 157
Eliot, George, 26, 97
Eliot, T. S., 5, 126, 146, 148, 153, 180
'Emerald Uthwart' (Pater), 34
empiricism, 24–43
  Hume and scepticism in 'The History
    of Philosophy', 32–4
  Hume's empiricism in *The
    Renaissance*, 27–32
  individualism and the 'aesthetic
    philosopher', 10, 17
  Locke's empiricism and 'The Child in
    the House', 34–7
  overview, 19, 24–7

Pater's rejection of constructive empiricism, 40–2
questioning Lockean empiricism, 37–9
sensuality, 89
subjectivity and imagination, 45–9, 52, 56, 61
English literature, 14–15
entropy, 20, 137, 138, 152
Epicurus, 86, 96, 107, 152, 177, 186
epiphanic moment, 20, 147, 150, 158, 163n
eroticism
desired body, 111, 112, 114
erotic touch, 108n, 115–18
Hellenism, 68
sensuality, 90, 93, 98, 101, 104, 154
An Essay Concerning Human Understanding (Locke), 19, 26, 35
Essays from the Guardian (Pater), 145n
An Essay Towards a New Theory of Vision (Berkeley), 26–7, 49
eternity, 144, 145, 161
Ethical Studies (Bradley), 63n
ethics, 165–82
and aesthetics, 21, 166–7, 174–6, 180
overview, 21, 165–7
Pater as 'aesthetic philosopher', 6, 18, 187
society, 167–73
violence, 175–81
Euphorion (Lee [Paget]), 7, 22n
Euripedes, 99
Evangelista, Stefano, 15, 20, 110
Evans, Lawrence, 23n
evil, 176, 177, 179, 180, 181
evolutionary theory, 130–45
empiricism, 28
ethics and violence, 180
evolutionary and dialectical history, 133–5
the moment, 146, 148, 149, 161
overview, 20, 130–3
the 'species', 138–45
spectacle of evolution and entropy, 136–8
see also Darwinism

female body, 127–9
Fête Champêtre (Giorgione), 104, 152–3
Feuerbach, Ludwig, 10
Fichte, Gottlieb, 10, 42–3n, 47, 54, 165
Field, Michael, 85, 174
film, 163n

First Principles of a New System of Philosophy (Spencer), 136
flame metaphor, 30
flaneur, 48
form, 75, 112, 132
Fortnightly Review, 63n, 108n
Four Quartets (Eliot), 146
Fox, George, 133
Fox Bourne, H. R., 35
'A Fragment on Sandro Botticelli' (Pater), 92
'The Function of Criticism at the Present Time' (Arnold), 51

Gagnier, Regenia, 21, 174
Garratt, Peter, 25
Gaskell, Elizabeth, 178
Gaston de Latour (Pater)
empiricism, 34
ethics, 166, 174, 175–6, 179
evolution and the 'species', 131, 144
Pater as 'aesthetic philosopher', 1, 22n, 23n
sensuality, 102, 107
subjectivity and imagination, 63n
Gautier, Théophile, 86, 107n, 111, 146
The Genealogy of Morals (Nietzsche), 181n
genius, 57–8, 70
The Germ (periodical), 59
German Idealism *see* idealism
Geschichte der Philosophie (*History of Philosophy*) (Schleiermacher), 43n
Gide, Andre, 163n
La Gioconda (*Mona Lisa*) (Leonardo da Vinci), 127, 128, 157–8
'Giordano Bruno' (Pater), 14, 22n, 40, 56, 63n, 72, 73
Giorgione, 104, 152–4, 156, 163n
Gissing, George, 22n
God
ethics, 169, 173, 177
metaphysics, 19, 65–7, 69–73, 77–81
subjectivity and imagination, 49, 53
Goethe, Johann Wolfgang von, 42n, 131, 147, 155, 163n
Gospels of Anarchy and Other Contemporary Studies (Lee), 183
Gosse, Edmund, 9, 13, 17, 22n, 82n, 102, 108n, 189n
Gould, Stephen Jay, 131
Greek Philosophy (Zeller), 43n
Greek Studies (Pater), 18, 108n, 145n
Green, T. H., 9, 10, 11, 54, 63n, 67, 72
Green, V. H. H., 82n
Grove, George, 39

habit, 40, 41, 42, 130
Hardinge, William, 101, 109, 115
Hardy, Thomas, 22n
Harper's Magazine, 124
Harvard University, 17
Heaven, 74
Hegel, G. W. F., 10–11, 22n, 55, 131,
    134, 171, 173, 187
Hellenism, 68–70, 80, 95, 120, 124
Heraclitus
    empiricism, 30, 32
    evolution and the 'species', 131,
        134–7, 139, 142, 144
    the moment, 160, 161
heredity, 140
Herodotus, 129n
Higgins, Lesley, 15, 23n, 62n
'The Historiography of *Studies in
    the History of the Renaissance*'
    (Bullen), 147
history, 89, 133–5, 137, 147, 159–61
*History of English Thought in the
    Eighteenth Century* (Stephen), 35
History of Philosophy (Lewes), 50
'The History of Philosophy' (Pater)
    empiricism, 19, 32–4
    metaphysics, 72, 79
    Pater as 'aesthetic philosopher', 1–2,
        11, 18, 189n
    the sensual moment, 154
    subjectivity and imagination, 45, 53,
        56
History of Philosophy (Schleiermacher),
    43n
Hobbes, Thomas, 24, 42n, 171, 173
Homer, 154, 155
homoeroticism, 82n, 83n, 109, 110,
    113, 115–18, 127, 167
homosexuality
    desiring body, 109, 110, 117, 127,
        129n
    ethics and violence, 176, 178
    Gide, 163n
    sensuality, 102
Hopkins, Gerard Manley, 9, 62n, 63n,
    64, 82n, 167, 181n
Hough, Graham, 22n
Houghton Library, Harvard University,
    17
Hugo, Victor, 62n
Hume, David
    empiricism and the imperilled self,
        19, 24–6, 42n, 43n
    ethics, 176–7, 181n
    history of philosophy, 186
    Hume and scepticism in 'The History
        of Philosophy', 32–4

Hume's empiricism in *The
    Renaissance*, 27–32
Pater as 'aesthetic philosopher', 11
Pater's rejection of constructive
    empiricism, 40–2
Philosophical Works, 24
sensuality, 20, 69, 86, 107
subjectivity and imagination, 45, 46,
    48, 54
A Treatise of Human Nature, 19, 26,
    42n, 43n, 54, 86
Hunt, William Holman, 83n
Huxley, Thomas Henry, 28, 62n
'Hymn to Proserpine' (Swinburne), 65

idealism
Berkeley's idealism in *The
    Renaissance*, 49–54
empiricism, 25
Kantian idealism and Paterian
    creativity, 54–8
Kantian idealism and subjective
    criticism, 58–61
metaphysics, 72
Pater as 'aesthetic philosopher', 9–10,
    11
subjectivity and imagination, 44, 46
Ideal Student (Fichte), 43n, 54, 165
identity
empiricism and the imperilled self,
    25–7, 29, 30, 35–7, 38, 40–2
evolution and the 'species', 140
individualism and the 'aesthetic
    philosopher', 15, 16
the sensual moment, 149
Imaginary Portraits (Pater), 186
imagination
empiricism and the imperilled self, 39
evolution and the 'species', 138, 144,
    145
metaphysics, 68, 69, 70, 73, 74, 81
the moment, 157, 161
Pater's post-Romantic individual,
    183, 187
scope of Paterian body, 127
sensuality, 98, 103–7
subjectivity and imagination,
    44–63: Berkeley's idealism in *The
    Renaissance*, 49–54; Humean
    subjectivity in 'Diaphaneitè', 47–9;
    Kantian idealism and Paterian
    creativity, 54–8; Kantian idealism
    and subjective criticism, 58–61;
    overview, 44–6
individual
empiricism and the imperilled self,
    26, 29–31, 35–7, 41

ethics, 166–71, 173, 174, 179, 180
evolution and the 'species', 135,
    138–44
individualism and the 'aesthetic
    philosopher', 2–4
metaphysics, 66, 67, 68–9, 78
the moment, 149, 150, 156, 157, 161
Pater's conception of individual, 1–2
Pater's post-Romantic individual,
    183–7, 189
subjectivity and imagination, 19, 47,
    51, 53, 56, 57, 60, 61
individualism
    the body, 20, 120
    ethics, 167, 172, 173, 178, 181
    evolution and the 'species', 138
    individualism and the 'aesthetic
        philosopher', 1–23: focus and
        argument, 15–19; late-Romantic
        individualism, 4–5; 'the mask
        without the face', 2–4; overview,
        1–2; Pater as the 'aesthetic
        philosopher', 5–7; structure of
        book, 19–21
    pantheism and creativity, 77
    Pater's post-Romantic individual,
        185, 187
    the sensual moment, 150
    subjectivity and imagination, 44
Individualism (Lukes), 4
Ingres, Jean-Auguste-Dominique, 94,
    128
Inman, Billie Andrew, 6, 22n, 23n, 28,
    42n, 43n, 101, 109, 171
Introductory Lectures on Aesthetics
    (Hegel), 10

James, Henry, 2, 9, 22n, 30, 102, 117,
    188
'Joachim du Bellay' (Pater), 151, 161
Johnson, Lee McKay, 147
Johnson, Lionel, 10
Johnson, Samuel, 90
Jowett, Benjamin
    the body, 109, 127
    evolution and the 'species', 130
    individualism and the 'aesthetic
        philosopher', 8, 9
    metaphysics, 64
    the sensual moment, 152
    subjectivity and imagination, 44, 54,
        62n, 63n
Joyce, James, 14

Kalip, Jacques, 20, 118, 127
Kant, Immanuel
    the body, 111, 118

Critique of Judgement, 46, 55, 86,
    137, 138, 168, 169
Critique of Practical Reason, 46
Critique of Pure Reason, 46, 55–6
empiricism, 32, 43n
ethics and society, 168, 169
evolution and the 'species', 137–8
Kantian idealism and Paterian
    creativity, 54–8
Kantian idealism and subjective
    criticism, 58–61
Pater as 'aesthetic philosopher', 11,
    186
sensuality, 86, 103, 107, 108n
Kaylor, Matthew, 82n
Keefe, Robert, 122, 126, 128
Kingsley, Charles, 111
knowledge, 27, 35, 51
Kompridis, Nikolas, 4, 184
Kritik der praktischen Vernunft (Kant)
    see Critique of Practical Reason
Kritik der reinen Vernunft (Kant) *see
    Critique of Pure Reason*

la Bruyère, Jean de, 181n
Laity, Cassandra, 67, 68
Lane, Christopher, 59
The Last Romantics (Hough), 22n
Leavis, F. R., 106
Lectures on the Philosophy of History
    (Hegel), 134
Lee, Vernon, 108n, 180, 183
Leighton, Angela, 5, 6, 13, 31–2, 61,
    75, 132, 140, 149, 150
Leonardo da Vinci, 127, 157, 160
'Leonardo da Vinci' (Pater), 157
Letters of Walter Pater (ed. Evans), 23n
Levey, Michael, 82n
Leviathan (Hobbes), 24, 42n
Levine, George, 28, 132
Levy, Michael, 18
Lewes, G. H., 26, 44, 49–50
Life and Death of Jason (Morris), 88
Life of John Locke (Fox Bourne), 35
The Life of Walter Pater (Wright),
    108n
light as metaphor, 19–20, 56, 67–72,
    78, 80–2, 168
Light of the World (Hunt), 83n
'Literary Communism: Pater and
    the Politics of Community'
    (Potolosky), 21, 108n
literature, 1, 14–15, 17
'Literature and Science' (Arnold), 46
Locke, John
    empiricism and the imperilled self,
        19, 24, 25, 43n

Locke, John (*cont.*)
  Locke's empiricism and 'The Child in
    the House', 34–7
  Pater's rejection of constructive
    empiricism, 40, 42
  questioning Lockean empiricism,
    37–9
  subjectivity and imagination, 48, 60
Loesberg, Jonathan, 43n, 52
London, 178
love, 115, 116, 118, 154
'The Love Song of J. Alfred Prufrock'
  (Eliot), 5
'The Lower Pantheism' (Pater), 63n
Lukes, Steven, 4, 77
Lyons, Richard, 89

McGrath, F. C., 25–6
Macmillan, Alexander, 96, 97
Macmillan's Magazine, 28, 39, 102,
  107, 108n, 131, 166
McQueen, John Ranier, 82n
Mademoiselle de Maupin (Gautier),
  107n
Madonnas, 127, 128, 169
male body, 110–16, 118
male-male desire, 6, 104, 109–10,
  153
Mallarmé, Stéphane, 159
Mallock, W. H., 97, 167
'The Man of the Crowd' (Poe), 165
Mansel, H. L., 87, 107n, 108n
manuscripts, 17–18, 23n, 188
Marius the Epicurean (Pater)
  desiring body, 111, 117, 121
  dying body, 123, 125
  empiricism, 34, 43n
  ethics, 21, 166, 174–5
  evolution and the 'species', 132
  individualism and the 'aesthetic
    philosopher', 7, 22n
  metaphysics, 77
  subjectivity and imagination, 61
*Masculine Desire: The Sexual Politics
  of Victorian Aestheticism*
  (Dellamora), 68
masculinity, 117, 119
matter, 74, 95, 112
Maxwell, Catherine, 22n, 61, 68
'Measure for Measure' (Pater), 125
Medusa, 94, 127, 128
Meisal, Perry, 43n, 52, 63n
memory, 31, 37, 38, 39, 162
Menander, 129n
Merimée, Prosper, 3
The Metaphor of Painting (Johnson),
  147

metaphysics, 64–84
  Christian soul in Pater's essays,
    77–80
  Hellenistic light in 'Diaphaneitè' and
    'Winckelmann', 67–72
  overview, 19, 64–7
  pantheism and creativity, 72–7
  philosophy and art, 188
  rejection of light in 'Apollo in
    Picardy', 80–2
  subjectivity and imagination, 45, 55
'The Metropolis and Mental Life'
  (Simmel), 165
Michelangelo, 90, 111, 112, 114, 115,
  118, 123, 127, 160
Mill, John Stuart, 17, 54, 91
mind, 72, 79, 111, 116, 120, 125
Miscellaneous Studies (Pater), 18, 44,
  145n
Les Misérables (Hugo), 62n
modernism, 17, 41
modernity, 3–6, 56, 180, 184, 185,
  187
the 'moment', 146–64
  the aesthetic moment, 155–9
  overview, 20–1, 146–8
  the sensual moment, 149–55
  time and discrimination, 161–3
  time and history in Pater's prose
    form, 159–61
Mona Lisa (Leonardo da Vinci), 127,
  128, 157–8
Monsman, Gerald, 16, 22n, 23n, 63n,
  145n, 165, 176, 181n
Moore, George, 104, 159, 176
Moorehouse, Matthew, 132
morality, 165–6, 168–71, 174, 176–7,
  179
Moran, Maureen, 43n
Morgan, Thaïs, 110, 113, 117, 129n
Morley, John, 58
Morris, William, 88, 92, 164n
mortality, 111, 122, 126, 129
music
  Anders-streben, 92–3, 163n
  evolution and the 'species', 139–40
  metaphysics, 74, 75, 83n
  the moment, 153, 159, 160, 163n
  Pater's post-Romantic individual,
    22n, 185, 187
  Pater's style compared to music,
    159–60
Myron, 111
'The Myth of Demeter and Persephone'
  (Pater), 108n
'The Myth of Dionysus' (Pater), 108n;
  see also 'A Study of Dionysus'

natural sciences, 19, 24, 27, 28, 131, 145, 149
natural selection, 142, 162
'new Ethick', 166, 167, 173, 174
Newman, (Cardinal) John Henry, 23n, 54, 64, 67
The New Republic (Mallock), 97
Nichol, John, 62n
Nietzsche, Friedrich
  Beyond Good and Evil, 181n
  ethics, 171, 172, 180–2
  The Genealogy of Morals, 181n
  metaphysics, 67, 71
  the moment, 156, 163–4n
  'On the Uses and Disadvantages of History for Life', 163–4n
  Pater as 'aesthetic philosopher', 6, 22n, 23n
  Thus Spoke Zarathustra, 71, 156, 172
Nietzsche in Anglosaxony (Bridgwater), 181n
Notes on Poems and Reviews (Swinburne), 114
'Notes on the Designs of the Old Masters at Florence' (Swinburne), 59

Of the Principles of Human Knowledge (Berkeley), 26
Old Mortality Society
  ethics, 165, 167, 168, 181n
  Fichte papers, 10, 43n, 54, 165
  metaphysics, 65, 82n
  subjectivity and imagination, 44–5, 47, 54, 62n, 63n
Oliphant, Mrs Margaret, 3, 151, 173
On Form: Poetry, Aestheticism, and the Legacy of a Word (Leighton), 6
On Liberty (Mill), 17, 91
On the Origin of Species (Darwin), 132
'On the Uses and Disadvantages of History for Life' (Nietzsche), 163–4n
'On Translating Homer' (Arnold), 62n
opposites, 116, 134–5
Original Sin, 25, 36, 71, 75
Østermark-Johansen, Lene, 15, 114, 116, 129n
Oxford and Cambridge Extension movement, 145n
Oxford Dante Society, 84n
'Oxford Life' (Pater), 64, 163n
Oxford Movement, 64

Oxford University
  Balliol College, 44, 62n, 63n, 104
  Brasenose College, 15, 45, 54, 111–12, 130, 167, 185, 187
  empiricism, 24, 35, 41
  metaphysics, 64–5, 66, 82n
  Pater and Hardinge, 109
  Pater as 'aesthetic philosopher', 8–11, 14, 15
  Queen's College, 9, 24, 45
  subjectivity and imagination, 44–5, 47, 54, 62n

paganism, 81, 116
Paget, Violet, 7, 22n
'The Painter of Modern Life' (Baudelaire), 48
Pall Mall Gazette, 14, 15
pantheism, 72–7, 143, 188
Pascal, Blaise, 125
'Pascal' (Pater), 77, 78, 125, 147, 185
passion, 69, 87, 96, 117, 176
Pater, Clara, 127
Pater, Hester, 127
Pater, Walter
  the body, 109–29: desired body, 111–15; dying body, 122–6; erotic touch, 115–18; overview, 20, 109–11; Pater's female bodies, 127–9; scope of Paterian body, 126–7; timeless body, 118–21
  conclusions on post-Romantic individual, 183–9
  death of, 9, 125, 184–5
  empiricism and the imperilled self, 24–43; Hume and scepticism in 'The History of Philosophy', 32–4; Hume's empiricism in *The Renaissance*, 27–32; Locke's empiricism and 'The Child in the House', 34–7; overview, 19, 24–7; Pater's rejection of constructive empiricism, 40–2; questioning Lockean empiricism, 37–9
  ethics, 165–82: ethics as aesthetics, 174–5; overview, 21, 165–7; society, 167–73; violence, 175–81
  evolution and the 'species', 130–45: evolutionary and dialectical history, 133–5; overview, 20, 130–3; the 'species', 138–45; spectacle of evolution and entropy, 136–8
  and Hardinge, 101, 109, 115
  health, 122–3, 124, 125, 129n, 184–5
  illustration of, xi

Pater, Walter (*cont.*)
   individualism and the 'aesthetic
      philosopher', 1–23: focus
      and argument, 15–19; late-
      Romantic individualism, 4–5;
      'the mask without the face', 2–4;
      overview, 1–2; Pater as 'aesthetic
      philosopher', 5–7; Pater falling
      between schools, 7–15; structure of
      book, 19–21
   'Joachim du Bellay' (Pater), 151, 161
   metaphysics, 64–84: Christian soul
      in Pater's essays, 77–80; Hellenistic
      light in 'Diaphaneitè' and
      'Winckelmann', 67–72; overview,
      19–20, 64–7; pantheism and
      creativity, 72–7; rejection of light
      in 'Apollo in Picardy', 80–2
   the moment, 146–64: the aesthetic
      moment, 155–9; overview, 20–1,
      146–8; the sensual moment,
      149–55; time and discrimination,
      161–3; time and history in Pater's
      prose form, 159–61
   sensuality, 85–108: history of
      sensuality in 'Poems by William
      Morris', 88–90; imaginative
      sensation, 103–7; overview, 20,
      85–8; Pater's Dionysus and the
      subversion of sensation, 96–102;
      touch and sensation, 90–3; Venus
      and sensual pleasure in *The
      Renaissance*, 93–6
   subjectivity and imagination,
      44–63: Berkeley's idealism in *The
      Renaissance*, 49–54; Humean
      subjectivity in 'Diaphaneitè', 47–9;
      Kantian idealism and Paterian
      creativity, 54–8; Kantian idealism
      and subjective criticism, 58–61;
      overview, 19, 44–6
   WORKS
   'The Age of Athletic Prizemen', 111,
      123
   'Apollo in Picardy', 20, 78, 80–2,
      84n, 102, 117
   'Art and Religion', 18, 23n
   'The Bacchanals of Euripides', 98,
      100, 108n, 175
   'The Child in the House', 19, 34–7,
      40, 153
   'Coleridge', 8, 27, 38, 40, 48, 133,
      139, 141, 185
   'Denys L'Auxerrois', 84n, 99–100,
      150
   Dionysus and Other Studies, 96, 97,
      102, 107, 108n, 119

Essays from the Guardian, 145n
'Giordano Bruno', 14, 22n, 40, 56,
   63n, 72, 73
Greek Studies, 18, 108n, 145n
Imaginary Portraits, 186
Miscellaneous Studies, 18, 44, 145n
'Oxford Life', 64, 163n
'Pascal', 77, 78, 125, 147, 185
'Poems by William Morris', 6–8, 18,
   87–92, 95, 105, 120, 135
'A Study of Dionysus', 84n, 98, 100,
   101, 108n, 142, 175, 178
'Style', 78, 79, 108n, 162
'Wordsworth', 48, 52, 53, 73, 74,
   83n, 109, 156
see also 'The Aesthetic Life';
   'Diaphaneitè'; *Gaston de Latour*;
   'The History of Philosophy';
   Marius the Epicurean; *Plato and
   Platonism*; *The Renaissance*;
   'Winckelmann'
'Pater's Reshuffled Text' (Shuter),
   145n
Pattison, Mark, 130
Pattison, Mrs Mark, 161
Pausanias, 97
Pearson, Karl, 132
'Le peintre de la vie moderne'
   ('The Painter of Modern Life')
   (Baudelaire), 48
Pensées (Pascal), 125, 147
personal identity *see* identity
personality, 2, 36, 67, 72, 79
Phenomenology of Spirit (Hegel), 22n
Philip of Croton, 114
Philosophical Romanticism
   (Kompridis), 4–5
The Philosophical Theory of the State
   (Bosanquet), 63n
Philosophical Works (Hume), 24
Philosophie der Griechen (*Greek
   Philosophy*) (Zeller), 43n
philosophy
   contradictions in Pater, 21
   empiricism and the imperilled self,
      24, 25, 27, 32–4
   ethics, 180
   evolution and the 'species', 132, 133
   individualism and the 'aesthetic
      philosopher', 1, 6–8, 10–14, 16–18
   Pater's post-Romantic individual,
      185–7
   sensuality, 107
'The Philosophy of Common Sense'
   (Sidgwick), 63n
photography, 154–5
Pico Della Mirandola, Giovanni, 160

The Picture of Dorian Gray (Wilde), 3, 124, 179
Pittock, Murray, 3–4
Plato, 12, 42n, 104–5, 118, 135, 171
Plato and Platonism (Pater)
   evolution and the 'species', 135–8, 140, 145n
   individualism and the 'aesthetic philosopher', 10, 18, 22n
   metaphysics, 83n
   sensuality, 90, 105, 152
Plautus, 129n
Plotinus, 71
Poe, Edgar Allan, 165
Poems and Ballads (Swinburne), 122
'Poems by William Morris' (Pater), 6–8, 18, 87–92, 95, 105, 120, 135
poetry, 49, 58, 74–5, 83n, 92, 163n
'The Poetry of Michelangelo' (Pater), 123
Pope, Alexander, 162
Positivism *see* Comte
Potolosky, Matthew, 21, 108n
Potts, Alex, 83n
Prélude à l'après-midi d'un faune (Debussy), 159
Prettejohn, Elizabeth, 55
Print in Transition 1850–1910 (Brake), 15
Problems of Life and Mind (Lewes), 44
Prolegomena to Ethics (Green), 63n
Promethean Man, 142–3
prose, 83–4n, 159–61
'Prosper Mérimée' (Pater), 55
Proust, Marcel, 5, 38, 145, 158
psychagogy, 39
'Psychoanalysis and Aestheticism' (Meisal), 43n
psychology, 16, 37, 38–9
publishing, 144, 147, 150–1
Purgatorio (Dante), 78, 84n
Pythagoras, 74, 83n, 140, 142

Quarterly Review, 87
Queen's College, Oxford, 9, 24, 45
queer theory, 23n, 109, 110, 115

Raphael, 14
Ravel, Maurice, 139
reason, 60, 69, 86, 106, 186
'Recent Scholarship on Walter Pater' (Hext), 23n
Reid, Thomas, 26, 63n
relativism, 17, 170–1, 176
relativity, 28, 41, 170, 173, 179–80, 183

religion
   ethics and violence, 181
   individualism and the 'aesthetic philosopher', 10, 16, 17
   metaphysics, 20, 64–5, 66, 77–80, 82n
   philosophy and art, 187, 188
The Renaissance (Pater)
   appearance of, 92–3
   the body, 112–13, 116–17, 123–5, 129n
   empiricism, 19, 27–32, 35, 38, 40–3
   ethics, 165
   evolution and the 'species', 140, 142, 145n
   individualism and the 'aesthetic philosopher', 3, 5, 13, 18, 22n
   metaphysics, 19, 64, 65, 68, 69, 71, 77, 84n
   the moment, 146, 149, 151, 152, 158, 160, 161, 164n
   Pater's post-Romantic individual, 186
   sensuality: imaginative sensation, 103–6; Pater's Dionysus and the subversion of sensation, 96–102; 'Poems by William Morris', 89; sensation, 86–8; the sensual moment, 149, 151, 152; touch and sensation, 91–3; Venus and sensual pleasure, 93–6
   spectacle of evolution and entropy, 137
   subjectivity and imagination, 49–54, 57, 59–61
Renaissance in Italy: The Age of the Despots (Symonds), 104, 116, 117
Republic (Plato), 171
Rereading Walter Pater (Shuter), 145n
The Rescue of Romanticism (Daley), 22n
reserve, 103–4, 107, 110, 116–17, 126, 176–7
'The Retreat' (Vaughan), 130
river metaphor, 136
Roach, J. P. C., 145n
Romanticism, 4–5, 12, 21, 60, 77, 138, 167, 184–5
Rossetti, Dante Gabriel, 58, 59, 75, 111
Rothenstein, William, 124
Ruskin, John, 26, 71, 164n, 166, 170
Russell, Bertrand, 24
Ryan, Judith, 107n, 108n

'The Salon of 1859' (Baudelaire), 59
'Sandro Botticelli' (Pater), 108n
Sartor Resartus (Carlyle), 8
scepticism, 32–4, 44, 49, 55

Schelling, F. W. J., 182n
Schiller, Friedrich
    The Aesthetic Education of Man,
        43n, 95, 162, 169
    empiricism and the imperilled self,
        43n
    ethics, 162, 168–70, 172–4, 177,
        180–2
    Pater as 'aesthetic philosopher', 11, 12
    sensuality, 95
Schleiermacher, Friedrich, 43n
'The School of Giorgione' (Pater), 75,
    92–3, 105, 108n, 156, 163n, 164n
Schopenhauer, Arthur, 21–2n, 82–3n
science
    empiricism, 24, 27, 28, 34, 43n
    evolution and the 'species', 131, 141,
        142, 144, 145, 149
    Pater as 'aesthetic philosopher', 8,
        19, 20
    subjectivity and imagination, 45, 46
'Science and Morals' (Huxley), 62n
sculpture, 113–16, 118, 119
Second Law of Thermodynamics, 28,
    137
Second Reform Bill, 91
Second Sight (Maxwell), 22n
self
    empiricism and the imperilled self,
        29–31, 37, 41
    ethics, 168, 179
    individualism and the 'aesthetic
        philosopher', 1–2, 5, 17
    Pater's post-Romantic individual,
        184
    sensuality, 91, 149
    the 'species', 140
    subjectivity and imagination, 49, 51,
        60, 61
self-culture, 165, 172, 180, 181n
self-identity *see* identity
sensation
    and art, 88
    ethics and violence, 177
    imaginative sensation, 103–7
    Pater's Dionysus and the subversion
        of sensation, 97, 98, 102
    Pater's post-Romantic individual, 186
    sensuality, 85–7, 88
    and touch, 90–3
    Venus and sensual pleasure in *The
        Renaissance*, 96
'Sensation Fiction', 151
sensation mania, 87, 150–1
Sensualist School, 35
sensuality, 85–108
    contradictions in Pater, 21

desired and desiring body, 109, 111,
    116, 117
erotic touch, 116, 117
ethics and violence, 176–7
evolutionary and dialectical history,
    134, 135
imaginative sensation, 103–7
overview, 20, 85–8
Pater as 'aesthetic philosopher', 16
Pater's Dionysus and the subversion
    of sensation, 96–102
in 'Poems by William Morris', 88–90
the sensual moment, 21, 149–55
subjectivity and imagination, 45
touch and sensation, 90–3
Venus and sensual pleasure in *The
    Renaissance*, 93–6
sexuality, 100, 104, 110, 117, 153, 167
Shadwell, Charles, 44, 78, 84n, 108n,
    176, 181n
Shakespeare, William, 125–6
'Shakespeare's English Kings' (Pater),
    74
Sharp, William, 98, 103
A Short History of Oxford University
    (Green), 82n
Shuter, William, 18, 23n, 71, 145n
Sidgwick, Henry, 55, 63n, 166
Simmel, Georg, 165
sleep metaphor, 88–9
Snell Exhibitioners, 62n
Snow, C. P., 131
social Darwinism, 20
'Social Organism', 132
society, 100, 166, 167–73, 180, 187
Socrates, 105, 118
solipsism, 49, 50, 52, 53, 158, 173
Solomon, Simeon, xi, 100, 101, 104,
    178
*The Sonnets of Michael Angelo
    Buonarotti and Tommaso
    Campanella* (tr. Symonds), 129n
soul, 67, 72, 77–80, 82, 121
'The Soul of Man Under Socialism'
    (Wilde), 172
space, 143, 144, 162
species, 138–45
speculative philosophy, 32–3, 63n
Spencer, Hubert, 20, 26, 132, 136
spirit
    the body, 120, 121, 125, 128
    evolutionary and dialectical history,
        135
    metaphysics, 66, 67, 69, 70, 72–7,
        81, 82
    sensuality, 95, 105
    subjectivity and imagination, 61

spirituality, 46, 56, 69–70, 76, 134–5, 180
statues, 112–16, 118, 119, 123, 153
Steiner, George, 182n
Stephen, Leslie, 35
Stewart, Balfour, 28
The Stones of Venice (Ruskin), 170
Strauss, David Friedrich, 10
Studies in the History of the Renaissance see The Renaissance
'A Study of Dionysus' (Pater), 84n, 98, 100, 101, 108n, 142, 175, 178
'Style' (Pater), 78, 79, 108n, 162
subjective idealism, 49, 52, 53, 76
subjectivity, and imagination, 44–63
  Berkeley's idealism in *The Renaissance*, 49–54
  Hellenism, 68
  Humean subjectivity in 'Diaphaneitè', 47–9
  individualism and the 'aesthetic philosopher', 1, 2, 5
  Kantian idealism and Paterian creativity, 54–8
  Kantian idealism and subjective criticism, 58–61
  overview, 19, 44–6
  Pater's post-Romantic indiviudual, 184
  self-identity, 31
sublime, 137–8, 145n
Swedenborg, Emanuel, 67
Swinburne, Algernon
  the body, 111, 114, 118, 122
  metaphysics, 65, 66, 67, 82n
  the moment, 146
  Pater as 'aesthetic philosopher', 9
  subjectivity and imagination, 58–9
Symonds, John Addington, 104, 116, 117, 129n
Symons, Arthur, 9, 14, 22n, 53, 84n, 92, 124, 172
Symposium (Plato), 105, 118

Tales of Ancient Greece, No 1, Eudiades and a Cretan Idyll (Symonds), 108n
Tennyson, Lord Alfred, 142
The Theaetetus of Plato (ed. Campbell), 24
Thomson, William, 20, 28, 137
Thus Spoke Zarathustra (Nietzsche), 71, 156, 172
time
  evolution and the 'species', 130–2, 143–5
  the moment: the aesthetic moment,

155, 156, 157, 158–9; overview, 146–8; the sensual moment, 149, 150, 151, 155; time and discrimination, 161–3; time and history in Pater's prose form, 159–61
  philosophy, 186
  teleologies, 181n
Time and Free Will (Bergson), 145n
timeless body, 118–21
Titian, 154, 163n
touch, 90–3, 108n, 115–18, 120
transcendental idealism, 11, 17, 25–6, 45–6, 54–6, 62n
Transfigured World (Williams), 6, 147
Les Travailleurs de la Mer (Hugo), 62n
A Treatise Concerning the Principles of Human Knowledge (Berkeley), 42n, 49
A Treatise of Human Nature (Hume), 19, 26, 42n, 43n, 54, 86
Tucker, Paul, 175
Tyndall, John, 28

Über die ästhetische Erziehung des Menschen (*The Aesthetic Education of Man*) (Schiller), 43n, 95, 162, 169
Uemura, Morito, 62n
unconscious, 38, 39
unity, 31, 42, 60, 73, 89, 170, 188
University Reforms Act (1854), 65

The Vanishing Subject: Early Psychology and Literary Modernism (Ryan), 108n
Varty, Anne, 62n
Vaughan, Henry, 130
Venus, 93–5, 97–9, 105, 127, 128
Venus (Botticelli), 128
Venus de Melos, 76, 94, 105
Victorian Aesthetic Conditions: Pater Across the Arts (Clements and Higgins), 15
The Victorian Critic and the Idea of History (Dale), 147
Victorians in the Mountains: Sinking the Sublime (Colley), 145n
'Victorian Universities and the National Intelligentsia' (Roach), 145n
violence, 175–81
The Vocation of Man (Fichte), 42–3n
Vorlesungen über die Philosophie der Geschichte (*Lectures on the Philosophy of History*) (Hegel), 134
The Vulgarization of Art (Dowling), 91

*Walter Pater and the Language of
    Sculpture* (Østermark-Johansen),
    15, 129n
'Walter Pater: A Portrait' (Gosse), 108n
'Walter Pater as Oxford Hegelian
    (Andrews), 10
Walter Pater: Lover of Strange Souls
    (Donogue), 16
'Walter Pater: Painting in the
    Nineteenth Century' (Higgins),
    23n
'Walter Pater's House Beautiful and
    the Psychology of Self-Culture'
    (Moran), 43n
Walter Pater's Reading (Inman), 6
'Walter Pater's Two Apollos' (Keefe),
    122
Walter Pater: The Idea in Nature
    (Ward), 10
Ward, Anthony, 10
Ward, Humphry, 7, 13, 112
Ward, Mrs Humphry (Mary), 23n, 78,
    162
water, 90–1, 92
Watteau, Antoine, 186
Die Welt als Wille und Vorstellung
    (*The World as Will and Idea*)
    (Schopenhauer), 21–2n, 82n
Westminster Review, 8, 87
Whiteley, Giles, 10
Wilde, Oscar
    'The Critic as Artist', 62–3n
    De Profundis, 111
    desiring body, 110–11, 117
    dying body, 123, 124
    ethics, 172, 179
    evolution and the 'species', 140
    individualism and the 'aesthetic
        philosopher', 1, 5, 6, 9, 14
    metaphysics, 66, 67, 83n

The Picture of Dorian Gray, 3, 124,
    179
    scope of Paterian body, 127
    'The Soul of Man Under Socialism',
        172
will, 2, 67, 72, 79, 82n
William Blake (Swinburne), 146
Williams, Carolyn, 2, 5, 6, 132, 147,
    150, 157, 158, 163n
Williams, Raymond, 185
Winckelmann, Johann Joachim, 42n,
    70, 83n, 111–12, 116–17, 120–1,
    160
'Winckelmann' (Pater)
    the body, 114, 119
    empiricism and the imperilled self,
        27, 40
    individualism and the 'aesthetic
        philosopher', 8, 10
    metaphysics, 19, 67, 68–70, 72, 80,
        81, 83n
    sensuality, 94, 95, 103, 153
    subjectivity and imagination, 60, 62n
Wise, J. R., 87
Wollheim, Richard, 6
Woolf, Virginia, 5, 14, 150, 158
'Wordsworth' (Pater), 48, 52, 53, 73,
    74, 83n, 109, 156
Wordsworth, John, 23n, 65
Wordsworth, William, 5, 48, 49, 52,
    74, 76, 131, 147
The World as Will and Idea
    (Schopenhauer), 21–2n, 82n
Wright, Thomas, 10, 63n, 77, 82n, 103,
    108n, 163n

Yeats, W. B., 14

Zeller, Eduard, 43n
Zeno, 32, 33